Bible
Speaks
today

the message of

THE SECOND COMING

Series editors:
Alec Motyer (OT)
John Stott (NT)
Derek Tidball (Bible Themes)

the message of

THE SECOND
COMING

Ending all things well

Steve Motyer

INTER-VARSITY PRESS
36 Causton Street, London SW1P 4ST, England
Email: ivp@ivpbooks.com
Website: www.ivpbooks.com

First published 2022

British Library Cataloguing-in-Publication Data
A catalogue record for this book is available from the British Library.

ISBN: 978–1–78974–406–4
eBook ISBN: 978–1–78974–407–1

Set in 9.5/13pt Karmina
Typeset in Great Britain by CRB Associates, Potterhanworth, Lincolnshire
Printed and bound in Great Britain by Ashford Colour Press Ltd, Gosport, Hampshire

Produced on paper from sustainable sources.

*Inter-Varsity Press publishes Christian books that are true to the Bible
and that communicate the gospel, develop discipleship and strengthen the church
for its mission in the world.*

*IVP originated within the Inter-Varsity Fellowship, now the Universities and Colleges
Christian Fellowship, a student movement connecting Christian Unions in universities
and colleges throughout Great Britain, and a member movement of the International
Fellowship of Evangelical Students. Website: www.uccf.org.uk. That historic association
is maintained, and all senior IVP staff and committee members subscribe
to the UCCF Basis of Faith.*

To Clare (daughter) and Lily (granddaughter):
you put up so patiently with me being shut away to write.
Now you can have me back! At least until Jesus comes again.
Then we'll be present to one another
in ways we can barely begin to imagine.

Contents

Bible Speaks today

GENERAL PREFACE

The Bible Speaks Today describes three series of expositions, based on the books of the Old and New Testaments, and on Bible themes that run through the whole of Scripture. Each series is characterized by a threefold ideal:

- to expound the biblical text with accuracy
- to relate it to contemporary life, and
- to be readable.

These books are, therefore, not 'commentaries', for the commentary seeks rather to elucidate the text than to apply it, and tends to be a work rather of reference than of literature. Nor, on the other hand, do they contain the kinds of 'sermons' that attempt to be contemporary and readable without taking Scripture seriously enough. The contributors to The Bible Speaks Today series are all united in their convictions that God still speaks through what he has spoken, and that nothing is more necessary for the life, health and growth of Christians than that they should hear what the Spirit is saying to them through his ancient – yet ever modern – Word.

ALEC MOTYER
JOHN STOTT
DEREK TIDBALL
Series editors

Author's preface

I am so glad to be contributing a volume to The Bible Speaks Today series, which has formed part of the backdrop to my life ever since my father became one of the founding editors of the series (with John Stott) in the 1970s. I learned from my father a deep love for the Bible, and in particular a love for its details, its particulars, asking the question 'why?' of every feature of the text, even the tiniest. I've had plenty of opportunity to indulge that love here.

Beyond just enjoying these texts, John Stott's principle of 'double listening' underlies the *raison d'être* of The Bible Speaks Today series, and this too has been written deeply into my life. We listen on the one hand to Scripture, and on the other to the world around us, and then we allow each to address the other. I discovered an opportunity to explore this 'double listening' in looking at 2 Peter 3 (chapter 16 of this book), because it turns out that Peter is doing the same! I find this very encouraging: amazingly, we hear God's voice through Scripture not in some kind of 'spiritual' way abstracted from real life, but as we carefully listen to the Bible using our own selves (our world, our worries and our woes) as lenses to give focus to the eternal Word for *today*.

This is how it works both on an individual level (as I read Scripture for myself) and on a wider level as we ask, 'What is God saying to the church today?' On both levels God actually uses the questions and agonies we bring, to help us understand both Scripture and himself more clearly. How wonderful. For the greatest scriptural example of this amazing hermeneutical principle, consider the book of Job!

The second coming of Jesus has been greatly neglected in the church generally, except in those churches where premillennialism holds sway and a literal Rapture of the church is taught and expected. I find many reasons, in the passages we look at in this book, not to believe in a literal Rapture (and therefore in a 'double' return of Christ). But I also find very many reasons to believe that the second coming is an absolutely crucial biblical doctrine, so that we cannot claim to be authentic, biblical believers unless the expectation of his coming is at the heart of our day-by-day faith.

And what's more, we will find many reasons to believe that the second coming is a deeply *political* doctrine, and this aspect of it thrills me deeply. Read on to find out what I mean!

I'm so grateful for the help of others on the way: not just for my father's influence (see above), but in particular for the fellowship of colleagues at London School of Theology, where I worked for many years. Robert Willoughby, Conrad Gempf and I once wrote a course on the theology of Paul for the now defunct Open Theological College, and the decision we took together to *begin* the course with Paul's eschatology, rather than finishing with it, expressed our shared conviction (which I think began with Conrad) that you can't properly understand Paul except from the End. Everything flows around and from his sense of where it's all heading, in God's purpose for the world in Christ. I think the same applies to the whole of biblical theology! Working with people like Robert and Conrad – and many others with them – has been an enormous blessing.

Derek Tidball was both our Principal at London School of Theology and my editor for this volume, and I am deeply grateful to him in both roles. He and the editors at IVP – Tom Creedy and before him Philip Duce – have added so much to this book and have shown enormous patience over its so-long-delayed production.

The dedication expresses my commitment and gratitude to the two ladies in my life, my daughter Clare and granddaughter Lily, and my prayer that with them I may be able truly to be ready for the coming of the Lord.

STEVE MOTYER

Chief abbreviations

ASV	American Standard Version
CEV	Contemporary English Version
ESV	English Standard Version
GNT	Good News Translation
J. B. Phillips	J. B. Phillips, *The New Testament in Modern English* (London: Geoffrey Bles, 1960)
JSNTSup	Journal for the Study of the New Testament Supplement Series
KJV	King James Version (Authorized Version)
The Message	Eugene H. Peterson, *The Message: The Bible in Contemporary Language* (Colorado Springs: NavPress, 2002)
NIV	New International Version
NKJV	New King James Version
NRSV	New Revised Standard Version
N. T. Wright	Tom Wright (tr.), *The New Testament for Everyone* (London: SPCK, 2011)

Select bibliography

The following is a selection of books not just on the second coming but also more broadly on the Christian hope and the last things, representing a variety of viewpoints.

Alexander, T. Desmond, *The City of God and the Goal of Creation*, Short Studies in Biblical Theology (Wheaton, IL: Crossway, 2018).
——, *The Message of the Kingdom of God*, The Bible Speaks Today (London: Inter-Varsity Press, forthcoming, 2023).
Alison, James, *Living in the End Times: The Last Things Re-imagined* (London: SPCK, 1997).
Blaising, Craig A., Kenneth L. Gentry and Robert B. Strimple, *Three Views on the Millennium and Beyond* (Grand Rapids, MI: Zondervan, 1999).
Blanchard, John, *Whatever Happened to Hell?* (Darlington: Evangelical Press, 1993).
Brower, K. E., and M. W. Elliott (eds.), *'The Reader Must Understand': Eschatology in Bible and Theology* (Leicester: Apollos, 1997).
Cameron, Nigel M. de S. (ed.), *Universalism and the Doctrine of Hell: Papers Presented at the Fourth Edinburgh Conference in Christian Dogmatics, 1991* (Grand Rapids, MI: Baker, 1992).
Carroll, John T., et al., *The Return of Jesus in Early Christianity* (Peabody, MA: Hendrickson, 2000).
Clouse, Robert G., *The Meaning of the Millennium: Four Views* (Downers Grove, IL: InterVarsity Press, 1977).
Fudge, Edward William, *The Fire That Consumes: A Biblical and Historical Study of the Doctrine of Final Punishment* ([Fallbrook, CA]: Verdict Publications, 2001).

Grier, W. J., *The Momentous Event: A Discussion of Scripture Teaching on the Second Advent* (London: Banner of Truth, 1970).

Hart, David Bentley, *That All Shall Be Saved: Heaven, Hell and Universal Salvation* (New Haven, CT/London: Yale University Press, 2019).

Hauerwas, Stanley, *Eschatological Reflections on Church, Politics, and Life* (Grand Rapids, MI: Eerdmans, 2013).

Holmes, Stephen, and Russell Rook (eds.), *What Are We Waiting For? Christian Hope and Contemporary Culture* (Milton Keynes: Paternoster, 2008).

Hunt, Dave, *When Will Jesus Come? Compelling Evidence for the Soon Return of Christ* (Eugene, OR: Harvest House, 1993).

MacArthur, John, *The Second Coming: Signs of Christ's Return and the End of the Age* (Wheaton, IL: Crossway, 2003).

McClymond, Michael J., *The Devil's Redemption: A New History and Interpretation of Christian Universalism* (Grand Rapids, MI: Baker Academic, 2020).

MacDonald, Gregory, *The Evangelical Universalist*, 2nd edn (Eugene, OR: Cascade, 2012).

Moltmann, Jürgen, *In the End – the Beginning* (London: SCM, 2004).

——, *Theology of Hope: On the Ground and Implications of a Christian Eschatology* (London: SCM, 1967).

Motyer, Stephen, *Come, Lord Jesus! A Biblical Theology of the Second Coming of Christ* (London: Apollos, 2016).

Perriman, Andrew, *The Coming of the Son of Man: New Testament Eschatology for an Emerging Church* (Milton Keynes: Paternoster, 2005).

Storms, Sam, *Kingdom Come: The Amillennial Alternative* (Fearn: Mentor, 2013).

Thiselton, Anthony C., *The Last Things: A New Approach* (London: SPCK, 2012).

Toon, Peter, *Heaven and Hell: A Biblical and Theological Overview* (Nashville, TN: Thomas Nelson, 1986).

Travis, Stephen T., *Christ and the Judgement of God: The Limits of Divine Retribution in New Testament Thought* (Milton Keynes: Paternoster; Peabody, MA: Hendrickson, 2009).

Wilkinson, David, *Christian Eschatology and the Physical Universe* (London/New York: T&T Clark, 2010).

Witherington III, Ben, *Jesus, Paul and the End of the World: A Comparative Study in New Testament Eschatology* (Downers Grove, IL: InterVarsity Press, 1992).

Wright, N. T., *Surprised by Hope* (London: SPCK, 2007).

Introduction

We live in an environmental crisis, which – with the accompanying issues of mass migration and conflict – is set to be *the* story of the twenty-first century on Planet Earth. Already the issues are clear: on the one hand, the urgent necessity to take action to mitigate the effects of global warming and pollution; on the other, the pressure to improve (or maintain) 'living standards' around the world, which have depended so much – both in so-called 'developed' and so-called 'developing' countries – on the use of fossil fuels, now accepted as the cause of the current warming of the planet.

Does the second coming of Jesus have anything at all to do with this crisis, so vital for humanity right now? Many will think it is completely irrelevant – an esoteric doctrinal interest of a few religious 'nuts' (like me). Others will go even further, and argue that it's a negative influence, distracting attention away from these pressing present problems to an other-worldly preoccupation – maybe even providing an excuse *not* to do anything about the environmental crisis, because Jesus is going to come again and remake the world anyway.

But I think – and this book sets out to show – that believing in the second coming of Jesus Christ is the best way to give a solid foundation to care for the creation around us, and for suffering humanity. It's the best way to *counteract* all the forces that undermine efforts to combat climate change and environmental degradation. Why? You need this book, to find the answer.

But you could get some hints in this introduction! Yes, Jesus is going to remake the world when he comes. But that's not a reason to step back from caring *now* for the world he will remake, and leave the job to him. Quite the opposite. The *object* of the work of salvation, in the Bible, is not just

1

sinful humankind but the *cosmos*, the whole of creation, into which God placed human beings as stewards. We've made a huge mess of that calling . . . but three cheers for that glorious human Jesus Christ, who represents the perfection of our humanity: when he remakes God's world he will fulfil *our* neglected and violated calling to care for it.

And in the meantime it hardly fits for us to go on deliberately neglecting and violating our environment, just because he is going to do what we should have been doing all along. Faith in the second coming of Jesus Christ gives us a solid reason to plunge in now, as his people, to care for the world in the fullest sense – the world of people and animals and plants, of homes and habitats, of industry and trade and politics and science and art. This is *his* world, and we must care for it, not just because he is its Lord, but more especially because 'when he appears we shall be like him',[1] and that means doing our best to look like him *now*. So if he is a world-rebuilder, we must be too.

Hope for – expectation of – the second coming of Jesus is right at the heart of New Testament faith. You'll discover the reasons for this as you take this tour around the main passages that teach about it. So here's the challenge: if you're going to be a faithful New Testament Christian, then you will need to believe in the second coming more than you (probably) do at the moment. 'Believing' in the second coming is more than just ticking it off the list of things Christians are supposed to believe, and then carrying on with your day. *This* faith will *make* your day – and then some: it will make it more effective, more purposeful, more joyful, more worth waking up for.

This book will change your life, if you let it transform your worldview around the second coming of Jesus.

Just a word about me. I've been teaching the Bible all my life, in a variety of settings, but especially at London School of Theology where I was privileged to work for over thirty years. During that time I developed special interests in John's Gospel, in Romans, in Hebrews and in the book of Revelation, and also in hermeneutics, the study of how we interpret. In later years I also trained as a psychotherapist and taught on LST's Theology and Counselling programme, and you will see the influence of that at several places in the book.

---

[1] 1 John 3:2, my translation.

I published an earlier book on the second coming, which bears quite a close relationship to this one: Stephen Motyer, *Come, Lord Jesus! A Biblical Theology of the Second Coming of Christ* (London: Apollos, 2016). That volume started life intending to be this book, but it grew and became too 'scholarly' and developed a life of its own. It looks at quite a few of the same passages as this book, but interestingly I often found I had different things to say when I came to write this one. I hope you enjoy reading this book as much as I have enjoyed writing it!

Unless I say to the contrary, I have used the New Revised Standard Version of the Bible (NRSV) when quoting biblical texts.

Part 1
The second coming in the Old Testament

Psalms 89 – 90

1. History and time

1. Getting started

This is surely an odd place to start our journey into the second coming of Jesus – with two psalms which mention neither Jesus, nor the second coming!

The reasons are important, and actually take us right into our topic. The second coming is not a detachable biblical 'theme' like the roof-bars on my car. It's more like the wheels or the pistons, things without which the car wouldn't be a car at all. It's rooted deeply in the Bible's view of God as Creator, Ruler and Redeemer of his world, and therefore (as we'll see in this book) the theme of the second coming brings us into close touch with all the central biblical themes. Without the second coming, God would not be the God of the Bible – because it's all about how God is bringing the world to its glorious destiny in Christ, and therefore it's about how God relates to *time* and to *history*, which is the record of time's story played out in the world.

In the Bible God's power and love are such that he doesn't back off when life falls apart and the world is unjust and cruel, but he truly hears our prayers and *comes to us*, even though sometimes his coming seems slow and we have to 'hold on' in faith to his promise. But come he will, both now as we pray, and (gloriously, powerfully) in the end to redeem his suffering creation. That's the journey ahead of us: to discover the biblical shape of that 'coming' of God which is at the heart of the *hope* that faith in Christ gives.

We start with these two psalms which, at first sight, don't seem to relate to each other at all. But they take us straight into two agonizing situations where God seems to have abandoned his people, and they show us how their authors coped: and it's all about displaying how God relates to history and to time. And thus we get launched into the theme of this book.

The two psalms could hardly be more different. Psalm 89 ends Book Three of the Psalms,[1] while Psalm 90 begins Book Four. In addition, they come from widely different times and settings. Psalm 89 belongs late in Israel's story: it's not a psalm of David, but is ascribed to 'Ethan the Ezrahite', and laments the awful events recorded in 2 Kings 25, when King Nebuchadnezzar of Babylon (the date is 587 BC) came against Jerusalem, laid siege to it for over a year until the inhabitants were starving to death, then captured King Zedekiah when he tried to escape, killed his sons in front of him, blinded him and carried him off to Babylon – and then destroyed the city. Terrible, awful suffering.

So we should imagine 'Ethan the Ezrahite' to be someone who has witnessed these appalling events, quite possibly someone who was carried away into exile, hearing the taunts of the victorious Babylonian soldiers (see 89:50). The Ezrahites were probably a guild of temple singers and musicians;[2] but because someone called 'Ethan the Ezrahite' was also a world-famous wise man in the time of Solomon,[3] the temple-singer Ezrahites (and perhaps Ethan especially) may also have had a reputation for wise teaching. Certainly this psalm (as we'll see) is full of amazing wisdom.

Psalm 90, on the other hand, is ascribed to 'Moses, the man of God' – the only psalm attributed to Moses – and is thus some seven hundred years older than Psalm 89! Some would doubt the ascription to Moses, though it's not difficult to trust the tradition of shared worship in Israel which could have preserved it, alongside the famous 'Song of Moses' in Deuteronomy 32 (the other psalm attributed to him in the Old Testament – not to mention all his teachings preserved in the 'books of the law'). To infer from the comments in 90:10 about the normal length of human life, we would have to surmise that Moses wrote this psalm while tending his father-in-law's sheep in the desert of Midian: in Exodus 7:7 we learn that he was eighty years old when he returned to Egypt, having met the Lord

---

[1] See 89:52; cf. 41:13; 72:18–20; 106:48.

[2] See the inscription over Ps. 88.

[3] 1 Kgs 4:31.

in the burning bush and received the commission to bring Israel out[4] – and he lived for another forty years after that.[5]

So, remarkably, Psalm 90 comes from 'way back when': not only from before the beginning of David's royal dynasty which came to such a terrible end after that Babylonian siege, but also before Jerusalem was the Lord's chosen 'place',[6] before they entered the Promised Land, before the events of the exodus which bound them together as a people under God's hand, before Moses' call to rescue them – in fact, when they were still a 'slave in the land of Egypt',[7] one tribal grouping among very many similar groups in the Ancient Near East, calling out to their God to rescue them from oppression.[8]

As we'll see, these huge differences in origin and setting between these two psalms are precisely the point. Because of these differences, and because of their juxtaposition at this 'hinge' between two books of the Psalms, a wonderful perspective emerges for us, which takes us to the heart of the biblical view of *time* and *providence*: that is, the biblical understanding of how God's purposes work out over the course of time, and *what we can trust him for* when we too – like Judah in the 580s BC, and like the tribes of Israel in Egypt – are stuck in a horrible place where God does *not* seem to be on the throne, indeed where he seems to be *absent*.[9]

And that is essential preparation for the biblical message of the second coming of Jesus Christ.

2. Psalm 89: 'Lord, will you hide yourself for ever?'

This question in verse 46 captures the pain and longing of the psalm. The final prayer of the Bible, 'Come, Lord Jesus!',[10] similarly expresses a longing that his hiddenness from the world should end. If you have ever felt abandoned by God, this is the psalm for you! Perhaps pause and read it now, knowing the background I've sketched above: this is the voice of

---

4 Exod. 3:1–10.

5 Deut. 34:7.

6 See Deut. 12:5–7.

7 Deut. 5:15.

8 Exod. 2:23.

9 I was first prodded in the direction of exploring the implicit 'dialogue' between these psalms by Christopher Seitz, 'Royal Promises in the Canonical Books of Isaiah and the Psalms', *Word without End: The Old Testament as Abiding Theological Witness* (Grand Rapids, MI: Eerdmans, 1998), pp. 150–167 (see p. 162).

10 Rev. 22:20.

someone who is being carried away from Jerusalem into Babylonian exile, having witnessed a period of prolonged, desperate suffering culminating in appalling slaughter and destruction. How does that change your 'hearing' of this psalm?

Against that background, verses 1–37 of the psalm become deeply *ironic*, and verses 38–52 devastating in their pathos. Ethan is wrestling, not so much with the awfulness of the physical suffering experienced by Israel at the hands of the Babylonian army (though that is very present), as with the *theological* trauma arising from God's apparent abandonment of his commitment to David and his throne. Verses 1–4 set the scene, with their repeated 'for ever': David's everlasting throne (3–4, *for ever . . . for all generations*) was meant to be an expression of the Lord's *steadfast love* (1–2, *for ever . . . to all generations . . . for ever*).

Then verses 5–37 fall into two sections, focusing first on God (5–18) and then on the promises made to David and his dynasty (19–37). God lacks nothing in power (5–13) or in commitment to Israel (14–18) to make good his promises to David. The irony continues to build as Ethan remembers the joyful covenant celebrations in which he took part (15–16), and probably also the coronation ceremonies in which he partici-pated – at which he, with the other singers, had doubtless recited the covenant promises which he trumpets in verses 19–37. Maybe he is actually quoting the very words of the coronation ceremony – words which go back to God's promises in 2 Samuel 7:8–16, when Nathan the prophet brought God's response to David's desire to build a 'house' for the Lord in Jerusalem. No, said Nathan, God does not want you to build him a temple. Rather, 'the LORD declares to you that the LORD will make *you* a house' (11 [emphasis added]): David's son will take care of building the temple, and the Lord will, for his part, 'establish the throne of his kingdom for ever' (1 Sam. 7:13).

Moreover, God's promises in 2 Samuel 7 took care of the possibility that one of David's sons might turn out to be a rotten egg, unfaithful and disobedient to the Lord – and Ethan unpacks this aspect of the promise at length in verses 30–34 of our psalm. The promise was 'When he [that is, one of David's sons] commits iniquity, I will punish him . . . But I will not take my steadfast love from him, as I took it from Saul, whom I put away from before you.'[11] So the case of Zedekiah, the last king, was covered by

---

[11] 2 Sam. 7:14–15.

this. According to 2 Kings 24:19, 'he did what was evil in the sight of the Lord', as did his brother Jehoiakim, who had also been king.

But that's what horrifies Ethan the Ezrahite! It seemed that the Lord had gone back on his promise to rescue and preserve Judah and its king *even if* they sinned. Yes, punishment (32) – but *this*? This is far more than a corrective scourging: this wholesale slaughter and destruction mean the end of the covenant. After the ironic recital of God's covenant commitment, the psalm reaches a moment of awful pathos in verses 38–39:

> But now you have spurned and rejected him;
>   you are full of wrath against your anointed.
> You have renounced the covenant with your servant;
>   you have defiled his crown in the dust . . .

– and then follow six further verses recounting the evidence that supports Ethan's conclusion that God has gone back on his promises to David's 'house' (40–45).

It is important to note that Ethan is not being sarcastic or cynical. He has not lost his faith. He still believes that God is as he describes him – totally sovereign, totally committed to his people, and totally faithful to his promises. He refers eight times to God's *faithfulness* to which, he says, God will never *be false* (33). That's the problem! But Ethan is still a worship leader, and this is a psalm. He's still singing. And his song comes from the darkness of his experience, from his confusion, his perplexity, and his *longing* for God actually to *be* the God he knows him to be:

> How long, O Lord? Will you hide yourself for ever?
>   How long will your wrath burn like fire?
> Remember how short my time is –
>   for what vanity you have created all mortals!
> Who can live and never see death?
>   Who can escape the power of Sheol?
>
> Lord, where is your steadfast love of old,
>   which by your faithfulness you swore to David?
> Remember, O Lord, how your servant is taunted;
>   how I bear in my bosom the insults of the peoples,

> with which your enemies taunt, O LORD,
>> with which they taunted the footsteps of your anointed.
> (46–51)

Knowing the events which evoked them, these are some of the most heart-rending words in the Bible: a cry for God to make his power and promise real at a moment when he seemed to have resigned the throne in heaven. And so ends Book Four of the Psalms, as well as the Davidic kingship in Jerusalem.

But this is not the last word!

3. Psalm 90: 'Lord, you have been our dwelling-place in all generations'[12]

Was Ethan already familiar with the wonderful *Prayer of Moses, the man of God* which we now have as Psalm 90? If so, maybe he too could console himself with the thoughts that come to us, as we meet it next in the Psalter. In an amazing way, Psalm 90 addresses the awful question with which Psalm 89 ends. It, too, talks about the terrible shortness of human life (5–6, 10), and the inescapability of death (3), and the power of God's wrath (7, 9, 11), and it utters the same cry 'How long, O LORD?' (cf. 13). In Psalm 90, too, God's *steadfast love* is a key term (14), and the two psalms begin with the same phrase, 'to/in all generations' (89:1; 90:1).

The juxtaposition of these psalms speaks volumes. It's important to realize that Psalm 90 doesn't provide 'the answer' to the terrible question with which Ethan wrestles in Psalm 89, but rather sets the question in a bigger context, and relates it more broadly to what human life is in itself. Ethan faces a terrible puzzle about how God is acting in a particular circumstance. Moses in Psalm 90 helps us to see that the same puzzle is *always* the case, whatever the circumstances, and gives us a way of facing it and dealing with it, even if we still don't know why things are the way they are: and, at the same time, he gives us a theology of *time* within which we can begin to understand how the second coming of Jesus fits into God's plan for his world.

Psalm 89 begins with *who God is* and how he relates to a particular, important human being and his family: David and his dynasty (1–4). Psalm

---

90 begins with *who God is* and how he relates to *all* of us human beings (1–6). And what a different picture emerges! We can trace some fascinating contrasts between the psalms:

- For Ethan, the Lord is the 'covenant' God who has committed himself in 'steadfast love' to David and his house, 'to all generations'. For Moses, God is the everlasting creator who has allowed himself to be *our dwelling-place in all generations* (90:1).
- For Ethan, the terrible frailty of 'David' before the Babylonian onslaught means that God has abandoned his covenant promise to protect and preserve. For Moses, we are all, always, terribly frail in this world – weak creatures of dust who are swept away like a dream, vanishing like grass dried up in the blazing Middle Eastern sun (90:3–6).
- For Ethan, God's 'wrath' is understandable (Zedekiah was not a close follower of the Lord), but at the same time deeply puzzling: why is it so fierce, burning like fire (89:46), exalting Judah's foes and hurling David's throne to the ground (89:42, 44)? Has God not promised to set aside his wrath and show mercy to David's sinful heirs? For Moses, God's wrath is written into the very fabric of being human: we cannot hide our sins (90:8), and so God's wrath consumes and overwhelms us (90:7) and sweeps us away like tender blades of grass in a fire-storm.
- For Ethan, the temple in Jerusalem, now destroyed, was the symbol of God's commitment to his people. He doesn't actually mention the temple specifically, but we can see it clearly behind 89:15–18 where he remembers the joy of the festival crowds worshipping and processing before the Lord and with their king. It was the 'dwelling-place' of the Lord himself.[13] But for Moses, there is no physical 'dwelling-place' for God on earth. Rather, God himself is *our dwelling-place in all generations* (90:1).[14]
- Finally, for Ethan, *permanence* was written into the covenant relationship: God had made David's house secure 'for ever' (89:36–37) – 'established for ever like the moon, an enduring

---

[13] See Ps. 26:8, 'O Lord, I love the house in which you dwell.' Ps. 132 gives another statement of this theology.

[14] He uses the same word that is used for the temple in Ps. 26:8.

13

witness in the skies'. For Moses, *impermanence* – in fact, terrible *brevity* – is written into our human experience: *the days of our life are seventy years, or perhaps eighty, if we are strong; even then their span is only toil and trouble; they are soon gone, and we fly away* (90:10). I know what he means: I am seventy now, as I write this, and I don't know how the years have slipped away. 'Soon gone' doesn't touch it. I shall be flying away before long.

4. Meeting of minds?

What are we to make of these contrasts? Actually Ethan would not disagree with any of Moses' perspectives here. For him, too, God's faithfulness rests in his awesome power and sovereignty as Creator (89:8–14), and God himself is the foundation of his hope – not the Davidic kingship or Jerusalem or the temple. Ethan too knows how frail and impermanent we human beings are – *Remember how short my time is – for what vanity you have created all mortals!* (89:47). The word translated *vanity* here means 'nothingness, uselessness, ineffectiveness'. It's only in relation to his specific circumstances that Ethan is in a different place, as he experiences this terrible theological disorientation, this quenching of his glowing confidence in the permanence of the Davidic kingship.

What does Moses say to this? It is as though he invites Ethan to climb upwards, to allow the specifics of Judah's experience in the 580s BC to shrink in size as the scene broadens out and he gains a much wider view. Beyond the pain of the recent events, beyond the founding of the Davidic kingdom and the establishing of Jerusalem as David's capital, beyond the entry into the land, even beyond the exodus and the call of Moses, indeed *before the mountains were brought forth, or ever you had formed the earth and the world* (90:2) – from that perspective, who is God? and who are we?

This is a perspective into which we constantly need to shift. We can get so stuck in our own local and immediate troubles and issues, even if we are deeply spiritual people of faith, like Ethan the Ezrahite. He was no spiritual slouch, no theological lightweight. He was a mature worship leader and lover of the Lord whom he had served for so long in the temple. But he was also deeply hurt – in fact, in agony over what had happened to Jerusalem and to his people. Doubtless he had lost many friends and family members to the Babylonians, whether through the famine caused by the siege or through the subsequent executions carried out by the

Babylonians. He had witnessed the wholesale destruction of the city and of Solomon's glorious temple, plundered for its precious metals.[15] And beyond and behind this he was in deep pain and perplexity about God's role in it all: where was he? Why did he not defend his anointed king as he had promised?

Lost in this pain, Ethan needs to rise up and embrace the bigger picture that Psalm 90 offers. So do we. What exactly is it? It has three elements to it:

- Big God, tiny humans (90:1–6)
- Angry God, nothing hidden (90:7–12)
- Compassionate God, reason for hope (90:13–17)

a. Big God, tiny humans (90:1–6)

Wandering through the Sinai desert with his sheep, the ageing Moses had plenty of time to reflect on who God is, and who he was in relation to that God. God is the Creator who pre-exists the grandeur around him, who called it into being, and who now is Moses' *dwelling-place*. He thought he had a home in Pharaoh's palace, a young Somebody with muscle and clout. But then he learned better. He lost that home, but he has found another one – and has learned that, in relation to the God in whom he now 'dwells', he is a passing moment in which dust gains a body and becomes conscious, and then slips back into being *just dust*. A wise man once said that Moses spent forty years learning he was Something; then forty years learning he was Nothing; then forty years learning that God is Everything.

We are towards the end of that second forty-year stretch in this psalm (see v. 10). The realization that God is Everything has yet to become concrete through the experience of the exodus – but he already sees and senses it in the mountains around him and in the unshakeable conviction that somehow he is *at home* in this God.

But . . . the desert faces him with his insignificance. *Utter* insignificance. Dust . . . a dream . . . a shrivelled blade of grass (3–6). We push these truths from us. There must be more to us humans than this – isn't there? No. In the desert there is no space for illusions, and Moses knows who he is. In our narcissism we big ourselves up and enjoy it when others confirm our size by their admiration – but what a deception that is. Shrink, little

---

humans. You are minuscule: whether you measure your physical, temporal or moral stature, you are tiny, and pass away insignificantly, ending like a sigh.

b. Angry God, nothing hidden (90:7–12)

The appearance of the theme of God's anger is surprising, after the picture of God as our 'dwelling-place' in verse 1. But Moses knows God well, and we need to listen. Moses was a murderer,[16] and that was why he was now wandering around the Sinai desert, and not swanning around in an Egyptian palace. The God who is 'home' for Moses is an uncomfortable Judge before whom everything is visible – not just the headline sins like murder, but also the *secret sins* (8) that no-one else sees: the sins of thought, the sins committed in solitude, and not least the sin which is our refusal to accept that verses 3–6 are true about *us*. Ethan might hear Moses tell him that his confidence in the Davidic kingship, and his belief in the indestructibility of Jerusalem – even though they rested in God's promises – were still sinful, because they were rooted in human realities and not solely in God himself.

God's anger roots out our hidden motives and instincts, and is uncompromising in its judgment. We stand condemned – and so the very brevity and insignificance of our lives, which we sinfully refuse to accept, become God's 'consuming' of us, 'overwhelming' us in his wrath (7).

c. Compassionate God, reason for hope (90:13–17)

Praise the Lord for these verses! The tension between 'dwelling-place' in verse 1 and 'fly away' in verse 10 is resolved, as Moses rests his hope in God's compassion. His wrath is not his last word. Each verse here brings out a different aspect of God's character towards us, which Moses prays he will activate: his *compassion* (the headline, 13), his *steadfast love* (14), his desire to give us joy (15), his *glorious power* (16), and his 'beauty' or *favour* which will cause us to flourish and our work to *prosper* (17).

This prayer, of course, was wonderfully answered some time later, when Moses met God in the burning bush, heard about his compassion for his people, and began to experience his power.[17] The prayer of verse 17 was amazingly confirmed as Moses began his life's work at the age of eighty!

---

[16] Exod. 2:11–12.
[17] Exod. 3:1 – 4:17.

So our hope, too, rests not in any specific evidence that we might claim as proof of God's power and reality. It may collapse, like the Davidic kingship in 586 BC. Churches rise and fall, movements come and go, present certainties collapse in ruin. Ethan saw the work of his hands go up in smoke, along with all his hopes and dreams. But like Moses he did not renounce his hope in God's *steadfast love* beyond his present experience (89:49). So our hope rests solely in God himself, in his character as *steadfast love*, and in his turning towards us in our frailty, insignificance and sinfulness.

5. Strung out on the line of time . . .

We meet two sorts of time in these psalms: time as *extent*, and time as *moment*. In Greek there are different words for these, which we will meet in later chapters: time as extent is *chronos*, time as measured by a clock, while time as moment is *kairos*, time as marked in an appointment diary. Think of 'time is passing so slowly today!' or 'where on earth has the time gone?' – this is *chronos*. But 'we had a terrible time last night!' and 'it's time we got together' are *kairos*, significant moments within *chronos*. Ethan was stuck in a terrible *kairos*-moment, the awful destruction of Jerusalem and of the monarchy, which challenged his faith to the core: and he needed to gain a *chronos*-perspective, a wider vision of God's longer relation to the world, beyond the immediate disaster. Moses gives this to him (and to us). But of course Moses, in contrast to Ethan, was stuck in a terrible *chronos*-experience – feeling his awful transience and insignificance before the vastness of God's universe and the power of God's wrath. He was longing for a *kairos*-moment, a spot in time when God would step in, show his compassion and save him from his frailty.

The second coming of Jesus is the ultimate *kairos*-moment in the long *chronos* story of our world. En route to that glorious event when God will finally step in to save us, we meet many other *kairos*-moments when we experience his compassion, steadfast love, joy, power and beauty – the things for which Moses prays here: 'burning bush' moments when *our* world shifts onto a new axis, as did his. A moment is coming when *the whole world* will shift and be remade, and that is the moment of Jesus' return.

So our journey has begun! These psalms together give us the *structure* of the biblical doctrine of the second coming of Christ. It's about God, and his creatorial rule over the universe he has made. It's about our total frailty and sinfulness and *nothingness* (89:47) apart from him. It's about how we have no hope apart from his *steadfast love* – his covenant commitment to us in Christ. It's about how sometimes we feel completely abandoned by him. It's about trusting, even desperate prayer, crying out to him for salvation. It's about those moments of great glory when he steps in to rescue us – and it's about how those moments foreshadow the greatest moment of all when he will transform his world and save us from that *nothingness* into his glory.

Psalm 18

2. Presence in power

1. Last will and testament

Our next passage is another psalm, one which takes us back to the beginning of the story of the Davidic kingship. This is David himself writing, and we discover from 2 Samuel 22, where it also appears, that this psalm was regarded as a kind of summary of David's testimony, looking back over his life. Hertzberg comments that the editor of 2 Samuel sees it as 'a theological commentary on the history of David', and includes it at that point because David has just withdrawn from the active military campaigning which he celebrates in the psalm.[1] It appears in 2 Samuel just before his 'last words'.[2]

This placement is slightly odd, because (to judge from verses 20–24, and especially verse 23) this psalm actually dates from David's younger days, before the awful story of Uriah the Hittite and his wife Bathsheba.[3] After that date, David could hardly have written

> I was blameless before him,
>> and I kept myself from guilt.
> Therefore the LORD has recompensed me according to my righteousness.
> (23–24)

The language of those verses is very different from that of Psalm 51, David's prayer of confession after the Bathsheba episode! So here in Psalm 18 it

---

[1] See 2 Sam. 21:17. H. W. Hertzberg, *I & II Samuel: A Commentary* (London: SCM, 1964), p. 393.

[2] 2 Sam. 23:1.

[3] 2 Sam. 11.

seems we actually meet David in his halcyon days – established as a new young king in Jerusalem and looking back over 'the story so far', reflecting on his experience of the Lord and giving thanks. The editor of 2 Samuel clearly felt, even so, that it could stand as David's spiritual 'last will and testament' in spite of his sin against Bathsheba and Uriah. Sin is never the last word, and God had forgiven him.[4]

Before we look at David's testimony – and in order to help us see how Psalm 18 fits into a book on the second coming! – we must pay a return visit to Ethan the Ezrahite. The last verse of Psalm 18 expresses the theology which, in Ethan's experience, has just been exploded by the Babylonians:

> Great triumphs he gives to his king,
>> and shows steadfast love to his anointed,
>> to David and his descendants for ever.
> (50)

If Ethan had read David's testimony again after 586 BC (as he may well have done), he would have experienced that sickening, hollow, stomach-churning feeling that must have been his constant companion as he walked through the ruins of Jerusalem. He would have heard verse 30 with particular poignancy – the promise of the LORD proves true – as well as the piled-up pictures of victory over enemies in verses 37–48. None of it was true for his Jerusalem.

As we have seen, Moses calls Ethan back to a bigger view of God as our 'dwelling-place' beyond and in spite of all terrible experiences of disappointment and abandonment which make us question him. We too can expand Ethan's view – but we will direct his attention not back, but forward to what is coming. How do we cope with the collapse of the Davidic dynasty in 586 BC, in spite of God's promises? Answer: because of Jesus. We would offer Jesus to Ethan, and encourage him to see in Jesus 'great David's greater Son',[5] the fulfilment of all the promises that surrounded the Davidic kingship. This is clearly the perspective of the New Testament writers, who pick up these promises and apply them to Jesus,[6] even though a huge change in perspective is involved. He was not going to be a king sitting on a physical

---

[4] 2 Sam. 12:13.

[5] This description is from James Montgomery's hymn 'Hail to the Lord's Anointed' (1821).

[6] E.g. Luke 1:32–33, 69; Acts 13:32–37; Rom. 1:3–4; Rev. 3:7.

throne in Jerusalem, in line with Ethan's view of the promise. Jesus as David's son was also David's *Lord*,[7] and therefore ruler over a much greater, worldwide kingdom with its roots in heaven, not on earth. What a shift! It's hard for us to feel the magnitude of this from the inside for people who, like Ethan, had grown up with a clear, fixed vision for the place of Jerusalem, and the Davidic king, in God's plan for the world. How might Ethan have responded if we could have told him about Jesus?

We can only imagine the conversation. We might start by quoting Psalm 18:43–45 to him:

> You delivered me from strife with the peoples;
>> you made me head of the nations;
>> people whom I had not known served me.
> As soon as they heard of me they obeyed me;
>> foreigners came cringing to me.
> Foreigners lost heart,
>> and came trembling out of their strongholds.

Head of the nations (43)? Ethan, when was such a wonderful position ever occupied by David? Never, he would reply, not in the strict meaning of the words – but surely David here is speaking just of his enemies whom he defeated. Well, perhaps, we would respond – but his language is bigger than that, in line with the words spoken over all the Davidic kings at their coronation, as you know, Ethan:

> [The Lᴏʀᴅ] said to me, 'You are my son;
>> today I have begotten you.
> Ask of me, and I will make the nations your heritage,
>> and the ends of the earth your possession.'[8]

Ethan, we know the glorious fulfilment of this vision in Jesus! It was never true of the Davidic kings in Jerusalem. God always had something bigger and more wonderful in mind. He has now brought that into reality through the outpouring of the Spirit on 'all flesh', because of the resurrection of Jesus . . .

---

[7] See Mark 12:35–37.

[8] Ps. 2:7–8. Psalm 2 is widely recognized as a Coronation Psalm, and is quoted and applied to Jesus in Acts 13:33 and Heb. 1:5; 5:5. It is also echoed in the Father's words to Jesus at his baptism (Matt. 3:17).

And so the conversation would go on. Would Ethan be convinced, and lift his eyes to see this bigger God? For us, this 'bigger vision' shapes our reading of Psalm 18. This is not just David celebrating his victories, but the Davidic king celebrating his office: hence his final description of himself as the Lord's *anointed*, and the final *for ever*, the very last phrase of the psalm (50). If the Davidic king is going to know the Lord's *steadfast love* and experience *great triumphs . . . for ever* (50), then after 586 BC God is going to have to do something very special indeed. Which, of course, he has – in Jesus.

So, for us, David's testimony is laced with a prophetic flavouring, because it describes an experience bigger than his own. His words foreshadow the experience of his 'greater Son', and actually make *more* sense when read in this bigger way. For instance, verses 20–24 make perfect sense when applied to Jesus as the Davidic son and heir. We don't have to qualify them, as we do in David's case. David was writing his testimony, but writing beyond himself.

2. An overview of the psalm

So what do we hear in this glorious psalm, especially as we read it in this bigger way – and particularly with the second coming in mind? Structurally, it falls into three sections, bracketed by a balancing introduction and conclusion:

> A. vv. 1–3 Rousing introduction: the Lord, David's confidence
> > B.   vv. 4–19 Glorious deliverance: David's testimony, part 1 – rescue
> > > C. vv. 20–30 Blameless righteousness: the root of the testimony
> > B'. vv. 31–45 Victorious strength: David's testimony, part 2 – equipping
> A'. vv. 46–50 Rousing conclusion: the Lord, David's hope (reiterating five themes or images from the introduction – rock, salvation, deliverance, victory over enemies, and praise)

What we see straight away is that the psalm is about *battle* from start to finish. This is true to David's life, of course – he was a warrior king. The whole sorry Bathsheba incident started with David staying in Jerusalem in the spring, when normally 'kings go out to battle'.[9] The first main section (4–19), which focuses on David's helplessness before, and deliverance from, his enemies, is balanced by the third section (31–45) where the focus is on David's strength and victory over them – but throughout the Lord is the great Actor: the architect both of David's rescue and of his strength and skill as a warrior.

Fascinatingly, the psalm starts with David the warrior being defeated – in fact, nearly being killed:

The cords of death encompassed me,
the torrents of perdition assailed me,
the cords of Sheol entangled me,
the snares of death confronted me.
(4–5)

Vivid language – and true to his experience when he was being hunted through the mountains by Saul and fleeing for 'safety' to his enemies the Philistines.[10] There were some very low moments indeed: most notably when he avoided being murdered by pretending to be mad,[11] and when he returned to Ziklag to find that it had been burned down by Amalekite raiders, who had carried off all the women and children belonging to David and his 'army'. On that occasion even his own men turned against him and threatened to kill him[12] – but, we read, 'David strengthened himself in the LORD his God',[13] and with tremendous resourcefulness and stamina he and his men pursued the Amalekites and retrieved their families and a lot of extra spoil.

David showed enormous courage and cleverness throughout this period of his life, and could have ascribed his victories to these qualities. But no:

In my distress I called upon the LORD;
to my God I cried for help.
From his temple he heard my voice,
and my cry to him reached his ears.
(6)

---

9   2 Sam. 11:1.
10   1 Sam. 21 – 30.
11   1 Sam. 21:10–15.
12   1 Sam. 30:1–6.
13   1 Sam. 30:6.

– and then follows a beautiful and deeply evocative passage describing the Lord riding to his aid *upon the wings of the wind* (10), using 'storm symbolism' to describe the Lord's dramatic intervention to save him. Earthquake, fire and smoke, storm clouds, torrential rain, thunder and lightning, hail, hurricane winds and even tsunami surges[14] roar across the psalm as David describes how

> *he reached down from on high, he took me;*
> *he drew me out of mighty waters.*
> *He delivered me from my strong enemy,*
> *and from those who hated me;*
> *for they were too mighty for me.*
> (16–17)

3. The special language of 'theophany'

Nothing like this ever literally happened, of course. The Lord certainly intervened to rescue David, on many occasions, but never literally by turning up on a cherub (10) or creating a mighty storm. David is using the traditional language of 'theophany', to give it its proper name – 'theophany' meaning 'God appearing'. It might be that this use of 'storm symbolism' to describe the Lord's arrival started with the stories of the exodus: maybe first with the stories of the plagues in Egypt (remember the hail, accompanied by thunder and fire?),[15] but then certainly with the story (Exod. 19) of the Lord's appearance in 'thunder and lightning, as well as a thick cloud' on Mount Sinai, while 'the whole mountain shook violently' and smoke went up 'like the smoke of a kiln'.[16] The only image in Exodus 19 that does not appear in Psalm 18 is the 'trumpet' which grew louder and louder as the Lord came down to speak with Moses on the mountain.[17]

Wherever David got it from, this storm symbolism for 'theophany' has a long biblical pedigree – maybe given a huge boost by David's dramatic use of it in Psalm 18. It appears elsewhere in the Psalms,[18] and in the hymn

---

[14] This seems to be the best way to understand the imagery in v. 15.

[15] Exod. 9:22–24; cf. Ps. 18:12–13.

[16] Exod. 19:16–18.

[17] Exod. 19:19.

[18] See e.g. Pss 50:3; 68:7–8; 97:1–5.

celebrating Deborah and Barak's victory over Sisera.[19] Isaiah has a special fondness for this kind of symbolism,[20] and Habakkuk develops it powerfully in his famous hymn of trust.[21] We often meet *cosmic* symbols being added to the storm symbols[22] – dramatic shifts in the heavenly bodies or the structure of the earth.[23] The point is, when God intervenes, it's *like* the whole world being shaken and stirred: everything shifts, nothing can be the same again, whether he comes to rescue (as in David's case) or to pour out his wrath in judgment.

And this takes us forward into the New Testament, where the same symbols appear frequently. In Revelation the symbolism of the plagues of Egypt lies behind the dramatic 'trumpet' and 'bowl' sequences (chs. 8 and 16), and 'storm and earthquake' symbols crop up regularly as markers of God's powerful presence and action.[24] Peter uses Joel's vivid symbols to underline the world-changing significance of God's outpouring of the Spirit on the day of Pentecost:

> I will show portents in the heaven above,
>> and signs on the earth below,
>>> blood, and fire, and smoky mist.
> The sun shall be turned to darkness
>> and the moon to blood,
>>> before the coming of the Lord's great and glorious day.[25]

Nobody complained that these cosmic happenings had not literally occurred, and therefore Peter's claim that Joel's prophecy was being fulfilled before their very eyes could not be true. They all knew – because of passages like Psalm 18:7–15 – that this kind of language fits perfectly when God steps in either to save or to judge (or both).

This language clusters around New Testament 'second coming' passages.[26] David gives us a clear steer on how to interpret them: it's likely that

---

[19] Judg. 5:4–5, 20–21.

[20] See e.g. Isa. 19:1; 24:23; 29:6; 30:25–28; 64:1–4.

[21] Hab. 3:3–15.

[22] Hinted at here in Ps. 18:9: *he bowed the heavens . . .*

[23] E.g. Judg. 5:20; Ps. 97:5; Isa. 13:9–10; 30:26; Joel 2:30–31; Hag. 2:6.

[24] See e.g. Rev. 6:12–14; 8:5; 11:19; 16:18–21; 20:11.

[25] Acts 2:19–20.

[26] E.g. Mark 13:24–27 (also 13:7–8); Luke 17:24; 1 Thess. 4:16–17 (Sinai's trumpet reappears!); 2 Pet. 3:10–12.

we should not interpret the language literally, but hear it as symbols underlining the world-shattering impact of the second coming. But of that, more anon.

We can certainly affirm David's experience for ourselves, when we look back on times – glorious *kairos*-moments – when the Lord intervened for us. Usually there are no external, 'out there' signs that some special encounter with the Lord has taken place in our lives. But *we* know. And often this has a hugely galvanizing effect on us. Faith is energized, love is rekindled, relationships or circumstances are transformed. For David, there were dramatic deliverances from Saul's pursuing forces. Even though so much depended on David's own courage and ingenuity (remember the incident with the corner of Saul's robe?),[27] he ascribes all his safety to the Lord:

> [*Those who hated me*] *confronted me in the day of my calamity;*
> > *but the* LORD *was my support.*
> *He brought me out into a broad place;*
> > *he delivered me, because he delighted in me.*
> (18–19)

The *inner* story was not of David's resourcefulness but of his helplessness, and of the Lord's amazing deliverance and equipping.

4. Reading the psalm with Jesus in mind

And the same is true, of course, of 'great David's greater son'. We can read the whole psalm on two levels, one applying to David himself and the other to Jesus the Davidic King of the new covenant. As we thought above, the central section (20–30, on the 'blameless righteousness' which prompted the Lord to act) is uncomfortable reading on the 'David' level. But applied to Jesus – no problem. That section can sit confidently at the heart of the psalm. In fact, looking at the psalm on this second level, we can see a whole-gospel perspective which carries us forward within biblical theology:

- Vv. 4–19 The King in need: rescued from death by the Lord.
- Vv. 20–30 The King in himself: loved and rewarded by the Lord for his blameless righteousness.

---

[27] 1 Sam. 24.

- Vv. 31–45 The King in victory: his victorious rule extending over the nations.

a. The King in need (18:4–19)

The New Testament does not hesitate to apply David's experiences of trouble and deliverance to Jesus' death and resurrection. See, for instance, Peter's quotation of Psalm 16:8–11 on the day of Pentecost, which he too reads on this double level:[28] David says, 'You will not abandon my soul to Hades, or let your Holy One experience corruption',[29] but Peter comments, 'I may say to you confidently of our ancestor David that he both died and was buried, and his tomb is with us to this day!'[30] In other words, read just on the 'David' level, this psalm makes little sense: at the very least we would have to say that David's confidence in deliverance from death was sadly misplaced. But applied to *Jesus*, the new Davidic King, it is gloriously true.

Or we might think of Paul's sermon at Antioch, where he applies the coronation Psalm 2 to Jesus' resurrection, alongside a repeat of Peter's verse from Psalm 16 – connecting it also to Isaiah's prophecy that God will reaffirm 'the holy promises made to David' when he delivers his people.[31] Or, supremely, we might think of Psalm 22, such a powerful and terrible poem of Davidic suffering and deliverance, which Jesus himself takes on his lips on the cross[32] – and to which Matthew then alludes, with great irony, in his description of the crucifixion. In casting lots over his clothes,[33] and in heaping mockery on this condemned, suffering figure,[34] the authorities actually confirm his identity as the Davidic King – right down to the detail of shaking their heads as they mock him.[35]

So we can certainly read verses 4–19 of our psalm as a glorious poetic and prophetic anticipation of the cross and resurrection of the Lord Jesus. Completely entangled in the *cords of death* and swamped by *torrents of perdition* (4), he cries out to the Lord, who crashes through all barriers and brings the skies down in order to rescue his Son and draw him *out of*

[28] Acts 2:25–32.
[29] Acts 2:27; cf. Ps. 16:10.
[30] Acts 2:29.
[31] Acts 13:32–37, quoting Isa. 55:3 as well as Ps. 2:7 and Ps. 16:10.
[32] Matt. 27:46, quoting Ps. 22.1.
[33] Matt. 27:35; Ps. 22:18.
[34] Matt 27:41–43 (cf. 29–31); Ps. 22:7–8.
[35] Matt. 27:39; Ps. 22:7.

mighty waters (16): as Paul puts it (less poetically), 'Christ was raised from the dead by the glory of the Father.'[36]

b. The King in himself (18:20–30)

This wonderful deliverance, we read, takes place *because he delighted in me* (19). 'Delight' is the same word as in Matthew 27:43, to which we referred above – the words of the mockers at the cross, quoting Psalm 22:8: 'let God deliver him now, if he delights in him!'[37] Of course God *does* delight in him, and will surely deliver him: and throughout the New Testament the basis for the resurrection is indeed the unbroken relationship of love between the Father and the Son. That is how the action of the cross and resurrection is one action in which all the persons of the Trinity are involved. God delights in his Son,[38] who always does his will,[39] and whose death constitutes an act of 'obedience' to the Father which is followed by a great divine 'Therefore!' as the Father raises him to life.[40] Paul calls Jesus' death an 'act of righteousness' which parallels Adam's 'trespass': Adam led the world into sin and death, but Jesus' 'act of righteousness leads to justification and life for all'.[41]

So Psalm 18:20–30 applies beautifully to the Lord Jesus as *his* testimony of his relationship to his Father, on the basis of which God first steps in to rescue him from death, and then appoints and equips him to be *head of the nations* (43). It is not completely inappropriate as a description of David either, if we restrict it to that period in his life when he was fleeing from Saul and living by faith (1 Sam. 21 – 31). He was ruthless and deceptive at times, but kept his relationship with God clear, and always sought to obey him rather than serve his own self-interest.

c. The King in victory (18:31–45)

This third main section of the psalm falls into three parts, with a sequence running through them:

---

[36] Rom. 6:4.

[37] NRSV translates 'let God deliver him now, if he wants to' – a possible translation, but one which misses the allusion to Ps. 22:8 (and indeed to Ps. 18:19).

[38] See also Matt. 3:17; 17:5 (cf. 12:18) – though a different word is used here.

[39] See e.g. John 5:30; 8:28–29.

[40] See the language in Phil. 2:8–9.

[41] Rom. 5:18.

- Equipping *for* battle (31–35)
- Victory *in* battle (36–42)
- Supremacy *after* battle (43–45)

Apart from the interesting exaggeration (see our conversation with Ethan above), this all fits as a summary of David's vigorous life as a military leader and campaigner. Once again it is striking how all the agency is ascribed to God. David was a very gifted battle commander, but he attributes all his giftedness, even his physical prowess, to the Lord's equipping of him, and takes no credit himself:

> *For who is God except the LORD?*
> *And who is a rock besides our God? –*
> *the God who girded me with strength,*
> *and made my way safe . .*
> *He trains my hands for war,*
> *so that my arms can bend a bow of bronze.*
> *You have given me the shield of your salvation,*
> *and your right hand has supported me;*
> *your help has made me great.*
> (31–35)

In line with this emphasis, David then ascribes his victories to God's agency, even though he did the actual smiting:

> *I struck them down, so that they were not able to rise;*
> *they fell under my feet.*
> *For you girded me with strength for the battle;*
> *you made my assailants sink under me.*
> (38–39)

And so finally David rejoices in the position these victories have given him, with people offering him obedience and submitting to his rule:

> *you made me head of the nations;*
> *people whom I had not known served me.*
> *As soon as they heard of me they obeyed me;*
> *foreigners came cringing to me.*

Foreigners lost heart,
  and came trembling out of their strongholds.
(43–45)

We must read all this with Jesus in mind, too. As we will see, the second coming is all about Jesus being acknowledged for who he is: he *is* the Lord, but when he comes again all will *see* that he is the Lord, and submit to him. In the meantime, the world is progressively submitting to his rule through the preaching of the gospel. His church does not beat people into submission by force of arms, but wins them into the kingdom; nonetheless there is a battle for their hearts and souls, and 'soul by soul and silently her shining bounds increase'.[42]

Paul gives us a steer on applying this to Jesus in Romans 15:9, where he quotes verse 49:

For this I will extol you, O Lord, among the nations,
  and sing praises to your name.

For Paul, this is one of a string of verses which show that, all along, God's plan was to draw the Gentiles (*the nations*) into membership of his people. Though he had chosen Israel to be his 'treasured possession out of all the peoples',[43] nonetheless that distinction is now being laid aside, Paul taught, and Jews and Gentiles are learning to worship the Lord together as equal members of the same body – the body of Christ. David's military victories, bestowed by the God who has *subdued peoples under me* (47), foreshadow the glorious day when this universal worship will ring out, as worldwide humankind will be united in the praise of the God who has appointed another great King to David's throne.

5. Pulling it all together . . .

So Psalm 18 points us forward, telling us that:

- God comes to us, when we cry out to him. We remember that the Bible ends on the great cry, 'Come, Lord Jesus!'[44]

---

[42] Cecil Spring-Rice (from the hymn 'I Vow to Thee, My Country').
[43] Exod. 19:5.
[44] Rev. 22:20.

- He comes now to rescue us, in our present experience – but his interventions in our lives are tokens of much more to come (and in particular of the final victory which will be his – though Psalm 18 doesn't look this far ahead).
- His victories are through his anointed king – who for us of course is Jesus the Lord.
- His coming can be described in wonderful, world-shaking imagery that underlines how awesome his arrival is.

There is so much to encourage us here. The fact that this is David's 'last will and testament' gives this a whole-life feel. And looking back now over my seventy years, I can certainly echo David's testimony to God's faithfulness, his rescue and his empowering. He has been 'my rock, my fortress, and my deliverer' (2), at every stage. But there is so much more to come! Our next passage moves us into this 'much more', because our individual lives are played out in big contexts – our people, our nation, our world.

Daniel 7:1–28

3. The beasts and the Son of Man

1. A vision at the heart of the Bible

Next we turn to an amazing vision which deeply influences the way the New Testament presents the second coming of Jesus. Daniel had a dream which he wrote down (1), and which left him feeling shocked and overwhelmed: *my thoughts greatly terrified me, and my face turned pale* (28). He felt this reaction during the dream itself: halfway through his account of it he writes that *my spirit was troubled within me, and the visions of my head terrified* me (15). It's important to let the imagery impact us. As you read it now, how does it make you feel?

At the heart of the vision is another theophany (9–14), and we notice some of the great symbols of Psalm 18 reappearing, most notably fire and clouds. But actually this is a vision not just of God but of the whole court that surrounds him as he sits on his *throne* (9–10) – and supremely it's a vision of a great and strange happening there in the throne room as *one like a human being* comes *with the clouds of heaven* to be presented before God (13). This 'humanlike figure'[1] – literally, 'one like a son of man' – then receives from God

> . . . *dominion*
> *and glory and kingship,*
> *that all peoples, nations and languages*
> *should serve him.*

---

[1] Goldingay's translation of 'one like a son of man': John E. Goldingay, *Daniel*, Word Biblical Commentary (Dallas: Word, 1991), p. 142.

His dominion is an everlasting dominion
   that shall not pass away,
and his kingship is one
   that shall never be destroyed.
(14)

We are on holy ground here! This chapter is alluded to some fifty-nine times in the New Testament, including six actual quotations from verses 13–14.[2] In addition, we remember that 'Son of Man' was Jesus' favourite way of referring to himself (thirty times in Matthew's Gospel alone) – a mysterious way of speaking which most people probably thought was just an odd idiosyncrasy. After all, it was God's favourite way of addressing Ezekiel: maybe Jesus was just making himself prophet-like by using this term?[3] But others (chiefly his disciples) began to hear an allusion to the 'one like a son of man' in Daniel 7:13, not least because it clearly connected to Jesus' proclamation of the kingdom of God: 'Repent, for the kingdom of God is arriving!'[4] Because Jesus *showed* the arrival of the kingdom by his own actions – healing, preaching, delivering – it seemed that the kingdom was arriving in and with him: that he had received the 'kingship', as it says in Daniel, and was now dispensing it liberally.

There is an interesting double focus in Jesus' use of the term 'Son of Man'. On the one hand, he uses it of his present activities – for instance, pronouncing forgiveness to the paralysed man who arrived through the roof: he heals him 'so that you may know that the Son of Man has authority on earth to forgive sins'.[5] (The watching 'scribes' were outraged, because they rightly felt that Jesus was exercising *God's* authority.)[6] But on the other hand, Jesus uses 'Son of Man' of a future coming in power, in a way that seems deliberately to recap Daniel's vision:

---

[2] These statistics are drawn from one of the main editions of the Greek New Testament, which includes tables summarizing the use of the Old Testament in the New: K. Aland et al. (eds.), *Novum Testamentum Graece*, 27th edn (Stuttgart: Deutsche Bibelgesellschaft, 1994), pp. 797–798.

[3] See e.g. Ezek. 2:1, 8; 3:1, 4, etc. NRSV translates 'son of man' in Ezekiel as 'mortal'. See how Jesus uses the term – e.g. to individuals (Matt. 8:20) and speaking to crowds (Matt. 11:18–19), to the Pharisees (Matt. 12:8), to his disciples (Matt. 13:37, 41), and supremely at his trial (Matt. 26:63–64).

[4] Matt. 4:17, my translation.

[5] Mark 2:10.

[6] Mark 2:7.

> Then the sign of the Son of Man will appear in heaven, and then all the tribes of the earth will mourn, and they will see 'the Son of Man coming on the clouds of heaven' with power and great glory.[7]

The NRSV puts quotation marks around the central phrase here, because it sees it as a deliberate reference to Daniel 7:13: so Jesus is saying that 'they' – that is, 'all the tribes of the earth' – will one day experience a rerun of Daniel's terrifying vision.

Matthew 24 is one of the central 'second coming' texts of the New Testament, and we will be back there soon![8] But we need to lay some foundations first, and it is important to spend time with this vital text, Daniel 7, so influential within New Testament theology. We notice immediately that Jesus applies its language to *both* his 'comings': to his coming in flesh, his earthly ministry of healing and forgiveness, and also to his coming in glory, his heavenly return. We are caught in the middle, between these two great Arrivals of the kingdom of God, but from the perspective of Daniel 7 these are *one* coming-in-power, by which the kingdom of God displaces the powers of this world – an exciting and powerful perspective, which we will need to revisit frequently in what follows!

2. An overview of the vision

So what exactly did Daniel see and hear? The vision falls into two halves, the division marked by the reference to Daniel's terror in verse 15:

1. The vision seen (2–14)
   a. The beasts and their awful power (2–8)
   b. The thrones and the Son of Man's authority (9–14)
2. The vision interpreted (15–28)
   a. Question 1 – all four beasts (16–18)
   b. Question 2 – the fourth beast (19–27)

The verses that top and tail the vision (1 and 28) are important: they let us know that we are reading an account of his dream which Daniel wrote down immediately afterwards (1), and also that he himself needed to keep *the*

---

[7] Matt. 24:30.

[8] See below, chapter 7.

matter in my mind (28). In other words, he was both terrified and deeply puzzled by what he saw. So he warns us that we may not fully understand it either. But the New Testament application of the vision to Jesus and to both his 'comings' may give us a head start which Daniel himself did not have.

He sees four beasts arising from a very stormy sea, all *different from one another* (3). The first, which *was like a lion and had eagles' wings*, might well have evoked 'Babylon' for his readers, because creatures like this (winged lions) were depicted on the famous Ishtar Gate which Nebuchadnezzar constructed in Babylon. But this 'beast' undergoes a transformation: it is humanized, given *a human mind* (4), just like Nebuchadnezzar in Daniel 4:34. There, actually, Nebuchadnezzar gained a *true* mind for the first time, because he came to see that the 'Most High' alone is sovereign. 'His sovereignty is an everlasting sovereignty, and his kingdom endures from generation to generation,' he says, after his 'reason returns' to him. That matches the view of sovereignty here in Daniel 7, where the 'Ancient of Days'[9] sits on the throne and bestows kingship on the Son of Man.

So maybe the first beast isn't too bad. But beasts 2, 3 and 4 get progressively worse. The second has huge teeth and is told to *Arise, devour many bodies!* (5). No humanizing here. The third is like a leopard with multiple wings and heads to make it more terrifying, and *dominion was given to it* (6). This whole chapter (indeed, the whole book) is about giving dominion – so what's going on, that these terrible beasts receive it? The fourth is the worst of all,

> *terrifying and dreadful and exceedingly strong. It had great iron teeth and was devouring, breaking in pieces, and stamping what was left with its feet. It was different from all the beasts that preceded it, and it had ten horns.*
> (7)

Daniel then witnesses a drama with the horns of this beast: three of them fall out and make room for another horn which has eyes and a mouth that speaks *arrogantly* (8, 11, 20). The first thing that happens when the thrones appear, and the heavenly court sits in judgment, is that this horn is silenced, and

---

[9] NRSV margin.

the beast was put to death, and its body destroyed and given over
to be burned with fire. As for the rest of the beasts, their dominion
was taken away, but their lives were prolonged for a season and
a time
(11–12)

– and then the Son of Man appears, and receives the dominion taken from the beasts (13–14).

But even though the beasts have been destroyed, Daniel is still terrified and puzzled, and the second half of the vision contains a fascinating *interpretation of the matter* given by one of *the attendants* (16) who first appear in verse 10 surrounding the throne. First this attendant explains that the four beasts are basically *four kings* that *shall arise out of the earth* (17), and then, when Daniel asks specifically about the fourth beast, the attendant explains that this beast represents

a fourth kingdom on earth
that shall be different from all the other kingdoms;
it shall devour the whole earth,
and trample it down, and break it to pieces.
(23)

The speaking horn stands for a particular king who will *speak words against the Most High*, and will gain power over *the holy ones of the Most High . . . for a time, two times, and half a time* (25), until *the court shall sit in judgement* and the beast will lose his *dominion* and be *totally destroyed* (26). So the interpretation in verses 19–27 unpacks the quick overthrow of the fourth beast in verse 11, and we realize that it's quite a complicated and painful process, involving much suffering for *the holy ones of the Most High* for a defined period of time. The climax of the interpretation is striking and intriguing:

[After the beast is destroyed] *the kingship and dominion*
and the greatness of the kingdoms under the whole heaven
shall be given to the people of the holy ones of the Most High;
their kingdom shall be an everlasting kingdom,
and all dominions shall serve and obey them.
(27)

Strangely, the rule of the Son of Man becomes here the rule of *the people of the holy ones of the Most High* – who are they? We will tackle this question shortly, but first let's ask, with Daniel . . .

3. Who are these 'beasts'?

What a fascinating question this is! The main option has been to try to identify four successive empires, perhaps starting from the clue that the first beast looks a little like Babylon. A popular solution has been the following:

1. The Babylonian Empire
2. The Medes and Persians
3. The Greek Empire (Alexander the Great)
4. The Roman Empire[10]

Roman rule was certainly cruel and brutal, in many respects, and would fit the picture of the fourth beast pretty well, except that it wasn't in essence atheistic or opposed to religion. Generally, Jews were well treated under Roman rule. Persecution both of Jews and of Christians broke out occasionally and locally, but it wasn't a central feature of Roman power, as the picture of the blasphemous horn and its victory might suggest. Actually a simple sequence of empires like this is hard to maintain in detail, as the careful discussion by John Goldingay shows.[11] In any case, Daniel's 'attendant' says that the beasts are *kings*, rather than empires (17), even though later he describes the fourth beast as a *kingdom* (23), and says that all of the ten horns, and the single blasphemous horn, are *kings* of this kingdom (24).

So it's complicated! Are they kings, or kingdoms? Or both? And how are we to account for the strange differences between the beasts, and for the particular role of the fourth beast in 'wearing out' (persecuting?) *the holy ones of the Most High* (25)?

I think that the book of Revelation comes to our aid here – and in so doing, reminds us that Scripture is its own best interpreter. John too sees

---

[10] See for instance Joyce Baldwin, *Daniel: An Introduction and Commentary*, Tyndale Old Testament Commentaries (Leicester: Inter-Varsity Press, 1978), p. 147.

[11] Goldingay, *Daniel*, pp. 173–176.

'a beast rising out of the sea'.[12] This one has 'ten horns and seven heads' – bizarre physically, but the point is that this is the total number of horns and heads shared by Daniel's four beasts: and as we go on through John's vision it becomes clear that his 'beast' is a careful amalgam of Daniel's four. It is 'like a leopard', with bear's feet and a lion's mouth.[13] It too speaks 'haughty and blasphemous words' against God and the inhabitants of heaven,[14] and is 'allowed to make war on the saints and to conquer them'.[15] The period of its rule is the same, too: 'it was allowed to exercise authority for forty-two months,' John says:[16] and if we take *a time, two times, and half a time* in Daniel 7:25 as years, the numbers correspond.[17] Truly, John's beast is a Big Beast, four made one.

John was a careful reader and interpreter of Scripture. Clearly, in reading Daniel 7, he did not feel challenged to identify four empires or individual tyrants as bestial candidates. Rather, he saw all four as *together* exemplifications of 'bestiality' – that is, as manifestations of the way in which secular power can conduct itself, from something quite mild and human (like Nebuchadnezzar at the end of Daniel 4, and indeed Cyrus the Persian who allowed the Jews to return from exile)[18] through to something truly horrendous, like the Rome he had seen in action under the emperor Nero, persecuting Christians as scapegoats for the fire of Rome and turning them into human torches to illuminate his gardens.

John's approach to the interpretation of Daniel 7 helps us greatly. Why should we not read it the same way? One very clear point of contact lies in the little phrase 'was given' – used in Daniel 7:4 and 6 about the *mind* and the *dominion* 'given' to the first and third beasts, and in Revelation 13:5 and 7 about the 'mouth' and the 'authority' given to the Beast to speak blasphemies and to wage war on 'the saints'.[19] Who is doing the giving, in both cases? Daniel's consistent position is that God alone, 'the God of

---

[12] Rev. 13:1.

[13] Rev. 13:2.

[14] Rev. 13:5–6.

[15] Rev. 13:7.

[16] Rev. 13:5.

[17] The same period appears as days in Dan. 12:11 and Rev. 11:9, 11; 12:6; cf. Rev. 11:2–3; 12:14. See Ian Paul, *Revelation*, Tyndale New Testament Commentaries (London: Inter-Varsity Press, 2018), pp. 195, 197–199.

[18] See Dan. 6:28.

[19] The NRSV has 'was allowed' in Rev. 13:5, 7, but the verb is the same as in the Greek version of Daniel 7 – 'was given'.

heaven', gives 'the kingdom, the power, the might, and the glory' which earthly potentates wield.[20] He is the one who

changes times and seasons,
  deposes kings and sets up kings;
. . . gives wisdom to the wise
  and knowledge to those who have understanding.
He reveals deep and hidden things[21]

– and all that is now happening in this vision.

So the beasts, I suggest, are not particular kings or kingdoms, but they stand for *all* secular rulers and powers, all governments and regimes, all democracies and autocracies, all monarchies and tyrannies, whether benevolent or oppressive or somewhere in the middle, and Daniel says to them all: God gave you your power, and will one day take it away and give it to the Son of Man. And if you misuse your power and persecute God's people, know that your days are numbered, and when your time is up, your *dominion* will be *taken away, to be consumed and totally destroyed* (26). You have been warned![22]

Daniel's interpretation of Nebuchadnezzar's dream in Daniel 2:31–45 lays the foundation for this. Nebuchadnezzar dreamed of a statue smashed by a stone 'cut from the mountain not by hands' (2:34, 45), which then expands to fill the whole earth. Daniel tells him that the stone represents a kingdom to be set up by 'the God of heaven' – which will crush all other kingdoms and then 'stand for ever' (2:44).

No wonder there is slippage between 'king' and 'kingdom' in the description of the beasts. They were pretty synonymous anyway, in Daniel's world. All secular rule has the potential to go the way of the fourth beast. Rulers can turn, and go 'rogue', and suddenly the earth is being devoured, trampled and broken by despotic power (7:23). But things can move in the opposite direction, too: awful tyrants like Nebuchadnezzar can change, and learn who gave them their power, and encourage the worship of 'the King of Heaven'.[23] And whatever rulers do, God is in

---

[20] Dan. 2:37; see also Dan. 4:17, 25, 32; 5:18, 21 – and then 7:6.
[21] Dan. 2:21–22.
[22] For a similar reflection on the 'dialogue' between Daniel and Revelation, see Paul, *Revelation*, pp. 234–235.
[23] Dan. 4:34–37.

charge. Daniel faithfully serves the tyrant king, underneath his prior loyalty to the 'God of heaven' who has called and equipped him to serve, because beasts are raised to power by God, and God will also bring about their demise, in due course.

So that's how Daniel's vision sets the scene for the second coming of Jesus. God's plan is to dethrone all secular authority and to establish his own kingdom under the dominion of the Son of Man. This essentially *political* vision of the second coming – its direct relation to human authorities as their *replacement* – will carry us right through the Bible. Daniel lays the foundation!

4. Who is the 'son of man'?

It would be easy to answer this question simply with, 'Jesus.' And of course that is true, looking back from a New Testament perspective. But we must first listen to Daniel himself, before we read him in the light of where his vision lands up later. And here in Daniel 7 we don't meet 'the Son of Man' at all. It's 'one like a son of man' (literally), or *one like a human being* (NRSV), 'a humanlike figure' (John Goldingay). And there is a most intriguing slippage around this figure also. The vague individual who appears in verse 13 then receives *dominion and glory and kingship – a kingship . . . that shall never be destroyed* (14), like the kingdom in Nebuchadnezzar's dream,[24] and the kingdom of the Most High himself.[25] So it seems that this 'human figure' will be a king!

But when the vision is then explained by the attendant, it's not an individual who receives the kingdom after the overthrow of the beasts: *But the holy ones of the Most High shall receive the kingdom and possess the kingdom for ever – for ever and ever* (18). Similarly, when the horn *made war with the holy ones and was prevailing over them* (21), *the Ancient One came; then judgement was given for the holy ones of the Most High, and the time arrived when the holy ones gained possession of the kingdom* (22). And finally, after the blasphemous 'horn' is overthrown, we read that *the people of the holy ones of the Most High* are to receive *the kingship and dominion and the greatness of the kingdoms under the whole heaven* (27).

---

[24] Dan. 2:44.

[25] Dan. 4:34.

Extraordinary! The 'son of man' is not mentioned again after verse 13, but is replaced by this wider group, *the people of the holy ones of the Most High*. Since they appear in the attendant's explanation, maybe the 'son of man' is just a symbol for this group. Daniel sees an individual human figure, but the attendant explains that this figure stands for a whole 'people' who are to be persecuted but then delivered, to enjoy an *everlasting kingdom* and the service and obedience of all other *dominions*.

What 'people' might this be? *The holy ones* could be angels, as we'll see in the next chapter.[26] But in this context that would not make much sense, and the addition of *the people* in verse 27 suggests that they are his people Israel. This would make glorious sense in Daniel's original setting, with Israel enslaved in Babylon and longing for release. But what about the universal rule promised to them? When release eventually came, at the hands of Cyrus king of Persia,[27] the exiled Israelites streamed back to Judah (42,360 of them, according to Ezra)[28] and immediately set about reinstating the worship of the temple. But it was hardly a glorious new start. Certainly not a release into dominion over former enemies. In the teeth of local opposition it took them years to rebuild the temple,[29] and decades later, when Nehemiah came on the scene, the city was still in ruins.[30] They could hardly have felt that their experience looked like a fulfilment of Daniel's vision. In fact, there was never a point, in all the following centuries, when Israel looked like a world-beating power. So it's not surprising that the New Testament authors, prompted by Jesus himself, began to read the chapter differently, interpreting the 'son of man' figure not as a symbol but as a real individual. *He* receives the dominion: and then, as a result of *his* exaltation, God's people are delivered too.

Paul never calls Jesus 'the Son of Man', but we can see the influence of this way of reading Daniel 7 behind, for instance, Ephesians 1:20–23:

> God put this power to work in Christ when he raised him from the dead and seated him at his right hand in the heavenly places, far above all rule and authority and power and dominion, and above every name that is named, not only in this age but also in the age to come. And he has put

---

26 See Zech. 14:5 (also 1 Thess. 3:13).

27 See Dan. 6:28; Isa. 44:24 – 45:7; Ezra 1:1–4.

28 Ezra 2:64.

29 Ezra 6:15.

30 Neh. 1:3.

all things under his feet and has made him the head over all things for the church, which is his body, the fullness of him who fills all in all.[31]

This is Daniel 7 in action. Jesus' exaltation to the highest dominion means that 'the church' (you and I!) are exalted there too, because we are his body. There is a kind of identity between 'the Son of Man' and *the people of the holy ones of the Most High*: in the end they share the same rule! What is left as a puzzle in Daniel becomes clear when we look at the relationship between Jesus, the exalted Son of Man, and his people, who are raised not just to new life but also to *rule* in him. Clinton Arnold has shown how the 'power' language in Ephesians – illustrated in this passage in Ephesians 1 – draws not just on Daniel but even more on the situation in Ephesus, which was a centre of magic and occult practices as well as of pagan religions. So the Christians there knew all about 'powers' at work around them, and 'names being named' in order to make magic spells work.[32]

We know all about that, too. In some parts of the world occult practices still carry great power, but *everywhere* people's lives are determined by powers beyond their control – powers political, military, economic, cultural and spiritual. In relation to all these powers Daniel offers us the 'Son of Man', Jesus Christ. His first coming forges that solidarity between him and his people, implicit in the fascinating 'slippage' we see in Daniel between the individual and the people. He takes our flesh as his own, and shares it completely, including our death.[33] He shares our suffering under the power of the beasts, whose lives are *prolonged for a season and a time* (12), even though the ultimate power is his. We are in that *season and . . . time* now: and like Paul's readers in Ephesus, we know that the 'powers' which seem to rule in the world around us now have a Ruler over them, the risen Christ whose power over them is 'for us'.

But his second coming is coming! On that day the ultimate rulership of Christ will be plain and realized by all, and we will rule in and with him:

> *The kingship and dominion*
> > *and the greatness of the kingdoms under the whole heaven*
> > *shall be given to the people of the holy ones of the Most High;*

---

[31] Other Old Testament passages are influencing Paul here too – most notably Isaiah 53 and Psalms 110 and 8.

[32] C. E. Arnold, *Ephesians: Power and Magic – The Concept of Power in Ephesians in Light of Its Historical Setting* (Cambridge: Cambridge University Press, 1989).

[33] Cf John 1:14; Heb. 2:14–15.

their kingdom shall be an everlasting kingdom,
   and all dominions shall serve and obey them.
(27)

The rest of this book is about exploring what this amazing vision means.

Zechariah 14:1–21

4. 'A day is coming for the LORD'!

We move on some years from Daniel – to 520 BC, in fact, when Zechariah begins to prophesy.[1] This is eighteen years after the end of the exile, but the story of the return to Judah and Jerusalem has not been glorious. It's been a tale of poverty and disillusion. Without effective leadership, the returning exiles have not rebuilt either the city or the temple, and have been scratching out an existence among ruins. But Zechariah is part of a renewal movement: two months before he begins to speak, the prophet Haggai was instrumental in gingering the people into action, to begin rebuilding the temple.[2] For both Haggai and Zechariah, it's about re-envisioning the people with a sense of their God as one who *acts*, and who will step in to rescue and rebuild his people. We can find the heart of Zechariah's message in 2:10–12:

> Sing and rejoice, O daughter Zion! For lo, I will come and dwell in your midst, says the LORD. Many nations shall join themselves to the LORD on that day, and shall be my people; and I will dwell in your midst. And you shall know that the LORD of hosts has sent me to you. The LORD will inherit Judah as his portion in the holy land, and will again choose Jerusalem.

This thought, that *God himself will come* to live with his people, is a keynote through Zechariah,[3] and forms the heart of the visionary prophecy in chapter 14 with which the book reaches its climax:

---

[1] See the date in Zech. 1:1; cf. 7:1.

[2] See Hag. 1:1–15.

[3] See Zech. 1:3, 16; 2:5, 10; 8:3, 23; 9:9; 14:4–5.

On that day his feet shall stand on the Mount of Olives, which lies before
Jerusalem on the east; and the Mount of Olives shall be split in two from
east to west by a very wide valley; so that half of the Mount shall withdraw
northwards, and the other half southwards. And you shall flee by the
valley of the LORD's mountain, for the valley between the mountains shall
reach to Azal; and you shall flee as you fled from the earthquake in the
days of King Uzziah of Judah. Then the LORD my God will come, and all
the holy ones with him.
(4–5)

For us, of course, the vital question is: what is this coming? – specifically, is it the second coming? Many writers apply this passage
without hesitation to the second coming of Christ, on the grounds that
(as John MacArthur puts it) 'nothing like that occurred at His first
coming', and therefore this prophecy 'awaits future fulfilment at the
Second Coming of Christ'.[4] If this is right, a second question then
becomes pressing: how literally should we interpret this prophecy (and
others like it)? Should we expect that the second coming will take place
at Jerusalem, and involve landscape remodelling and flight from the city,
as described here?

These are difficult questions. We need careful sensitivity to what
Zechariah writes, and in particular a careful sense of the way in which
these prophecies were 'heard' and used by New Testament writers. As
with Daniel 7, the New Testament use of the passage gives us a good steer
as we seek to hear the message of Zechariah 14 for today.

1. An overview of Zechariah 14

As Joyce Baldwin points out,[5] the chapter has a dramatic chiastic structure,
pivoting around the wonderful 'coming of the Lord' in the centre:

A. Battle, defeat and plundering (1–2)
(The nations gather to overcome Jerusalem.)

---

[4] John MacArthur, *The Second Coming: Signs of Christ's Return and the End of the Age* (Wheaton, IL:
Crossway, 2003), p. 33. MacArthur sees these verses as a description of 'the millennial kingdom, which Christ
will establish immediately in the wake of His coming' (p. 131).

[5] Joyce G. Baldwin, *Haggai, Zechariah, Malachi: An Introduction and Commentary*, Tyndale Old Testament
Commentaries (London: Tyndale Press, 1972), p. 199. The analysis that follows differs somewhat from
Baldwin's, however.

B. The Lord intervenes! (3–9)
- in the battle (3–5)
- in the world (6–9)

A'. Peace, restoration and holiness (10–21)
- peace and security (10–11)
- battle reversed, plunder restored (12–15)
- the nations gather for worship in Jerusalem (16–21)

So the chapter begins and ends with *the nations* gathering at Jerusalem – first to battle against it and loot it (2), but then (after the Lord's intervention) to *worship the King, the LORD of hosts, and to keep the festival of booths* (16). The opening picture of battle, rape, pillage and new exile is truly horrifying. The returned exiles, newly launched on their temple-building project, might well feel deeply despondent about this – but might then ask, Is Zechariah actually talking about what we've been through already? Indeed, earlier in Zechariah the suffering is *past*, and the blessing future:

> Just as you have been a cursing among the nations, O house of Judah and house of Israel, so I will save you and you shall be a blessing. Do not be afraid, but let your hands be strong.
>
> For thus says the LORD of hosts: Just as I purposed to bring disaster upon you, when your ancestors provoked me to wrath, and I did not relent, says the LORD of hosts, so again I have purposed in these days to do good to Jerusalem and to the house of Judah; do not be afraid.[6]

The double command here, 'Do not be afraid',[7] is undermined by this later prophecy of coming defeat – unless the future tense in 14:2 actually reflects their past experience. Having said this, however, the terrible events of sixty years before, when the Babylonians sacked Jerusalem, were but the first of many occasions over the centuries when Jerusalem was 'surrounded by armies . . . taken away as captives among all nations' and 'trampled on by the Gentiles', as Jesus puts it.[8] So, even if Zechariah's first hearers could legitimately read this prophecy as reflecting their *past* experience, future

---

[6] Zech. 8:13–15.
[7] Zech. 8:13, 15.
[8] Luke 21:20–24.

generations of readers know that terrible, repeated suffering lay ahead for Jerusalem.

But the real burden of this prophecy is not the coming suffering, but the glorious future that the Lord will unfold for his people. Specifically:

- His victory over all attacking forces and his rescue of his people (3–5a).
- His personal presence, transforming night into perpetual day (5b–7).
- A stream of perpetual *living waters* flowing out from Jerusalem to east and west (8).[9]
- Further landscape transformation – hills flattened to north and south, and Jerusalem lifted up in perpetual security (10–11).
- Terrible suffering for *all the peoples that wage war against Jerusalem* (12) – reminiscent of the defeat of Sennacherib's army two hundred years before[10] (12–13).
- The restoration of all the plunder, and more besides: wealth pours into Jerusalem from *the surrounding nations* (14).
- A beefed-up *festival of booths* (Tabernacles), now an international festival for all *the families of the earth* (17), with an ironic re-enactment of the plagues of Egypt: previously, the plagues were a punishment on Egypt for stopping Israel from leaving to worship the Lord;[11] now, they are a punishment on Egypt for refusing to leave to worship the Lord themselves (16–19).
- And finally, universal holiness: spreading even to the harnesses of the horses that bring the worshippers. No longer will *traders* be needed to help visitors comply with temple regulations (21b), because all will be holy already (20–21).

What a superb and gripping picture! We can well imagine the impact on Zechariah's hearers. Confidence grew, and the temple restoration was completed two years after this prophecy.[12]

But what does it mean for us today? Written on such a grand scale, Zechariah's prophecy has migrated out of its original setting and become

---

[9] In Ezekiel's similar (and more detailed) vision, the water flows only to the east: Ezek. 47:1–12.

[10] 2 Kgs 18 – 19; Isa. 37.

[11] See e.g. Exod. 7:15–17.

[12] See Ezra 6:14–16.

'the word of the Lord' for all God's people, not just for his first hearers. And this is not least because, written on such a grand scale, it could never be fulfilled in the limited and local conditions of the sixth century BC! There was then no mechanism by which 'all the nations' could be gathered to fight Jerusalem – there was no 'international world order'[13] which could organize this. And there was certainly no point, either then or in the succeeding centuries, when verse 9 became true – *And the LORD will become king over all the earth; on that day the LORD will be one and his name one*, that is, Yahweh, Israel's Lord, is recognized as the one King and God of all the earth – so that *the surrounding nations* start donating their *wealth* to Jerusalem (14), and *all who survive of the nations* begin trekking up to Jerusalem for the feast of Tabernacles (16). It never happened. So maybe John MacArthur is right: because this has never yet been fulfilled, it must refer to events surrounding the second coming of Christ. Is he right?

To get a handle on this, we need to look more widely, particularly at the impact of this passage on New Testament writers. But we will start by thinking about a very important expression in this passage:

2. 'The day of the Lord'

Zechariah is latching onto a widespread prophetic theme by his repeated reference to 'the day' that is coming. After his opening *See, a day is coming for the LORD* (1), he uses the phrase *on that day* seven times,[14] including the very last words of the chapter (21), so that the vision begins and ends with references to this coming 'day'. Similarly 'on that day' occurs nine times in the preceding oracle, chapters 12–13. The full phrase 'the day of the Lord' occurs twenty-two times in the prophets, with countless further references to 'the day' or 'that day' when some significant event will occur.

Thomas McComiskey comments: 'The day of the Lord in prophetic literature designates any time when Yahweh steps into the arena of human events to effect his purposes.'[15] It does not, therefore, have to mean 'the end times' or 'the last day', but simply points to some clear and decisive intervention by God in fulfilment of his purposes. For instance, Lamentations calls the events of 586 BC (when Jerusalem fell to the Babylonians)

---

[13] Joyce Baldwin's phrase: *Haggai, Zechariah, Malachi*, p. 200.

[14] Vv. 4, 6, 8, 9, 13, 20, 21.

[15] Thomas E. McComiskey, 'Zechariah', in T. E. McComiskey (ed.), *The Minor Prophets: An Exegetical and Expository Commentary*, vol. 3 (Grand Rapids, MI: Baker, 1998), p. 1227.

48

'the day of the anger of the LORD'.[16] This is why – as we have already seen – such interventions are often described with 'world-bending' language, storm symbols or images of earthly and cosmic disruption: and Zechariah 14 is no exception. The landscape reshaping in verses 4–5 and 10, and the change in the normal procession of night and day (6–7),[17] and the living waters flowing even in the parched summer months (8) – all these have that quality of 'divine presence' symbols like those we met in Psalm 18. The point is that God steps in to rescue his people, and a gloriously vivid way of underlining his determination is to picture him knocking a huge valley through the Mount of Olives so that they can easily flee to the east. His 'day' is the day when he acts to fulfil his covenant promises to his people – in judgment or salvation, or both – and to work out his plans for the earth.

What are those purposes, as we see them in Zechariah 14? There are five of them:

- Unite his people with himself in a shared life in which he is personally present with them (5b).
- Fully provide for his people's needs – symbolized here by the never-failing *light* (7), the ever-flowing *living waters* (8) and the *gold, silver, and garments* collected *in great abundance* for them (14).
- Overcome all forces that seek to frustrate his plan to save his people (3, 12–13).
- Extend his rule worldwide, drawing all the nations into his kingdom alongside Israel (9, 16).[18]
- Bring people of all nations together into worship which celebrates his saving actions for them, making them as *holy to the LORD* (20) as the temple is (16–21).

So here's the thing: whenever we see or experience the fulfilment of any of these purposes, that moment is 'the day of the Lord', in prophetic terms! And Zechariah would say to us: Yes, that's what I meant. This

---

[16] Lam. 2:22.

[17] The Hebrew is difficult in v. 6: it says (literally), 'And it will be in that day that there will be no light; the glorious things will congeal' (this is McComiskey's translation: 'Zechariah', p. 1232). The references to 'cold' and 'frost' in NIV and NRSV are drawn from the Septuagint. We can probably understand 'the glorious things' to be the great heavenly lights, which cease to work and are replaced by the Lord's own continuous light.

[18] Cf. Zech. 2:11; 8:20–23; 9:10.

means that we should not primarily look for literal fulfilment of these prophecies: for instance, monumental earthworks on the Mount of Olives, or two literal rivers flowing east and west from Jerusalem – amazing though such happenings would be. Actually, as summarized in these five points, we look for greater things than these. And I believe that the way in which Zechariah 14 is used in the New Testament encourages us in this approach.

3. The New Testament helps our interpretation

Zechariah is widely quoted and alluded to in the New Testament. In fact, among the prophets, only Isaiah and Daniel are more influential (in proportion to length). There are some very significant quotations of verses from earlier chapters – most notably the prophecy about the lowly king riding into Jerusalem on a donkey, which Jesus took steps to fulfil when he entered the city just before his death,[19] and the two verses in chapters 12–13 which are applied to the crucifixion: that the inhabitants of Jerusalem shall 'look on the one whom they have pierced',[20] and 'strike the shepherd, that the sheep may be scattered', quoted by Jesus of the disciples deserting him at his arrest.[21]

Focusing on chapter 14, it is remarkable that *all five of God's purposes, listed above, are picked up and unpacked, in different ways, in the New Testament* – in three cases with clear allusion to our chapter. We see the fulfilment of Zechariah's vision explained to us, as we read the New Testament, and this should firmly guide us as we read Zechariah 14 for today. We will take each of the five in turn.

a. The Lord comes to live with his people

The glorious promise in verse 5b summarizes this: *Then the Lord my God will come, and all the holy ones with him.* Since his feet have already landed on the Mount of Olives (4), this must be like a triumphal entry into the city, from which all enemies have now been expelled. The *holy ones* here are probably angels – the vast host of 'attendants' whom we met in Daniel 7,

---

[19] Zech. 9:9: see Matt. 21:1–6. It may be that the Gospels' emphasis that this took place on 'the Mount of Olives' (Matt. 21:1; Mark 11:1; Luke 19:29) alludes to Zech. 14:4a.

[20] Zech. 12:10: quoted in Rev. 1:7 with reference to the second coming (alluded to also in Matt. 24:30), and in John 19:37 with reference to the piercing of Jesus' side at the crucifixion.

[21] Zech. 13:7, quoted in Mark 14:27 // Matt. 26:31.

and who now accompany their Lord as he comes to live with his people. Paul echoes this verse in 1 Thessalonians 3:13, where he prays for the Thessalonians, 'May he so strengthen your hearts in holiness that you may be blameless before our God and Father at the coming of our Lord Jesus with all his saints.' Here 'saints' and 'holy ones' translate the same word. Paul could also mean angels, because Jesus teaches that angels will accompany the 'Son of Man' when he comes in glory.[22] But Paul is also going to tell the Thessalonians that their already-dead loved ones will not miss out on the coming of the Lord, but will accompany him when he comes.[23] So they are probably the 'holy ones' in 3:13. The NRSV, by translating it 'saints', has opted for this interpretation.

So we can certainly apply Zechariah 14:5b to the second coming! That is when, supremely, the Lord will come to live with his people. But we need to add three important observations.

First, Paul clearly did not believe that the Lord will come again *at Jerusalem*. He does not tell the Thessalonians (who lived about 930 miles from Jerusalem, as the crow flies) that they will *hear tell* of the Lord's arrival there, and if they quickly pay the hefty fee and jump on a ship they will be able to set eyes on him. Hard luck if you can't afford it. Paul believed that the Lord's return will be *to the earth*, and not to a particular place on it.

Second, how amazing it is that, for Paul, the 'Lord' who comes is *the Lord Jesus*. In 1 Thessalonians 3:13, as in many New Testament verses, Old Testament scriptures originally about Yahweh, Israel's 'Lord', are applied to *Jesus* the Lord.[24]

Third, it would be a very poor deal for Zechariah's hearers if the second coming of Jesus was the *only* way in which the Lord will 'come' to be with his people. He comes in many other ways – not least through the ministries of Haggai and Zechariah, and through others like Ezra and Nehemiah who led the rebuilding of temple and city. In the person of his Son his feet came to stand on the Mount of Olives, and he lives among us still in the person of his Spirit. But only that final, climactic coming will remodel the landscape of Planet Earth in the way Zechariah foresaw, and unite the nations around their Lord!

---

[22] See Matt. 24:31. Paul echoes this teaching in 2 Thess. 1:7.

[23] 1 Thess. 4:14.

[24] The same Greek word *kurios* is used of both. See Larry Kreitzer, *Jesus and God in Paul's Eschatology*, JSNTSup 19 (Sheffield: Sheffield Academic Press, 1987). He discusses 1 Thess. 3:13 on pp. 117–118.

b. The Lord meets his people's needs

The picture of the plundering of the nations (14) is picked up in Revelation 21:24–26, where 'the glory and the honour of the nations' are brought into the heavenly city: all that is great and wonderful about this world, including its great human achievements, is preserved and celebrated in the new creation. We must wait to see what that will mean! But it is the images of *continuous day* (7) and the *living waters* flowing from Jerusalem which chiefly capture the Lord's provision for his people here. *Living* means 'life-giving', and it is easy to feel the meaning of this if you stand in a parched Middle Eastern landscape longing for water.

Both these images are picked up in Revelation as features of the new Jerusalem. John tells us that 'the city has no need of sun or moon to shine on it, for the glory of God is its light, and its lamp is the Lamb . . . There will be no more night!'[25] Similarly the city is nourished by 'the river of the water of life, bright as crystal, flowing from the throne of God and of the Lamb through the middle of the street of the city'.[26] Both images point outwards also: 'the nations will walk by its light',[27] we hear, and the river feeds the tree of life whose leaves 'are for the healing of the nations'.[28] As in Zechariah, Jerusalem's rebuilding is for the blessing of all.

But it is not just a blessing for the end times. Jesus famously picks up Zechariah's *living waters* image in his words in John 7:37–38: 'Let anyone who is thirsty come to me, and let the one who believes in me drink. As the scripture has said, "Out of the believer's heart shall flow rivers of living water."'[29] About which John comments, 'Now he said this about the Spirit, which believers in him were to receive; for as yet there was no Spirit, because Jesus was not yet glorified.'[30]

'Living water' is a gift given by Jesus the Messiah, as the Samaritan woman learned in her conversation with Jesus by the well:[31] and as we enter into the full enjoyment of the life of the Spirit *now*, we are beginning to experience that life-nourishment which we will fully experience only when the waters of the new Jerusalem are flooding out into the world.

---

[25] Rev. 21:23; 22:5. 'Night' is a symbol of evil and separation from God.

[26] Rev. 22:1–2.

[27] Rev. 21:24.

[28] Rev. 22:2. We look at these passages in chapters 18 and 19 below.

[29] The Greek is hard to translate here, and it could be that Jesus himself is the source of the 'living water', rather than the believer. Also, no scripture says exactly this, so probably Zechariah is one of several Old Testament passages in mind – see also Exod. 17:6; Ps. 46:4–5; Isa. 44:3–5; Jer. 2:13; Ezek. 47:1–12.

[30] John 7:39.

[31] John 4:10, 14.

c. The Lord will overcome all opponents

The Lord is a warrior. He fights for his people and of course wins the battle (3, 12–13). The language in verse 12 is gruesome, and reflects what soldiers have seen on many a battlefield after the battle: except that Zechariah pictures the decay setting in before death! This underlines the absolute certainty of the Lord's victory. As we will see in coming chapters, the second coming is closely associated with final judgment as an essential element in setting the world to rights, and 'battle' is often used as a picture of this process.

However, what are we to make of the fact that, sadly, Jerusalem has not been immune from defeat as apparently promised here? Before the destruction of the city by the Romans in AD 70, which Jesus prophesies in Matthew 24, Jerusalem was overcome by the Syrians in 167 BC and by the Romans in 63 BC – not to mention the Persians in AD 614, the Muslims in 637 and the Crusaders in 1099! We need to look for a bigger fulfilment of this promise, looking especially to Revelation which teaches us to see this impregnable Jerusalem differently: she's a *heavenly* city adorned like a bride for her wedding![32]

d. The Lord will draw all nations into his worldwide rule

And the LORD *will become king over all the earth; on that day the* LORD *will be one and his name one* (9). This reflects the famous language of the 'Shema', the confession in Deuteronomy 6:4 which Jews recited morning and evening: 'Hear, O Israel, the LORD our God, the LORD is one!'[33] But whereas the Shema is an affirmation of a *present* truth, Zechariah has made it a *prospect* as if it is not yet true: as if the Lord cannot truly be 'one' while his world is divided and the nations gather to fight his people. Interestingly, Paul appeals in a similar way to the Shema when expounding his doctrine of justification by faith:

> Is God the God of Jews only? Is he not the God of Gentiles also?
> Yes, of Gentiles also, since God is one; and he will justify the
> circumcised on the ground of faith and the uncircumcised through
> that same faith.[34]

---

[32] Rev. 21:2.

[33] Literal translation. The word 'shema' is the first word in the Hebrew, 'hear!'

[34] Rom. 3:29–30.

God's *oneness* is the foundation on which rests his treatment of all people on the same basis, in spite of the covenant distinction that made Israel different. Finally, he is 'the LORD of all the earth',[35] not just the God of Israel.

e. The Lord will bring all peoples into united holiness and worship

Zechariah pictures a magnificent international feast of Tabernacles with free access for all, and – amazingly – no restrictions based on the *impurity* of the Gentile participants (16–21). This amazing vision brings his whole prophecy to an almost unbelievable conclusion. Really? – in spite of the fact that so much of the law is devoted to separating the impure from the holy, so that the holy things and places at the heart of the worship are not contaminated? Actually – as with Jesus touching the leper[36] – in Zechariah's vision the 'infection' is running in the opposite direction: the holy is infecting the impure, spreading outwards, touching even the bridles and bells on the horses that bring the worshippers to Jerusalem (20).

And that's who we are: 'saints', 'holy ones'. How delighted Paul must have been, against this background, to use the word 'saints' as his usual description of Gentile believers in Jesus – no fewer than thirty-eight times in his letters![37]

Zechariah's final comment takes us straight into Jesus' ministry: *And there shall no longer be traders in the house of the LORD of hosts on that day* (21). Jesus must have had this verse in mind when he entered the temple, fired up with Isaiah's vision that it should be 'a house of prayer for all the nations',[38] and started driving the traders out. The traders were actually meant to be helpful to visitors, enabling them to buy the necessary supplies for their worship using the special temple currency. But their presence simply accentuated the separation of the 'holy' from the worshippers who could not participate without the necessary coins and provisions: and in any case, Gentile worshippers could not progress beyond the first court because of their 'impurity'. All this is to be overthrown, as we Gentiles pile into the (heavenly) temple courts with no restriction.

When is *that day* (Zechariah's very last words)? It's *any day of God's intervention*. It was the day when Jesus overthrew the tables. It's the day

---

35 Zech. 6:5.

36 Mark 1:40–42.

37 See e.g. Rom. 1:7; 1 Cor. 1:2.

38 Mark 11:17, quoting Isa. 56:7.

whenever Gentiles worship the God of Israel with awe and love.[39] And it will be the glorious day when Jesus comes again and 'every knee [shall] bend, in heaven and on earth and under the earth, and every tongue . . . confess that Jesus Christ is Lord, to the glory of God the Father'![40]

So we leave the Old Testament braced by the hope that Zechariah communicated to his generation: hope of the *day* that is *coming for the* LORD when the Lord himself will stand upon the earth and transform it by his ruling presence. It has not yet come, and we hope for it still – but how does the New Testament teach us to frame our hope?

---

[39] See Rom. 15:8–12.

[40] Phil. 2:10–11.

Part 2
The second coming in the Gospels and Acts

Acts 1:6–11; 3:17–21

5. Refreshments to follow

Into the New Testament! We start with two fascinating passages in Acts that point forward to the second coming right at the beginning of Luke's history of the earliest church. Interestingly, these passages contain the only references to the second coming in the whole of Acts: after the prominent prediction of it by the angels at the start (passage 1), and Peter's subsequent reference in his sermon in Acts 3 (passage 2), the second coming disappears from view in Luke's narrative. He never mentions it again. Why is this? An interesting answer emerges in passage 1, as we'll see.

1. Passage 1 (Acts 1:6–11): quick overview

Luke tells us that, after the resurrection, Jesus 'presented himself alive' to the apostles 'by many convincing proofs, appearing to them over the course of forty days and speaking about the kingdom of God'.[1] This was no passing contact with Jesus – Luke actually uses an interesting and unusual word in verse 4 which is best translated 'while staying with them'. He didn't just pop in from time to time. In fact, verse 6 begins in a way which suggests that they made arrangements to meet at specific times: *So when they had come together, they asked him, 'Lord, is this the time when you will restore the kingdom to Israel?'* Jesus deflects them from this question, even though it is specifically about 'the kingdom' (their main topic of discussion), and then gives them their mission marching orders, first

---

[1] Acts 1:3.

promising the Holy Spirit's power: *you will receive power when the Holy Spirit has come upon you; and you will be my witnesses in Jerusalem, in all Judea and Samaria, and to the ends of the earth* (8).

This sets the agenda for Luke's whole story, which traces this geographical spread of the gospel as far as Rome – through many hardships and difficulties, not least the challenge of taking a very Jewish and Israel-centred gospel (as reflected by the disciples' question about Israel and the kingdom) out into the Gentile world. But just as Jesus is giving them this incredible commission, the conversation is suddenly broken off:

> *When he had said this, as they were watching, he was lifted up, and a cloud took him out of their sight. While he was going and they were gazing up towards heaven, suddenly two men in white robes stood by them. They said, 'Men of Galilee, why do you stand looking up towards heaven? This Jesus, who has been taken up from you into heaven, will come in the same way as you saw him go into heaven.'*
> (9–11)

Daniel's cloud suddenly reappears (last seen on the mount of transfiguration)[2] and Jesus rises and fades into it – and then two of Daniel's 'attendants' are suddenly present, to explain this extraordinary happening to the disciples, as one of them did to Daniel. There are three puzzling things about what these angels say:

- First, why do the angels address the disciples as *men of Galilee*? Why not as 'followers/friends/apostles of Jesus'?
- Second, what is the connection between their question ('Why are you looking into heaven?') and the promise of the second coming that follows? Surely, if Jesus is coming again, that might be a reason *for* looking into heaven, not for stopping doing that!
- And third, what do they mean by *in the same way* (11)? What aspect of Jesus' departure will be matched by his return?

We'll tackle these questions shortly. But first, let's capture our second passage.

---

[2] Luke 9:34–35; remember Dan. 7:13.

2. Passage 2 (Acts 3:17–21): quick overview

The mission is now well under way in Jerusalem, the Holy Spirit has been given as promised,[3] and Peter has performed an amazing healing on 'a man lame from birth'.[4] This has not unnaturally caused a crowd to gather, and Peter seizes the opportunity to speak. He insists that this healing has occurred by faith in the name of Jesus, the crucified but now glorified 'Author of life, whom God raised from the dead'.[5] 'The faith that is through Jesus has given him this perfect health in the presence of all of you,' Peter declares.[6] Having previously accused them of being murderers,[7] Peter then mitigates the charge a little and underlines God's purpose at work: *And now, friends, I know that you acted in ignorance, as did also your rulers. In this way God fulfilled what he had foretold through all the prophets, that his Messiah would suffer* (17–18). And then, rather than use the healing of the lame man as evidence just for Jesus' resurrection, Peter draws in his second coming as well:

> *Repent therefore, and turn to God so that your sins may be wiped out,*
> *so that times of refreshing may come from the presence of the Lord,*
> *and that he may send the Messiah appointed for you, that is, Jesus, who*
> *must remain in heaven until the time of universal restoration that God*
> *announced long ago through his holy prophets.*
> (19–21)

This emphasis on the fulfilment of the prophets' words then launches Peter into a string of prophecies which are being fulfilled through Jesus in 'these days'.[8] For 'you', he says, 'are the descendants of the prophets and of the covenant that God gave to your ancestors'.[9]

So Peter is operating within a firmly Old Testament and Jewish context here, as he addresses these Jerusalemite 'descendants of the prophets'.

---

[3] Acts 2:1–13.

[4] Acts 3:1–10.

[5] Acts 3:15.

[6] Acts 3:16.

[7] Acts 3:15 (cf. 2:23).

[8] Acts 3:22–26. In the fuller chapter on this passage in *Come, Lord Jesus!* (pp. 171–182) I look at this fascinating sequence of quotations and ask why Peter chose them.

[9] Acts 3:25.

We will need to bear this in mind as we tackle the fascinating questions which his words prompt:

- First, what exactly are these *times of refreshing* (20)?
- Second, are the *times of refreshing* the same as *the time of universal restoration* (21)? – bearing in mind that actually the Greek in verse 21 uses the plural, 'times' *of universal restoration*, rather than the singular used by the NRSV.[10]
- And third, why *must* the Messiah *remain in heaven* until God's appointed time? What's the reason for the delay? We would all like the Lord to come and rescue this struggling world tomorrow, if not sooner! Does this passage help us at all with this teasing question?

So both passages leave us with some really interesting issues to unpack. We'll start with this last one:

3. Why 'must' the Messiah remain in heaven (3:21)?

The little word *must* in 3:21 is a favourite of Luke's. He uses it more frequently in his Gospel than Matthew or Mark, and in Acts it appears no fewer than twenty-four times – often with the subtle flavour that something 'must' happen because it is part of God's plan. For instance, God sends Ananias to visit Paul, hot from his encounter with the risen Christ on the Damascus road, to show him 'how much he *must* suffer for the sake of my name'.[11] Similarly Paul himself, having been stoned and almost killed in Lystra, returns to the fledgling church there and 'encouraged them to continue in the faith, saying, "It is through many persecutions that we *must* enter the kingdom of God."'[12]

But why *must* it be like that? Specifically, why *must* Jesus stay in heaven until the 'times of restoration' arrive (21)? Actually, we can shift the question a little and ask why the ascension takes place at all. It's Jesus' ascension, described in our first passage (1:9), that means that he withdraws from the scene so that the second coming becomes necessary! Why does he not bring in the kingdom straight away, with his resurrection?

---

[10] Among the main translations currently used, only NKJV correctly has the plural 'times' in v. 21.

[11] Acts 9:16; emphasis added.

[12] Acts 14:22; emphasis added.

This is what the disciples are clearly expecting when they ask the question in 1:6, *Lord, is this the time when you will restore the kingdom to Israel?*

It's not hard to imagine ourselves into the disciples' heads here. They've been reading Zechariah 14! – along with many other prophetic passages which foretell the Lord's restoration of Israel or Jerusalem.[13] Fed from their mothers' arms with passages like these, they are expecting the Lord to step in and liberate Israel from all foreign forces and foes, and establish Jerusalem as an international centre of renewal, with Gentile nations coming to worship Israel's God. They are not yet applying Zechariah's vision to the new Jerusalem coming down from heaven, as John does in Revelation 21 – 22.[14] They know that the vision has not yet been fulfilled, and they are still hoping and trusting that it will be fulfilled for the physical Jerusalem they know and love. Now Jesus' resurrection has given them new expectation: *has the moment actually come?*

It is interesting that they use the Greek word *chronos* in their question. This is the word that means 'period of time' (as measured on a calendar), rather than the word *kairos* which would point to a special moment or intervention.[15] So their question *Is this the time when . . . ?* means 'Is this the *period during which* you will restore the kingdom to Israel?' Jesus' reply is then very interesting: *It is not for you to know the times* [chronoi] *or periods* [kairoi] *that the Father has set by his own authority* (7).

Personally, I would reverse the translations here, and use *periods* for *chronoi* and *times* for *kairoi*. But this does not matter much. The point is: Jesus does not deny their hope or expectation, but prepares them for a delay by leaving God's plans in God's hands: it is not for them to know whatever ages (*chronoi*) and interventions (*kairoi*) he may be planning in order to fulfil those prophecies. But in the meantime there is a great *kairos*-moment just around the corner – *you will receive power when the Holy Spirit has come upon you* (8a) – and this will then lead into a great *chronos*-period stretching away in front of them: *and you will be my witnesses in Jerusalem, in all Judea and Samaria, and to the ends of the earth* (8b).

What a task! Clearly, before the Lord 'restores the kingdom to Israel', this huge venture must be undertaken and fulfilled. As Jesus had said before, 'The good news must first be proclaimed to all nations.'[16] The

---

[13] See e.g. Isa. 2:2–4; Jer. 31:23–40; Ezek. 37:21–28; Joel 3:16–21; Hag. 2:1–9; etc.!

[14] See above, pp. 52–53.

[15] See above, p. 17.

[16] Mark 13:10.

kingdom is not going to be brought in just by *divine* action, but by *divine–human* action, including the preaching of the gospel. I think this is probably why the angels address the disciples as *men of Galilee* in 1:11 – geography is important here! They are going to have to go back to their home area and bear witness to Jesus there, before ever the kingdom will come. And the same is still true today: our witness *at home* is still our primary responsibility.

Peter has clearly grasped this message, preaching his heart out in Acts 3, because his reference to *universal restoration* (21) picks up the same word from the disciples' question in 1:6. In 1:6 we have the verb, in 3:21 the noun – but it is the same word, appearing only in these two places in Acts (and actually this is the only occurrence of the noun *restoration* in the New Testament). It's as though Peter is answering his own question, with the experience of Pentecost behind him. Peter tells his hearers that *the time of universal restoration that God announced long ago through his holy prophets* will not come until God sends *the Messiah appointed for you* – and somehow his hearers' repentance is essential in paving the way for this coming. Notice the string of three 'so thats' following his call to *repent . . . and turn to God* (19):

- *so that your sins may be wiped out* (19),
- *so that times of refreshing may come from the presence of the Lord* (20a),
- *and [so] that he may send the Messiah appointed for you, that is, Jesus* (20b).

In some mysterious way the coming of the Lord follows from their repentance – and we can see the reason for this in the Great Commission in 1:8: first the gospel must be preached *to the ends of the earth*, bringing about 'repentance and forgiveness of sins' among all nations,[17] and then the Lord will come.

What does preaching the gospel to all nations look like? When might we suspect that it's been achieved, or nearly achieved? When it comes to the *timetable* of the Lord's return, the Bible gives no clearer indication than this. So this is a most important question, which we'll come back to later.

---

[17] See Luke 24:47.

4. What are these 'times of refreshing' (3:20)?

When it comes to using unique words, Peter was having a field day. The word translated *refreshing* is also used only here in the New Testament. It means 'breathing space, relaxation, relief, rest'. Imagine a hectic day working, and you quickly catch a moment outside to pause, breathe in the fresh air and recharge your batteries with a cup of coffee. That's this word! But although the meaning is clear (and vivid), the experts disagree about whether this is an alternative description of the *times of universal restoration* of the next verse, or whether Peter has something different in mind. The fact that the word 'time' is in the plural in both phrases might suggest that the *times of refreshing* are the same as the *times of universal restoration*. After all, both come *from the presence of the Lord* (20) as gifts of his grace. When Jesus comes, the whole universe will breathe again as he refreshes and restores God's creation.

A wonderful picture! But actually I don't think this is right. The *times of refreshing* are things like the wonderful miracle just performed, which is the prompt for Peter's sermon. What a 'refreshment' for that man, as his legs came to life and he 'entered the temple with them, walking and leaping and praising God'![18] And for all who witnessed it, it was a refreshing, invigorating glimpse of the power and grace of God manifested through the name of the risen Jesus Christ.

It's interesting that the words for 'time' are again different in the two phrases. Both our words for 'time' appear, as in 1:7: when people repent, the Lord sends *times* [*kairoi*] *of refreshing* (20) – that is, wonderful interventions of his grace that lighten the load and cheer the dark day. But ultimately the *times* [*chronoi*] *of universal restoration* will arrive when the Messiah comes (21) – the ages of a renewed earth that the prophets foresaw: no momentary refreshment, but a permanent transformation of all things. The fact that Peter uses the different words for 'time' here convinces me that he (and Luke) have different things in mind.

'Moments of refreshment' – like those experienced by Hagar in the desert,[19] Moses at the burning bush,[20] David when Jonathan came to visit,[21]

---

[18] Acts 3:8.
[19] Gen. 21:17–19.
[20] Exod. 3 – 4.
[21] 1 Sam. 23:15–18.

Paul in that sinking boat[22] – and Peter when he walked beside the lake with Jesus.[23] When we need refreshment, God will give us the strength to go on – and will send these moments of re-creation *because* Jesus has ascended to heaven and *because* we therefore have this enormous mission task to fulfil, this huge journey to bring the news of Jesus to *the ends of the earth*.

But clearly there is a connection between these moments of refreshment and the coming *times of . . . restoration*. We could put it like this: our present lovely experiences of God's renewal, his touches of reinvigoration on the dusty road – moments when God charges out of heaven to rescue us, as for David in Psalm 18 – are foretastes of what is coming. They anticipate the much greater moment when he will *send the Messiah appointed for you, that is, Jesus,* and usher in a wholesale remake of the planet, as the prophets foresaw: evil defeated, nations united, peace proclaimed, worship ringing out, and God himself dwelling in our midst.

5. How will he come again?

Though the second coming is not a strong theme in Acts, the words of the angels in 1:11 are unique in the New Testament and very important, and we must spend some time with the disciples as they stand gazing into heaven, trying to catch another glimpse of Jesus who has just disappeared into the cloud – their jaws dropping at this sudden departure. And then they hear strange words from a couple of strange men who appear out of nowhere, just as Jesus disappears: *Men of Galilee, why do you stand looking up towards heaven? This Jesus, who has been taken up from you into heaven, will come in the same way as you saw him go into heaven* (11).

It's not unnatural to assume that the second half of their words gives the reason for the first half: they should not look upward, because Jesus will come back in the same way he left. But if he left by rising into a cloud, would it not make sense to keep sneaking glimpses heavenwards, in case they catch the first sign of the returning Lord?

The angels' discouragement of this upward looking is a word for us too. It is possible to get preoccupied with details of the 'end times' that might be teased out of the Bible: dates, timetables of end-time events, the Rapture, the great persecution, Armageddon, the millennium, the signs

---

22 Acts 27:22–25.
23 John 21:15–19.

of the end – and on and on![24] This kind of 'heavenward gazing' is discouraged by the angels' words here. In Acts they had no such pre-occupation. Even the *fact* of the Lord's return fades from view in Luke's narrative, so focused is he (and the church) on spreading the gospel to the ends of the earth.

But it's perfectly OK to ask exactly what the angels mean here. Their phrase *in the same way* suggests a similarity between Jesus' departure and his arrival: he will come back *in the same way* as he left. But what exactly is the similarity? There are several possibilities. Let's review them.

a. On the very spot!

Here in Acts Luke doesn't say where this took place, but in his earlier account he locates the ascension at Bethany, on the Mount of Olives:[25] and not a few people link this with Zechariah 14:4 and suggest that *in the same way* means 'in the same place'. Jesus will return onto the very spot just vacated.[26] But as we saw above, this is not how Paul reads that prophecy: he expects the Thessalonians to witness the return of the Lord hundreds of miles from Jerusalem. In fact, he doesn't seem to think in literal, spatial terms at all: the Lord will return *to earth*, and Paul doesn't ask 'where, exactly?'

b. What goes up must come down!

The usual understanding of the angels' words is that, just as Jesus rose visibly into the cloud, so he will descend visibly from the clouds when he returns. Thinking of Paul again, it looks as though this is how he understood it:

> For the Lord himself, with a cry of command, with the archangel's call and with the sound of God's trumpet, will descend from heaven, and the dead in Christ will rise first. Then we who are alive, who are left, will be caught up in the clouds together with them to meet the Lord in the air.[27]

---

[24] Just one book to illustrate this very understandable and widespread interest: Dave Hunt, *When Will Jesus Come? Compelling Evidence for the Soon Return of Christ* (Eugene, OR: Harvest House, 1993). Hunt dedicates his book to 'all those citizens of heaven for whom this world has lost its appeal. And who, loving Christ with their whole heart, long to be at home with Him in His Father's house.' Well, Luke would tell us that this world must never lose its appeal, because God loves it and we must remain focused on *his* mission to save it!

[25] Luke 24:50.

[26] So e.g. Hunt, *When Will Jesus Come?*, p. 206.

[27] 1 Thess. 4:16–17.

But the language of 'up', while clearly present, is not emphasized in the angels' words. The word 'up' has been added in the NRSV (it's not in the Greek).[28] Actually, here in Acts, Jesus' *destination* seems to be more important than his *direction* – perhaps this is more precisely the focus of the angels' words:

c. Straight into God's presence, and back again!

F. F. Bruce emphasizes the significance of the cloud that receives him, pointing to its earlier appearances in Daniel 7, at the transfiguration, and as the cloud of the 'Shekinah glory' that filled the tabernacle and the temple when the Lord took up residence there.[29] It is the cloud of God's presence. Bruce quotes Michael Ramsey who comments that the disciples were granted 'a theophany: Jesus is enveloped in the cloud of the divine presence'.[30] As with David in Psalm 18, God is bending the heavens and riding the clouds to rescue his servant: and in due course Jesus will do the same for us.

The angels use the word *heaven* three times in their words to the disciples. And while the Greek word can mean 'sky', its much more usual meaning in the New Testament is 'heaven', the dwelling-place of God. That is surely what it means here. A literal translation would be 'Why are you standing there peering into heaven?' 'Peering' gives a better idea of the word than just 'looking': the Greek word carries the notion of *intent* looking, trying to see *into* something. The disciples are trying to see the heavenly scene through the cloud – a scene which now includes the risen Jesus. Stephen is granted this vision just before his lynching: Luke tells us that he 'gazed into heaven' (exactly the same phrase as in Acts 1:10) 'and saw the glory of God and Jesus standing at the right hand of God'.[31]

So when Jesus returns, it will be straight from the presence of God, symbolized by the cloud that received him.

d. You were just saying . . . ?

A fourth possibility is that *in the same way* could refer to what Jesus was doing when he disappeared. He was taken away in the middle of a

---

[28] It is added also in CEV, GNT and NKJV. NIV implies 'up' by translating the first *heaven* as 'sky': 'Why do you stand here looking into the sky?'

[29] Exod. 40:34; 1 Kgs 8:10–11; F. F. Bruce, *Commentary on the Book of the Acts*, New London Commentary (London: Marshall, Morgan & Scott, 1962), pp. 40–41.

[30] Bruce, *Acts*, p. 41.

[31] Acts 7:55.

conversation with the astonished disciples, who are left with questions trembling on their tongues. *When he had said this* (9) gives the impression that Jesus had finished what he was saying, but the Greek doesn't carry this implication – and for sure, the disciples would have been bursting with questions about the bombshell that Jesus had just dropped on them. *Power . . . the Holy Spirit . . . witnesses . . . to the ends of the earth – ?!?* But without warning, the conversation which has been continuing for forty days (3) is cut off.

So maybe the angels mean that he will come in a way that cuts right across what we expect – suddenly and without warning. This would chime with both Jesus' and Paul's words elsewhere.[32] If this is right, the angels are saying: there's no point in trying to anticipate his coming, because by definition he's going to come when you don't expect him, right in the middle of 'life as normal'. Keep your eyes on your everyday discipleship: that's what matters!

Maybe there's another aspect, too. The conversation between Jesus and his disciples doesn't actually end, it just changes its *mode*:

- Mode 1 – during his ministry, before he ascended – was 'normal' face-to-face dialogue. But according to Acts 1:1, this was only what Jesus '*began* to do and to teach'.[33]
- So Mode 2 – after his ascension – is continuing conversation through the medium of the Holy Spirit, as Jesus carries on 'doing and teaching' in his church.
- Then – at his return – Mode 2 will shift back into Mode 1 again. We will see him and speak with him face to face.

What richness there is here! The first possibility (on the Mount of Olives) can't be right, but I think numbers 2, 3 and 4 all have validity and truth, filling out our understanding of the second coming in wonderful ways.

6. Bursting with questions

It's not only the disciples who have lots to ask, and who are left struggling to find answers. We are in exactly that place with the second coming.

---

[32] See Matt. 24:36–44 (Luke 17:26–35); 1 Thess. 5:2–4.

[33] Strangely NRSV omits the word 'began' in Acts 1:1.

When it comes to the 'how' of Jesus' return, the Bible is extraordinarily shy. It's not surprising that writers like Dave Hunt (see footnotes above) do their best to coax the facts out of hiding by putting together biblical texts in order to 'discover' a timetable of end-time events which goes beyond anything the Bible says in one place.[34] I think we have to be gentle in interpretation, and not press the Bible to say more than it wants to say by combining verses from different passages in this way. We need to let each passage speak in its own terms, and give special attention to the way in which the New Testament directs our interpretation of the Old.

But the Bible is not in the least shy about the *fact* of Jesus' return! Nor about its *significance* for the world and for our lives now. Just being told that he will surely come again once the gospel has reached *the ends of the earth* launched the first apostles into lifetimes of sacrificial mission and obedience: and it must have the same effect on us, too!

---

[34] I look at the background to such prophetic schemes, and how they are put together, in the introduction to *Come, Lord Jesus!* (pp. 15–25).

Luke 17:20 – 18:8

6. Will he find faith on the earth?

1. Three questions

What a fascinating passage this is. It tackles three frequently asked and vitally important questions about the second coming: when, where and why? – its *timing*, *location* and *purpose*.

The Pharisees ask the first one. *Once Jesus was asked by the Pharisees when the kingdom of God was coming, and he answered . . .* (17:20). The coming of the kingdom was a key article of faith for the Pharisees, who longed with glowing expectation for the day when God would step in to deliver the Jews from their enemies, and fulfil the prophets' vision of a vindicated Israel at the heart of a submissive world. Approaching Jesus as a rabbi (not all the Pharisees were hostile to him), they wanted to know *when* he thought this might happen. Interest in the timing of the end-time events goes right back to the first century! Their question was essentially the same as the disciples' question that kicks off the second-coming passage at the beginning of Acts, albeit without the experience of the resurrection that makes the disciples ask 'Is it *now*?'[1]

In reply Jesus puts a spin on the coming of the kingdom that would never have crossed the Pharisees' minds (21).

Jesus' surprising reply then leads into an even more surprising private conversation with the disciples (22–37), which culminates in the second question: *Then they asked him, 'Where, Lord?' He said to them, 'Where the corpse is, there the vultures will gather'* (37). Jesus certainly has the capacity to leave us wondering what he means!

---

[1] Acts 1:6 – see above.

Actually the question 'Where?' is not dropped, but underlies the next paragraph too (18:1–8), the so-called parable of the unjust judge. As we will see, here 'where?' is linked to 'why?' as we discover that the purpose of the second coming is to *grant justice* to God's suffering people as they cry out to him in faith and patience (8).

We have a feast in store as we wrestle with this intriguing section of Luke's Gospel, seeking to hear it speaking to us today. We will tackle the three questions in turn – but first:

2. A quick overview of the passage

The passage begins and ends with a question about 'coming'. The Pharisees' question in 17:20 about *when the kingdom of God was coming* is balanced by Jesus' own question in 18:8, *When the Son of Man comes, will he find faith on earth?* The balance between the questions reveals something vital, namely that for Luke, as for Jesus, the coming of the kingdom is equivalent to the coming of the Son of Man. This is hardly surprising, granted the background in Daniel's vision which we have already looked at: the power of the 'beasts' is overthrown and 'everlasting dominion' and 'kingship' is given to the Son of Man.[2] So it's as though Jesus' question in 18:8 is his ultimate answer to the Pharisees' question in 17:20: instead of concerning themselves with *when* the kingdom will come, why don't they busy themselves making sure that they are ready for the Son of Man to come – living out the *faith* that he looks for?

Faith is an important theme throughout this section of Luke. The parable of the dishonest manager[3] issues the challenge to be 'faithful' in our use of money: 'if . . . you have not been faithful with the dishonest wealth, who will entrust to you the true riches? . . . You cannot serve God and wealth.'[4] God knows what's really going on in our hearts, and whether we, like the Pharisees, are dominated by 'love of money'.[5] Then the famous parable of the rich man and Lazarus[6] adds an extra dimension to this challenge about faith: if we will listen rightly to 'Moses and the

---

[2] Dan. 7:12–14.
[3] Luke 16:1–9.
[4] Luke 16:11, 13b.
[5] Luke 16:14–15.
[6] Luke 16:19–31.

prophets', we'll be protected from falling into the terrible snare of money and its deception. Otherwise, not even someone rising from the dead will be enough to rescue us.[7]

Chapter 17 then opens with Jesus underlining how tough it is to get through life without messing up, especially without messing up other people's lives: so it's not surprising that 'the apostles' then ask him to 'increase our faith!'[8] In what follows Jesus seeks to do just that, and our passage fits into a sequence of passages with that purpose. We could analyse them like this:

- The *needful size* of faith: a mustard seed is enough! (17:6).
- The *core activity* of faith: just get on with serving! (17:7–10).
- The *essential heart* of faith: be thankful for grace received! (17:11–19).
- The *vital focus* of faith: look for the coming of the kingdom! (17:20 – 18:8).

We can best analyse our passage, therefore, around this underlying theme of faith. Taking the cue from the punchline in 18:8, it unpacks the kind of faith that the Son of Man wants to see when he comes:

A.   17:20–25: Faith that sees the presence of the kingdom, but longs for more.
   B.   17:26–33: Faith that rejects material security.
   C.   17:34–37: Faith that expects and endures unbearable loss.
D.   18:1–8: Faith that holds on in prayer and hope for justice.

Paragraphs B and C in the middle are both about *faith that suffers* and bears loss. On the other hand, paragraphs A and D (the bracket around them) are about *faith that hopes* and lives with courageous expectation. They are not alternatives: hopeful, expectant faith is always faith that endures suffering and loss, and is not bowled over by them.

Paragraphs A and B address the first of our questions – the 'when' of the kingdom. Then paragraph C addresses 'where?' and paragraph D 'why?'

---

[7] Luke 16:31.
[8] Luke 17:5.

3. When will the kingdom of God come? (17:20–33)

Our passage starts with this amazing exchange between Jesus and the Pharisees:

> *Once Jesus was asked by the Pharisees when the kingdom of God was coming, and he answered, 'The kingdom of God is not coming with things that can be observed; nor will they say, "Look, here it is!" or "There it is!" For, in fact, the kingdom of God is among you.'*
> (20–21)

The word *once* has been added at the start of verse 20 by the NRSV (also by NIV) – it is not in the Greek. The addition tends to distance this conversation from the story that precedes it, the healing of the ten lepers. But as we will see, it is vital to keep the connection! 'Then' would be better – or nothing at all.

I love theology: it's the pursuit of loving God with all our minds.[9] But theologians can get caught up in the pursuit of intellectual knowledge (and reputation) rather than true understanding which touches the whole person. The Pharisees were Israel's theologians, but Jesus has already accused them of being lovers of money whose hearts are not right before God:[10] so it is likely that their question in verse 20 falls into this 'intellectual' category. They've been debating a point of theology, and they would like Jesus' perspective on it. Is it possible to tell when the kingdom of God will arrive?

What a contemporary question that is! The second coming is the great *kairos*-moment that hangs over human history in God's purposes for us and our world: but is it possible to tell *when*, within the great sweep of *chronos*-time that carries us forward, this *kairos*-moment will occur? The temptation to try to do so is very strong! The Wikipedia article 'Predictions and Claims for the Second Coming' contains a very sobering list of some fifty different estimations or dates given over the course of Christian history, all of which of course have so far proved false.[11] Many of these have been made by groups and preachers on the fringes or outside

---

[9] See Mark 12:28–31.

[10] Luke 16:14–15.

[11] <https://en.wikipedia.org/wiki/Predictions_and_claims_for_the_Second_Coming>, accessed 8 June 2022.

'orthodox' Christianity, but even John Wesley (according to the sources cited in the article) committed himself to the view that the second coming would occur before 1836.

In this mini dialogue with the Pharisees we have Jesus' fascinating response to this question. He doesn't respond (as he might have done) by saying, 'Only God knows that, and it's not for us to know.'[12] Rather, he redirects the questioners to something their question implicitly denies, namely the fact that the kingdom *has already come* – as just demonstrated, gloriously, in the magnificent healing of the ten lepers of Samaria.[13] Were they truly to *see* that healing, the Pharisees' theology would be shaken. Kingdom power is *among you*, already on the loose, prowling round the countryside, and pulling into kingdom blessing people whom the Pharisees would never have approached or spoken to. It's there for the Pharisees to see and grasp – will they do so?

Rather than 'among you', some translations have 'within you', suggesting that somehow the kingdom of God is in the Pharisees' hearts.[14] This is a possible translation, but it seems very unlikely that Jesus would mean this, to judge from his highly critical words about the Pharisees' hearts elsewhere.[15] We will discover that this is the consistent focus of the New Testament: not on *when he is coming*, but on *how we are living* as we prepare for his appearance. If we truly see the presence of the kingdom in the healing of the ten lepers, what impact will that have? Well – speaking just for myself – I'd be longing for more. If the power of the kingdom can do that, would it not be wonderful to see it again and again and again? In fact – as Jesus puts it to his disciples – I'd be 'longing' *to see one of the days of the Son of Man* (22), desperate to see more of his ministry of putting things right, rescuing the lost and delivering the oppressed. Will the Pharisees begin to think and feel like that?

However, as Jesus unpacks his conversation for the disciples from verse 22 onwards, it is interesting that his emphasis falls not on the presence of the kingdom but on its futurity. He doesn't only believe that the kingdom is present, of course – in fact, he would fundamentally agree with the Pharisees that the kingdom is yet to come. He just doesn't want them speculating about *when*.

---

12 See Acts 1:6–7; cf. Mark 13:32.
13 Luke 17:11–19.
14 So e.g. KJV, NKJV, GNT.
15 See Mark 7:6–8.

What does he say to his disciples in these verses? Basically, six things:

a. People will long for the kingdom, and be constantly disappointed

The lovely phrase *one of the days of the Son of Man* (22) means 'one of those refreshing days when the Son of Man's kingdom power is truly shown in the overthrow of his enemies and the blessing of his people'. Such days can either precede his full coming – as with the ten lepers – or follow it! To *long* to see his power at work is one of the marks of discipleship, and so another mark of discipleship is the frustration of *not* experiencing what we long for. We will see what this means in practice when we look at 18:1–8.

b. Its coming will not be signalled in advance

As Jesus puts it to the Pharisees, the kingdom *is not coming with things that can be observed* (20). *Nor will they say* (21) means 'nor will they *justifiably* say'. Jesus knows that his disciples will certainly hear claims of this sort – to be able to spot the coming of the King in advance. But *do not go*, he says, *do not set off in pursuit* (23). Because, when the kingdom comes . . .

c. It will come suddenly, and universally

. . . like lightning flashing right across the sky from one horizon to the other (24). Lightning, of course, does not generally do that – it usually strikes downwards. But it is not hard to imagine lightning completely filling the sky. *So will the Son of Man be in his day* – unheralded, and overwhelming.

d. There will be much suffering first

But first he must endure much suffering and be rejected by this generation (25). This is true as spoken within the context of Jesus' ministry. He is heading towards the cross. But what about us? Must we expect suffering, too, before he comes? We remember Daniel 7 and the way in which the experience of the Son of Man became the experience of 'the people of the holy ones of the Most High': they gained kingship and dominion like him, but first they had to endure suffering under the power of the fourth beast. So maybe Jesus' words here extend out beyond his own sufferings, because his sufferings were actually ours. He was stepping into our experience, as the Son of Man. We know that this is true, anyway: every day that passes, as we long for him to come, we endure all the sufferings that go with having him in our hearts, and not seeing him.[16]

e. It will mean sudden judgment in the midst of 'ordinary' life

Jesus then uses two scriptural examples to illustrate his meaning: the stories of Noah (26–27) and of Lot (28–30). In both cases – while Noah was building the ark, and while Lot was living in Sodom – life carried on as 'normal' for all the people around them. *They were eating and drinking, and marrying and being given in marriage . . . buying and selling, planting and building,* until the moment when *the flood came and destroyed all of them* (27) or *it rained fire and sulphur from heaven and destroyed all of them* (29).

The repeated *destroyed all of them* is horrifying: for all those who carry on in forgetful materialism, devoted to the absorbing business of getting and providing, the coming of the Son of Man will not be good news. Far from it.

f. So they must not get attached to their stuff!

Verse 31 is a powerful challenge to the disciples. When the Son of Man comes, where will they want to be? Rushing out to meet him, or dashing back inside to pick up the essentials? To what are our hearts attached? The Pharisees have already been accused of being 'lovers of money', as we saw,[17] so they would be thoroughly given to the vital business of *buying and selling*. But the disciples could fall into the same trap: will they be willing to give it all up, without a second thought, when the Son of Man appears? Lot's wife (32) illustrates the consequence of holding on: she didn't want to leave Sodom and 'looked back', and was turned to salt.[18]

It's not just 'stuff', of course. Jesus is calling us to abandon everything on which we might depend for our security. *Those who try to make their life secure will lose it, but those who lose their life will keep it* (33). What a paradox! This means that we have to 'lose our lives' now, in our hearts – we can't leave the decision until suddenly he is here and we feel torn.

---

[16] See 1 Pet. 1:6–9.
[17] Luke 16:14.
[18] Gen. 19:26 (cf. 19:17).

4. Where will the Son of Man come? (17:34–37[19])

'I tell you, on that night there will be two in one bed; one will be taken and the other left. There will be two women grinding meal together; one will be taken and the other left.' Then they asked him, 'Where, Lord?' He said to them, 'Where the corpse is, there the vultures will gather.'

Here's an interesting thing: what is it about Jesus' words in verses 34–35 that prompts the disciples' question in verse 37? Jesus' earlier reference to Lot and Sodom pointed to God's judgment falling on a particular place. Will the coming of the Son of Man be like that? These new, vivid pictures of people being separated – two in a bed, two working together – also suggest a particular location. Lot and his family were 'taken' from Sodom, Noah and his family were 'taken' away in the ark, and in both cases the rest of the inhabitants were 'left'.

The issue of the *place* of the judgment has now been given a particular twist because of the way these verses have been used as the basis of the Rapture, an end-time event based on a particular understanding of what 'taken' means, combined with 1 Thessalonians 4:17 and John 14:3, and turned into a mini doctrine: without warning, this teaching says, Jesus will snatch all true believers away to heaven – dividing married couples and business partners and leaving the non-believers behind.[20] Within the premillennial scheme of things, the Rapture begins seven years of 'tribulation' during which the Antichrist appears, and which end with the coming of Christ to begin his thousand-year reign on earth (the millennium).

Belief in this Rapture doctrine is widespread, especially among American evangelicals. The 'Left Behind' series of novels and films dramatizes it and the subsequent events as laid out in premillennial expectation, and their sales show the popularity of the ideas: 9 million copies of the first volume[21] have been sold (in which the Rapture takes place, leaving planes plunging to the ground without pilots, cars without drivers causing massive motorway pile-ups and patients abandoned to die on operating tables),

---

[19] Verse 36 is missing in nearly all translations – only NKJV includes it. It is not in most ancient manuscripts, but became part of the 'Received Text' on which NKJV is based.

[20] See Hunt, *When Will Jesus Come?*, pp. 125–136.

[21] Tim LaHaye and Jerry B. Jenkins, *Left Behind: A Novel of the Earth's Last Days* (Wheaton, IL: Tyndale House, 1995).

and 63 million copies of books in the series as a whole, according to the publishers.[22] Tele-evangelist Jerry Falwell rated the impact of the first volume on Christians as 'probably greater than that of any other book in modern times, outside the Bible'.[23]

But the Rapture is a fictional doctrine spun out of the biblical texts with no solid basis in them. A basic principle of interpretation is at stake here. Interpretations of any text must at least be possible for the first hearers to grasp! – even if fuller meanings emerge later. But there is simply no way in which Jesus' first hearers (his disciples) could possibly have heard him teach this. There is nothing in the text to suggest that one of the pair, in each case, is a believer or disciple and the other is not. Nor is there anything to suggest that 'taken' means 'whisked off to heaven, like Enoch or Elijah'.[24] Nor is there anything to suggest that this Rapture is a separate event from the coming of Christ. (This is required by the premillennial scheme summarized above, and is explicitly defended by, e.g., Dave Hunt.)

Rather, the picture in verses 34–35 (what would have struck the disciples) is of *sudden death*, and therefore of the awful impermanence, unpredictability and insecurity of life. To wake to find your spouse dead beside you! To have your partner suddenly die while working alongside you! We *know* that such horrors are possible. We have all heard of them or know people to whom they have happened. One of my neighbours recently came home from work deeply sobered because a colleague had suddenly died at work that day. The coming of the Son of Man, says Jesus, will be like that – literally (see verse 24!) a bolt from the blue, robbing people of everything in which they have found place and security.

This is what Jesus means! His teaching is far more sobering and challenging than this fictional 'Rapture' doctrine, which is designed to make believers feel *comfortable* about their future. Increasing our sense of comfort could not be further from Jesus' intention here. The way to be ready for the coming of the Son of Man, he says, is *already* to give up dependence on this world for security – even dependence on the closest relationships, with those in bed with us. The Pharisees thought that the

---

[22] See 'Left Behind', Tyndale House Publishers, <https://www.tyndale.com/sites/leftbehind/>, accessed 11 January 2022.

[23] Cited in the article '*Left Behind*', Wikipedia, <https://en.wikipedia.org/wiki/Left_Behind>, accessed 11 January 2022.

[24] These are the scriptural examples of rapture cited as precedents: Gen. 5:24; 2 Kgs 2:11.

coming of the kingdom would be glorious.[25] No, says Jesus: it will mean fearful division and terrible loss.

No wonder the disciples ask, 'Where?' Does this really apply everywhere, or just to the Sodoms of the world? Jesus replies with a (slightly gruesome) proverb – a saying which leaves the hearers (us!) with the challenge of working out how it applies: *Where the corpse is, there the vultures will gather* (37). What does this mean?

Jesus deliberately (I think) uses an image which further pricks the bubble of those who think of the coming kingdom with rosy-glow cosiness. There's nothing cosy about vultures. People notice them wheeling in the sky, and infer that below them lies a corpse on which they will prey. The point is: this could happen anywhere. All that's needed is a corpse, and animals die unpredictably and universally. So the Son of Man will come wherever his world needs and calls him, as surely as vultures land on their prey. And where are there not people sharing beds, and working side by side? These are universal images. Judgment will therefore be universal, and unpredictable, and sudden, and deeply uncomfortable.

How can we be ready to meet this Son of Man? The following parable tells us, as it brings before us *what he looks for*, when he comes.

5. Why will the Son of Man come? (18:1–8)

He comes looking for *faith* (8): supremely, faith expressed in persistent and heartfelt prayer – prayer which amounts to a *cry for him to come* and to bring the justice which he alone can provide: precisely, the justice which will give the poor the redress they cry to him for.

There is no justice in this world – is that not true? There may be elaborate justice systems in many countries, but even where 'human rights' are protected people often end up feeling that justice has been denied them. In first-century societies there was no police service and no public criminal justice system. There were only civil courts. If you were a victim of crime, it would be up to you to approach a judge to adjudicate on your behalf – and of course there would be no guarantee of redress, even if the judge decided in your favour. So the picture of a judge who is not interested in justice (2) rings horribly true. That's the reality of life, in fact.

---

[25] Cf. Luke 14:15.

But along comes a widow who is not satisfied with that! Widows were the weakest in society, the poorest and most vulnerable to exploitation.[26] If they had no man to speak for them, they had no voice – unless, that is, they raised their voices in prayer. The woman in this story is a widow who has found her voice and will not be silenced. She makes herself a complete nuisance to this lazy and indifferent judge – even threatening to give him a black eye[27] if he goes on refusing to *grant me justice against my opponent* (3)! She simply *kept coming* (3), whatever his response, so great was her desire for justice.

She was 'longing' for *one of the days of the Son of Man* (17:22)! She illustrates what that looks like. Our hope for justice in this world is fixed not on the feeble and failing resources of human authority – that way lies great disappointment. Our hope is fixed on the Son of Man, whose judgment will finally and infallibly bring justice to those who cry out to him. *Will not God grant justice to his chosen ones who cry to him day and night?*, asks Jesus. *Will he delay long in helping them? I tell you, he will quickly grant justice to them* (7–8).

The word translated *justice* here and in verses 3 and 5 means 'vindication', even 'vengeance'. It is translated 'vengeance' in Romans 12:19, where Paul urges us, 'Never avenge yourselves, but leave room for the wrath of God; for it is written "Vengeance is mine, I will repay, says the Lord."' It is that justice which finally sets things right, and which finally only God can give, because finally only he knows exactly where justice lies. We may have ideas about what that justice may look like, but in the end only he can define it – and part of our faith is submitting to him and leaving it in his hands: and not rushing back into the house to grab our ideas of what justice means, and certainly not grabbing anything else to give us security. Our security rests in his hands, not in ours.

This fills out the 'where' question, also. He will come wherever his *chosen ones* are crying out to him – that's where the vultures will circle! He is not deaf to our cries. He hears and knows. And he will come. A sceptic might point out that the question *Will he delay long in helping them?* (7) should really be answered, 'Yes, he sure will – two thousand years and counting!' – but this would miss the point. As we have seen so often, his 'coming' is a very subtle thing. He comes to us in all sorts of

---

[26] See Mark 12:40.

[27] That's the literal meaning of the verb NRSV translates as 'wear out' in v. 5.

ways, touching our experience with *kairos*-moments that point ahead to the great and final *kairos* when he will transform the whole world and not just our lives.

So why does he come? This passage gives three answers:

a. He comes because we pray

Our persistent prayer is the focus of the faith that he looks for, and we must make sure that he finds it on earth when he comes (8)! The whole Bible ends with the prayer 'Come, Lord Jesus!'[28]

b. He comes because we are his 'chosen ones'

This little description of us in verse 7 slips in almost unnoticed. God's *chosen ones*, his 'elect' people, are those to whom he is committed by covenant and in love.[29] He is in *relationship* with them – an unbreakable relationship which will bring him 'storming' in to rescue them, just as he rescued other 'chosen ones' like David. This subtle and passing reference to our 'election' is actually the basis of everything. The Son of Man comes because of *his* commitment to *us*.

c. He comes because he is committed to justice in his world

We can be confident that it is worth holding on, like the widow in the story. It's worth hanging on in there, fighting for good and truth and mercy and justice, because he is committed to these things too – and one day he will come and bring them to full realization on this lovely planet which he died to save.

So the Son of Man comes because he responds to committed, heartfelt prayer that arises from longing for justice and a passionate desire to 'see his day' (17:22): prayer generated out of suffering, loss, poverty and above all out of *faith* in him. How might – should – this passage impact our prayer, and our lives, in this in-between time before he comes?

We turn next to Matthew's Gospel for more answers!

---

[28] Rev. 22:20.

[29] Deut. 7:6–10 is a passage that might well lie in the background behind this parable, maybe providing the expression 'chosen ones'.

Matthew 24:1–44

7. The coming of the Son of Man

We land in Matthew's Gospel, for this chapter and the next. As is well known, Jesus' teaching in Matthew is focused into five chunks, often called 'discourses', and Matthew 24 – 25 together form the fifth discourse – known as the 'Olivet Discourse', because Jesus delivers it sitting on the Mount of Olives with his disciples. The theme of these two chapters could be summarized as 'Preparing for the Coming of the King': making sure that we are ready to welcome him, and knowing what challenges we face in doing that. In the first part (Matt. 24:1–44) – this chapter – we hear powerful and deeply moving teaching from Jesus on *what happens* in the period leading up to the coming of the King. In the next chapter we will look at the second part (Matt. 24:45 – 25:46), on *how to be ready* for the coming of the King. We have a feast in store!

1. What's going on in Matthew 24?

This section of the discourse is quite closely parallel to Mark 13 and Luke 21. It's really interesting to read the three chapters alongside one another; sometimes the differences are illuminating.

There was a stunning view of the temple from the Mount of Olives, and the disciples comment on it as they leave the city. In Mark they say, 'Look, Teacher, what large stones and what large buildings!'[1] Jesus' response, however, is not glowing admiration but horrifying prediction: *You see all these, do you not? Truly I tell you, not one stone will be left here upon*

---

[1] Mark 13:1.

another; all will be thrown down (2). This prophecy was fulfilled some forty years later, when the Romans sacked the city and destroyed the temple after a four-year siege (the date was AD 70), causing appalling suffering for the inhabitants of Jerusalem. Not surprisingly, the disciples ask Jesus about this awful prediction, in an interestingly complicated question: *Tell us, when will this be, and what will be the sign of your coming and of the end of the age?* (3).

The end of the age gets thrown in because, if the temple is going to be destroyed, then that will surely mean 'the end of the age'. The temple is so central to Israel's whole existence and sense of self as God's people that, if it is going to disappear, Israel must cease to be who they currently are. *The end of the age* does not mean 'the end of the space–time universe' but simply 'the end of the current order of things' – usually, of course, the moment of final judgment and the arrival of the kingdom. It's fascinating that they add in *the sign of your coming* also: this must be because of Jesus' teaching in Matthew 16:27–28, where he links 'the coming of the Son of Man' to final judgment (which takes place at the end of the age), and adds, 'Truly I tell you, there are some standing here who will not taste death before they see the Son of Man coming in his kingdom.'[2]

So they have already heard the Son of Man say that he will be coming in glory and as Judge, bringing the kingdom, within the lifetime of at least some of them. Now they connect all that with these new words about the destruction of the temple. It's a powerful mix.[3]

One of the issues that we must face, of course, is that these things were not all connected, in fact – even though Jesus reiterates in this chapter that *this generation will not pass away until all these things have taken place* (34). The temple was destroyed within the lifetime of many hearing him, but the Son of Man did not come at the same time, and final judgment (the end of the age) has not yet taken place. We'll tackle this problem later.

Jesus' response has teased interpreters. Specifically, when is he responding to the disciples' question about the destruction of the temple, and when to their question about the coming of the Son of Man? And – even more important – how does he think these two events are related to

---

[2] Matt. 16:28.

[3] This background in Matt. 16:28 helps us to see that the 'coming' of the Son of Man in 24:27 (his *parousia*) is the same as his 'coming' in 24:30, where a different Greek word is used (reflecting the language of Dan. 7:13). Some have argued that a different word implies a different coming. But the disciples' question in 24:3 – using *parousia* – naturally picks up Jesus' promise in 16:28 which also echoes Dan. 7:13.

each other? Scholars have been all round the houses and uphill and down again on this, and many different suggestions have been made. However, I'm not going to join that debate, except at a couple of points. Having looked at it all, I'm simply going to expound what I think is the best approach. For the technically interested, I'm following the approach suggested by Don Carson and David Wenham (with some adjustments).[4]

2. A quick overview

I love the challenge of analysing the shape of biblical passages. Once again we notice a general chiastic structure here, with sections on 'signs' bracketing the two central sections on the destruction of the temple and the coming of the Son of Man. In addition, the whole section begins and ends with balancing commands to 'watch out!'[5] and 'keep awake!' (4, 42) so as not to be deceived or fall asleep while we wait for the Son of Man.

A. Signs of the end, 24:4–14
    a. General, vv. 4–7
    b. Specific, vv. 8–14
B. The destruction of the temple, 24:15–28
    a. The need to flee, vv. 15–22
    b. The need to keep focus, vv. 23–28
C. The coming of the Son of Man, 24:29–31
    a. His appearance, vv. 29–30
    b. His gathering of his people, v. 31
D. Signs of the end, 24:32–44
    a. Signs you can see, vv. 32–35
    b. Signs you can't see, vv. 36–44

There is tremendous encouragement here, to sustain us so that our love doesn't *grow cold* (12) and so that we can *endure to the end* and be saved (13). We need that. There is also great realism about the pressures and difficulties we face, to sustain faith in our coming Messiah when the world

---

[4] D. A. Carson, 'Matthew', in *The Expositor's Bible Commentary*, vol. 8 (Grand Rapids, MI: Zondervan, 1984), pp. 488–495; David Wenham, *The Rediscovery of Jesus' Eschatological Discourse*, Gospel Perspectives 4 (Sheffield: JSOT Press, 1984). For more detail see Motyer, *Come, Lord Jesus!*, ch. 4 (pp. 93–123), which is on Mark 13.

[5] NRSV has *Beware* in v. 4. 'Watch out' is a more literal translation.

around us is offering so many alternative 'christs' – so many tempting and more immediate offers of 'salvation'. Let's be encouraged by each section in turn.

3. Signs of the end (24:4–14)

The last words of verse 14 give us the focus of this section: *and then the end will come.* This picks up the disciples' question in verse 3 about signs of *the end of the age.* En route to verse 14 we notice *but the end is not yet* in verse 6 – in other words, this section tells us what to expect during the course of this age until *the end* comes. And tough it is going to be. But the very fact that all these terrible things are predicted – told in advance – means that they are part of a plan. *This must take place*, says Jesus (6), using the same Greek phrase that Daniel uses to King Nebuchadnezzar (in the Septuagint) when he reveals the meaning of his dream: 'The revealer of mysteries disclosed to you *what must take place.*'[6] Somehow, God is behind that 'must'.

And so, whatever we are facing – political upheaval, war, famine, natural disasters (6–7), torture, persecution, execution, the apostasy and betrayal of our friends, the rise of false prophets (9–11) – Jesus' word to us is *see that you are not alarmed* (6), literally, 'don't be shaken'. These things *must* happen, and they are 'signs' of the approaching *end of the age*, or as Jesus puts it in verse 8, *the beginning of the birth pangs.* What a perspective: the sufferings of the church are in themselves *signs* of their coming end, because they *must take place*, a vital part of the endgame like the first labour pains signalling the end of pregnancy.

The church of Christ is facing all of this at the moment. According to the Open Doors website, 4,761 Christians were murdered for their faith in 2020, and 4,472 churches and Christian buildings were attacked.[7] It's not surprising that *because of the increase of lawlessness, the love of many will grow cold* (12). It is incredibly difficult to keep one's faith and love alive at such great cost. But there's no alternative to simply finding the strength to keep going: *anyone who endures to the end will be saved* (13).

Why is all this necessary? Why *must* the church of Jesus Christ endure all this? The climax in verse 14 tells it all: *And this good news of the*

---

6 Dan. 2:29. NRSV has 'what is to be'.
7 See Open Doors, <https://www.opendoorsuk.org>, accessed 16 January 2022.

kingdom will be proclaimed throughout the world, as a testimony to all the nations; and then the end will come.

The trouble is, we can't hide away! The gospel has to be proclaimed *to all the nations* before the end can come – and so the church has to stay public, and visible, and as vocal as possible. That's why the persecution comes. And (as we saw above in thinking about Acts 1:6–11 and 3:17–21) that's why this whole 'end is not yet' period is necessary: to give space for the preaching of the gospel. Both Mark and Luke, at this point in the discourse, refer to the empowering of the Holy Spirit who gives us the words to speak when we are called to account before a hostile world.[8] To find the strength not to be 'shaken' in the face of all this must be down to his presence within us. It can't come from us.

What does it actually mean, to preach the gospel *to all the nations*? This is much more difficult to answer now, because of the huge growth in world population. When Jesus spoke these words, the number of human beings who made up *the nations* was relatively static – about 230 million.[9] By the year 1000 it was still only about 320 million. When the modern missionary movement was born (in about 1800), world population stood at approximately 980 million. By the time I was born in 1950 it had increased to 2.5 billion. Today it is nearly 8 billion. World population has increased more than threefold in my lifetime. God clearly loves people-making. What will count as *a testimony to all the nations* (14) in these circumstances? The Son of Man will not come, the 'age' will not end, until this task of proclamation is finished – but how might we measure what that 'finishing' looks like?

A glance at Paul's missionary strategy will give us a steer.[10] The phrase *all the nations* (14) is elsewhere translated 'all the Gentiles' – as for instance in Romans 1:5, where Paul writes of his specific call 'to bring about the obedience of faith among all the Gentiles for the sake of his name'. For Paul, 'the Gentiles' had a personal face: they were not vaguely 'the nations'. He goes on: 'including yourselves who are called to belong to Jesus Christ, to all God's beloved in Rome, who are called to be saints . . .'[11]

---

8 Mark 13:11; Luke 21:15.

9 This figure and the statistics that follow are given under 'World Population Growth' on the website Our World in Data, <https://ourworldindata.org/world-population-growth>, accessed 16 January 2022.

10 An old but famous book is helpful here: Roland Allen, *Missionary Methods: St Paul's or Ours?* (London: Robert Scott, 1912).

11 Rom. 1:6–7.

For Paul, 'the Gentiles' were *people*: members of the Roman church whom he longed to visit so that he could build them up in their faith.[12] Spreading the word like this was a shared task in which Paul was a 'co-worker' with the Lord.[13] This shaped his missionary strategy. He travelled extensively, led by the Lord, and at great personal cost.[14] He planted churches wherever he went and appointed local leaders. But he also planted himself, in the big centres of population with access to crowds of people both living there and travelling through (Antioch, Corinth, Ephesus – and, later, Rome), and made himself as visible and vocal as he could. He must have been greatly shaped by his early experience in Antioch, where he joined Barnabas as a teacher in the church, and (as Luke summarizes it) 'the hand of the Lord was with them, and a great number became believers and turned to the Lord'.[15]

Because this was a mission shared with God himself, amazingly Paul did not complain when he was locked up in prison for long periods and was unable to travel and speak publicly. The Lord was in charge! Paul did what he could,[16] and in particular, while locked up, he wrote letters.

What would Paul say to us, facing the challenge of communicating the gospel to the vast and increasing number of humans inhabiting the planet today? Five things, I believe, which also all rest in this passage and its parallel passages in Mark and Luke:

- Trust the Lord, and seek to be led at all times by the Spirit. This is *his* task.[17]
- Embrace suffering gladly, for Jesus' sake and the gospel's (9–13).[18]
- Take care not to be 'led astray' from the core confession of Jesus as the coming Son of Man (4–5, 10–11).[19]
- In particular, make sure that love does not *grow cold* as the core motivation of all you do and say – love both for the Lord and for those you serve (12).[20]

---

[12] Rom. 1:11–12.

[13] See 1 Cor. 3:9: a very dramatic statement of partnership (unjustifiably toned down in NIV and NRSV).

[14] See 2 Cor. 11:23–28.

[15] Acts 11:21.

[16] See Acts 28:30–31; Eph. 6:19–20; Phil. 1:12–14.

[17] Mark 13:11; Luke 21:14–15. Cf. Acts 16:6; 19:21; Rom. 1:10; 2 Cor. 2:14–17.

[18] Cf. 2 Cor. 1:5–7; Col. 1:24; 2 Tim. 2:3.

[19] Cf. Rom. 16:17; Gal. 1:6; 3:1; 2 Thess. 2:15; 1 Tim. 1:3–4.

[20] Cf. 1 Cor. 13:1–13; Col. 3:14; 1 Thess. 3:12–13.

- Use every possible means to speak the good news, and thus to build the church up in love and faith (14). Maximize your audience! For Paul that meant using his status as a rabbi to teach in synagogues, hiring other venues, speaking in open spaces, using homes (others' and his own) and seizing all opportunities with groups and with individuals, as well as writing letters:[21] surely today he would be using all available media to spread this gospel-for-the-world as widely as possible!

Fascinatingly, at the time of writing Romans Paul thought that he had 'fully proclaimed the good news of Christ' across half the northern Mediterranean area 'from Jerusalem and as far around as Illyricum' (modern Croatia).[22] Actually, this remarkable achievement was not his but 'what Christ has accomplished through me'.[23] Paul had certainly not travelled to every centre of human population across that vast area. Rather he had preached the gospel in a representative way, by focusing on the main centres, so that every human being had the *chance* to hear, either first-hand or second-hand.

Paul's example is powerful and suggestive. As human populations increase, we (that is, the church of Christ) need to think ever more creatively about how we too can make the gospel accessible in every human society, while letting the Lord direct the task by his Spirit. We must leave to the Lord the decision about *the point at which* it can be truly said that the *good news of the kingdom* has been *proclaimed throughout the world* (14). He will not come until that moment arrives.

Let us take full note of this solitary piece of scriptural teaching about the *timing* of the Lord's return! He will come when the job is done. This is why the church suffers, this is why we cry out day and night for justice and he *seems* to delay, this is why nearly two thousand years have elapsed since first he spoke these words! Craig Keener points out that this is not just a prediction, it is also a promise 'that some generation will succeed in finishing the task others have begun'.[24]

---

[21] See Acts 17:2–3; 19:9–10; 17:17; 20:7–8; 28:23; 17:22; 26:1ff.; cf. Phil. 2:15.

[22] Rom. 15:19.

[23] Rom. 15:18.

[24] Craig S. Keener, *Matthew*, IVP New Testament Commentary (Downers Grove, IL: InterVarsity Press; Leicester: Inter-Varsity Press, 1997), p. 347.

Keener also does not flinch from the speculation that 'the Lord's return has been delayed and the world's suffering prolonged by the church's disobedience to the Great Commission'.[25] I don't think I agree with this, for it is not just suffering that has multiplied. The world's population has multiplied too! – and we surely cannot maintain that several billion humans exist only because of the church's disobedience. God's plan must have something to do with it. The point is, it's his decision, in every respect, and we do not know when *the Lord* will reckon that this great precondition has been fulfilled. He will not be restricted by the church's faithlessness, although for sure he uses the church's faithfulness. All we can say is: one day the Day will dawn! – and it could be today.

4. The destruction of the temple (24:15–28)

So when you see the desolating sacrilege standing in the holy place, as was spoken of by the prophet Daniel (let the reader understand), then those in Judea must flee to the mountains . . . (15–16). The strange language of verse 15 brings us straight back to the Jerusalem temple, *the holy place*. But before we think about what this actually means, it's important to notice the little word *So* with which the verse begins. *So* connects what Jesus is going to say about the temple with the general picture of 'life before the end' in verses 4–14. What he predicts for the temple fits with that picture – it will hold no surprises, whenever it will actually take place. Of course, Jesus' hearers had no inkling of what we know: that the end would be postponed beyond the destruction of the temple by many, many years.

The suffering described in these verses is thus an *instance* of the suffering that heralds the end. The events surrounding the destruction of the temple were truly awful, as reflected in verse 21: *At that time there will be great suffering, such as has not been from the beginning of the world until now, no, and never will be.* On the basis of the description of the fall of Jerusalem by the Jewish historian Josephus, Carson comments that, while greater numbers of people have perished in other dreadful events, 'never [was] so high a percentage of a great city's population so thoroughly and painfully exterminated and enslaved as during the Fall of Jerusalem'.[26] Jesus' prophecy came horribly true.

---

[25] Keener, *Matthew*, pp. 346–347.

[26] Carson, 'Matthew', p. 501.

In response to Jesus' command in verse 16, Christians in Jerusalem at the beginning of the siege (while it was not yet total) fled from the city and relocated themselves across the Jordan at a place called Pella. Josephus also helps us to understand their flight, for he too thought that events in the temple at that time constituted a *desolating sacrilege* of the kind that Daniel describes: two Zealot factions fought each other for possession of the temple, leading to great bloodshed, including the deaths of innocent worshippers. Josephus comments that the temple could no longer be 'God's place', having become a tomb for the bodies of God's own people.[27] This is what *desolating sacrilege* means: a *sacrilege* that causes God to desert his house, so that it becomes 'desolate'. *Let the reader understand* (15b) points to the judgment made by the Christians at that time: like Josephus, they deemed that this was, indeed, a *sacrilege* signalling the end of the temple as God's house.

It was a four-year period of terrible uncertainty, with many dawns of false hope (23–24). But Jesus encourages people to set their hope on the coming of the Son of Man: *For as the lightning comes from the east and flashes as far as the west, so will be the coming of the Son of Man* (27).[28] When he comes, there will be no doubt about it!

Jesus immediately moves on to unpack that hope.

5. The coming of the Son of Man (24:29–31)

Immediately after the suffering of those days

> *the sun will be darkened,*
> *and the moon will not give its light;*
> *the stars will fall from heaven,*
> *and the powers of heaven will be shaken.*

Then the sign of the Son of Man will appear in heaven, and then all the tribes of the earth will mourn, and they will see 'the Son of Man coming on the clouds of heaven' with power and great glory. And he will send out his angels with a loud trumpet call, and they will gather his elect from the four winds, from one end of heaven to the other.

---

[27] Josephus, *Jewish War* 5.19.
[28] Cf. Luke 17:24.

I think that *immediately after the suffering of those days* is best taken to refer to all the sufferings described in verses 4–28 – not just those associated with the fall of Jerusalem, but more widely all the sufferings of the church in this age of proclamation. Once that's all done and dusted, and as soon as the gospel has been proclaimed to all nations (14) and all the suffering endured, then *immediately* (no delay) the Lord will come. Some have taken the 'cosmic collapse' language of verse 29 to refer specifically to the fall of Jerusalem, because the language is drawn from Isaiah, where it is used of the fall of Babylon and of Edom.[29] Mighty political 'earth-shattering' events can certainly evoke this kind of language in the Bible – but in this case, so closely connected to verse 30, it seems that this earth-shattering event is even greater than the fall of Jerusalem. In response, 'all' *the tribes of the earth will mourn* (30),[30] not just one affected people, because the Son of Man comes – as we know from Daniel 7 – to displace *all* the powers of earth, to set up a kingdom 'not [made] by human hands',[31] a universal kingdom which the Most High has given to him.

And then – surprise, surprise – we get the key quotation from Daniel 7:13 (30b)! He will come, for sure, when the sufferings of the gospel age are complete, and all have heard the good news. The good news of course *includes* the glorious message that he is the Son of Man who fulfils the vision and expectation of Daniel 7!

We are helped in understanding verse 31 by looking back to Matthew 13:36–43, where Jesus explains the parable of the 'wheat and tares' to his disciples: he says that 'at the end of the age' (same phrase as in the disciples' question in 24:3) 'the Son of Man will send his angels' to gather in the harvest and to separate out the weeds from the wheat.[32] The *loud trumpet call* echoes several places where a 'trumpet' is God's summons to his people to gather, or to all the inhabitants of the earth to listen.[33] The final judgment, ushered in by the appearance of the Son of Man, will mean a gathering of his people – *his elect* – from the four corners of the earth.[34]

---

[29] Isa. 13:10 (Babylon); 34:4 (Edom). Cf. also Ezek. 32:7; Joel 2:10. Influenced by those who want to make these verses a description just of the fall of Jerusalem, the NIV margin proposes an alternative translation: 'all the tribes of the land' rather than 'all the peoples of the earth'. This is a possible translation (the Greek *ge* can mean 'land' or 'earth'), but the global action in verse 31 supports us in giving it its wider meaning here.

[30] The language echoes Zech. 12:12.

[31] Dan. 2:34.

[32] Matt. 13:41.

[33] Isa. 27:12–13; 18:3. Cf. Psalms of Solomon 11:1–3, where the sounding trumpet is called a 'sign' or 'signal'.

[34] Cf. Zech. 2:6–13.

The *sign of the Son of Man* may be this great trumpet call. If so, we probably should not expect to hear a literal trumpet blast, but rather experience what it signifies: the nations will *hear*, and their life will be rounded up under the glorious rule of the Son of Man, the judge and saviour of all.

So we see that the coming of the Son of Man will be:

- Universal and visible to all (*all the tribes . . . will see*, 30);
- A cause of mourning as well as joy;
- The moment of his 'coming into his kingdom';
- The bringing home of all his people, back from exile;
- A multicultural unifying of the whole earth: *all the tribes* will mourn, and *from the four winds* the elect will come.

6. Signs of the end (24:32–44)

As we noted above, this last section falls into two interestingly different parts: first Jesus emphasizes the things that presage the coming of the Son of Man (*when you see all these things, you know that he is near, at the very gates*, 33), but then he underlines that there will be no advance indications, as for the flood in Noah's day: *For as . . . they knew nothing until the flood came and swept them all away, so too will be the coming of the Son of Man* (38–39). This seems strange – so much so that some have thought Jesus must be referring to different events. A clever suggestion, supported by quite a few,[35] is that in verses 32–35 he is talking about the fall of Jerusalem, which will be heralded by all the sufferings summarized in verses 19–25, but in verses 36–44 he is talking about the coming of the Son of Man, which will be completely unexpected, like a thief in the night (43–44). This view points to the 'but' at the beginning of verse 36 – Jesus is turning to a different topic, it says: *But about that day and hour no one knows, neither the angels of heaven, nor the Son, but only the Father.*

However, this makes it all unnecessarily complicated – not least because it asks us to believe that the description of the coming of the Son of Man in verses 30–31 is actually apocalyptic language referring to the fall of Jerusalem. This might work for the 'cosmic collapse' language in

---

[35] E.g. R. T. France, *Matthew*, Tyndale New Testament Commentaries (Leicester: Inter-Varsity Press, 1985), pp. 333–335, 347.

verse 29, but it's a very big stretch to take this view of verses 30–31 as well.[36] As we saw, verses 30–31 describe a coming which will impact the whole world, not just Israel.

The relationship between the coming signalled in advance (32–33) and the coming unknown ahead of its time (36–37) is not a great problem. The *all these things* which presage his coming (33) are all the sufferings of his people in this gospel age – including (but not limited to) the sufferings that surrounded the destruction of the temple, the issue of particular concern to the disciples. Everything we go through, including all the things summarized in verses 5–12, is a step towards the harvest, like leaves that say 'summer is coming' (32). But the *precise timing* of his coming is as mysterious as the precise moment at which the gospel of the kingdom will have been proclaimed to all the nations. We know both are coming – but when? Only the Father can judge this. And so only the Father can know the timing of his coming.

This helps us with the particular difficulty posed by verse 34: *Truly I tell you, this generation will not pass away until all these things have taken place.* In the context here Jesus is talking about the *signs* that presage the end, not about the end itself. So *all these things* doesn't mean 'all the things I've described so far', which would *include* the coming of the Son of Man. Rather, *all these things* means 'all the kinds of things I've described as signs of the end'. Every generation, including the generation that actually experienced the fall of Jerusalem, has experienced *all* the things (the sufferings) that presage his coming, so that at every and any moment during the gospel era it could be said that *he is near, at the very gates* (33). But the precise moment of his coming is unknown – *an unexpected hour* (44).

Jesus' teaching in verses 37–41 about the suddenness and unexpected-ness of his coming is a shortened version of the teaching in Luke 17 which we looked at in the last chapter.[37] As there, so here: we need to hold the two truths in glorious tension, that *on the one hand*, we do not know when he is coming, but *on the other hand*, our very sufferings, the things that make us cry out for his deliverance, are signs of his coming, because he will not delay in answering our prayer![38]

---

[36] See France, *Matthew*, pp. 344–346.

[37] Luke 17:26–36.

[38] Luke 18:7–8.

7. Watch out . . . keep awake . . . be ready! (24:4, 42, 44)

These encouragements bracket the chapter, as we noticed. There is a progression between them which we should take to heart:

- To 'watch out' is to do our theological work: to think about what Jesus' second coming means, how to understand it, how to reject false theologies, and how his coming relates to 'the kingdoms of this world' and his purposes of salvation and judgment.
- To 'keep awake' is to let it impact us, so that our theology moves out of theory and starts to affect how we live from day to day: we become people whose lives have a new horizon – his coming!
- To 'be ready' is to take steps to shape our lives practically, in the light of the Coming Dawn.

How do we get ready? As Jesus' discourse continues, he answers this question! Let's listen . . .

Matthew 24:45 – 25:46

8. Parables of preparation

How much does the second coming impact our lives, from day to day? You may be like me: I have to confess that for most of my life the answer would be 'hardly at all'. The business of everyday life carries a pressing agenda, and if 'thinking about or preparing for the second coming' appears at all, it would be under 'Any Other Business' at the bottom, certainly not up among the main items of the day.

But that's not where Jesus thinks it should be. His teaching on the *fact* of his coming (Matt. 24:1–36) flows seamlessly into a long section on *preparing* for it.[1] I included the first part of this section in the last chapter, because 24:37–44 seems to belong chiefly with Jesus' answer to the disciples' question in 24:3. But already, in talking about his coming without warning like Noah's flood, Jesus is moving towards the themes of this next section. And verses 42–44 give us the two main focuses that we will meet. Compare verse 42 and verse 44:

Keep awake, therefore, for you do not know on what day your Lord is coming.
(42)

Therefore you too must *be ready*, for at an hour you don't expect the Son of Man is coming.
(44)[2]

---

[1] Matt. 24:37 – 25:46.

[2] This is my translation of v. 44, designed to bring out the close parallel between the two verses.

We don't know when he is coming – day (42) or hour (44) – and therefore we must 'be ready'. These two themes (wakefulness and readiness) weave through the four parables in this section:

- The faithful and wise servant (24:45–51)
- The wise and foolish bridesmaids (25:1–13)
- The talents (25:14–30)
- The sheep and the goats (25:31–46)

How can we be ready for a coming which might happen at any moment? We will look at each of these parables in turn, and will discover that they follow on from one another as they expand our thinking about being ready for the Lord's return.

1. The faithful and wise servant (24:45–51)

This little parable sets the scene for the three great parables that follow in Matthew 25. It focuses for us the basic idea expressed in verse 50: *the master of that slave will come on a day when he does not expect him and at an hour that he does not know* – so we must be constantly wakeful and ready to receive our returning Lord.

It would be tempting to think that this parable is just for those in leadership, because *the faithful and wise slave* at the heart of the story is *put in charge* of his master's household to make sure that the house runs smoothly and the other slaves are well cared for (45). But that would be a mistake. It's for all who have a task to perform for the Lord while we wait for him to come. The slave's comment in verse 48 is interesting – *My master is delayed*: it suggests what we now know so clearly, that the second coming has not happened as soon as we might have expected. Hence the opportunity to serve him! – in fact, hence the opportunity to be involved in that worldwide mission to take the gospel to all the nations. Within the church of Jesus Christ, we all have a job to do which is part of that great purpose.[3] So this head slave has . . .

a. A clear task to fulfil (24:45)

This is a question we must all ask ourselves: in what ways does the Lord want us to serve him, to help manage his world until he returns?

---

[3] Cf. 1 Cor. 12:7–11.

b. A happy reward to expect (24:46–47)

Jesus has already spoken emphatically about the reward awaiting those who put their relationship with God ahead of all human reputation and status.[4] Paul develops the same theme in 1 Corinthians.[5] What this will actually look like, after the Lord returns, is hard to know, but the teaching is very clear: the *quality* of our service for him really matters! We meet the same theme shortly, in the parables of the talents and the sheep and the goats.

c. A constant decision to take (24:48–49)

Will the servant continue to let his master's return shape the way he lives – day after day after day? Jesus imagines a downward spiral, to the point where his master's coming has so faded from focus that he begins to treat the household as his own, and to behave in a way completely at odds with his master's trust in him. His position and status become more important to him, and he starts to exploit them in order to indulge his own desires rather than fulfil his master's. Sadly, in recent years there have been reports of several high-profile Christians who (it turns out) were drawn down this route.

The key lies in the words *My master is delayed* (48). The Greek verb is based on our old friend *chronos*, time as measured by the calendar: as *chronos* ticks along, hour by hour and day by day, the expectation fades, and loses its force to shape our behaviour. But in God's eyes, the chronological extension of time is the vital backdrop to those billions of choice-moments which will enable us – the world – to prepare for Christ's return: within *chronos*, every moment is a *kairos*-opportunity to choose either for or against the coming Lord. The servant in this parable starts off *faithful and wise* (45), choosing *for* his master. But gradually it all changes as he starts to *beat his fellow-slaves*, and he *eats and drinks with drunkards* (49).

d. A terrible fate to fear (24:50–51)

Jesus' words are stark:

> *The master of that slave will come on a day when he does not expect him and at an hour that he does not know. He will cut him in pieces and put*

---

4   Matt. 6:1–24.

5   See 1 Cor. 3:5 – 4:5.

him with the hypocrites, where there will be weeping and gnashing
of teeth.

Straight and clear! The master steps in dramatically on behalf of the slaves who have been cruelly exploited and mistreated (and who, we can imagine, have been longing and praying for him to return and give them justice).[6] The reference to *the hypocrites* takes us back to the first part of this long discourse in Matthew 23, where Jesus accuses the 'scribes and the Pharisees' of being hypocrites, because they present a facade of uprightness which conceals a very different inner reality.[7] God's judgment will surely fall on such hypocrisy, Jesus roundly tells them.[8] Just so for the head slave: the beating, gluttony and drunkenness have been hidden behind closed doors, but the master knows. And all will be revealed, and avenged.

The *weeping and gnashing of teeth* reappears at the end of the parable of the talents, summarized as *eternal punishment* at the end of the Sheep and Goats.[9] The reality of final judgment and punishment at the return of Christ is a prominent theme in our passages, as we will see.

How can we avoid slipping into the wrong choices, so as to make sure that we are *ready* for his return? That's the focus of the next story.

2. The wise and foolish bridesmaids (25:1–13)

'At that time the kingdom of heaven will be like ten virgins who took their lamps and went out to meet the bridegroom' (1, NIV). This opening makes clear that Jesus is thinking of the moment of his return – 'at that time'. He invites us to imagine a wedding, with ten bridesmaids waiting to greet the groom as he arrives at the bride's house to 'collect' the bride. Normally there would then be a procession to the groom's house where the banquet would take place, and we should probably imagine this happening in verse 10: *those who were ready went with him into the wedding banquet.*

But, says Jesus, the groom was *delayed* (same *chronos*-word as in 24:48), and the bridesmaids all went to sleep. Some people think that the early

---

6 Remember Luke 18:7!

7 See e.g. Matt. 23:27–28.

8 Matt. 23:35–36.

9 Matt. 25:30, 46.

church was really troubled by what's called 'the delay of the parousia',[10] that is, that Jesus did not return as quickly as they expected, and they had to adjust their theology on the hoof to take account of his non-appearance. I think there is very little evidence for this, and it's plausible only if they had not been listening to this parable (among others). Jesus makes his *delay* in coming part of his teaching about it!

'He's here!' the cry goes up (6). All ten lamps need tending, but five bridesmaids are *foolish* and don't have spare oil, and so need to dash off to buy some. The five *wise* ones have thought ahead and – here's the vital thought – have *anticipated the delay* and equipped themselves with extra oil. So they are ready to join the procession and enter the feast, while the five foolish ones arrive late and are shut out, hearing these horrifying words from the groom: *Truly, I tell you, I do not know you* (12). His not knowing them, however, started with their not knowing him: unlike the wise, they did not suspect that he might be delayed. The wise knew him well enough to know that, and acted accordingly.

I'm fascinated by the punchline to this parable in verse 13: *Keep awake therefore, for you know neither the day nor the hour.* But all ten bridesmaids fell asleep, the wise as well as the foolish! We might have expected something like 'So make sure you're *ready* to join him when he arrives!' 'Awakeness' and 'readiness' are the two themes running through all these stories, as we noted above. But this punchline seems to highlight the wrong one!

Thinking about this takes us into the heart of the parable. Because they had anticipated the delay and made preparations, it didn't matter that the wise dozed off like the foolish. Like the *faithful and wise slave* in the previous parable (before he went bad), they had done what they were supposed to do, and were therefore *blessed* like him.[11] God is gracious! It doesn't matter if the second coming slips from our conscious attention, as we're immersed in the business of living from day to day, provided that our lives are oriented around serving him, keeping our focus on him. That's keeping awake: staying *alert* to his claim on us and *alive* to the call of our relationship with him.

---

[10] *Parousia* is the Greek word translated 'coming' in Matt. 24:3, 27, 37 and 39. It literally means 'presence', but then by extension 'becoming present, arriving'. 'The parousia' is a technical term for the second coming in theological discussions.

[11] Matt. 24:46.

That leads us to a realm of meaning here lying behind the words *wise* and *foolish*. These words take us back into the Old Testament contrast between 'wisdom' and 'folly'. In one of the ancient Greek translations of Daniel, King Belshazzar addresses Daniel like this: 'I have heard about you, that God's Spirit is in you, and awakeness and understanding and abundant wisdom were found in you'[12] – and he goes on, of course, to ask Daniel to interpret the writing on the wall. Awakeness, wisdom and possessing God's Spirit all go together in Daniel. 'Awakeness' is having eyes open to understand the Lord, so that we know how to respond to him and to live before him.[13] In Proverbs Wisdom herself appeals to people to seek her:

For waywardness kills the simple,
    and the complacency of fools destroys them;
but those who listen to me will be secure
    and will live at ease, without dread of disaster.[14]

Indeed, if you 'keep sound wisdom and prudence', then

If you sit down, you will not be afraid;
    when you lie down, your sleep will be sweet . . .
The wise will inherit honour,
    but stubborn fools, disgrace.[15]

So we are meeting two sorts of 'sleeping' in this parable: on the one hand, the sweet rest of the wise, who have done all and are trusting the Lord to come when he will; on the other, the ignorant complacency of the foolish, who don't know their Lord and therefore don't understand what they must do. To be 'awake' is, at heart, to know that our heavenly bridegroom is one who breaks the rules and doesn't turn up when he is supposed to – so we are ready for the delay and content that we *know neither the day nor the hour* (13). The foolish are those who think they know when he is coming and don't prepare for his delay. But they don't know him as the wise do.

---

[12] Dan. 5:14, my translation. The word 'awakeness' is the noun form of the verb to 'keep awake' which Jesus uses. NRSV has 'enlightenment'.

[13] Cf. Eph. 1:17–18.

[14] Prov. 1:32–33.

[15] Prov. 3:21, 24, 35.

As the wisdom tradition developed, the connection between wisdom and the Holy Spirit became clearer. The wise possess and are led by God's Spirit.[16] It's not a good practice to allegorize the parables, but there might be just a hint of the Holy Spirit pictured in the *oil* that fuels the bridesmaids' lamps.[17]

So what is the essential activity involved in being prepared? How should we actually live while the Son of Man delays his coming? The next parable tackles this question, and with it the even more important underlying question: what kind of Lord is he – so that we can be sure that what we're doing is pleasing to him?

3. The Talents (25:14–30)

This parable follows straight on from the last without a break: *For it is as if a man, going on a journey, summoned his slaves and entrusted his property to them . . .* (14). But whereas the parable of the bridesmaids starts at the end of the story, with the Lord's return, this one starts at the beginning, with his departure. And immediately it poses a problem, or rather leaves a question open: what does *entrusted his property to them* mean? Did he actually give them these huge sums of money,[18] or is he simply giving them the job to 'make his money work' for him while he is away?

The Greek leaves it open, though the three servants understand it in the latter sense. The third servant, resentfully returning his talent from its hiding place in the ground, says, *Here you have what is yours* (25). And servants numbers 1 and 2 are clearly ready to give back to their Lord not only his original stake but also all that they have earned with it (20, 22).

But at the end of the parable we learn something different. Responding to their report, the delighted Lord says the same words to both servants 1 and 2: *Well done, good and trustworthy slave; you have been trustworthy in a few things, I will put you in charge of many things; enter into the joy of your master* (21, 23). *Enter into the joy* means 'receive the joy that I give you in response', and the punchline of the parable reveals what this *joy* is, at least in part: here servant number 1 is called *the one with the ten*

---

[16] In addition to Daniel's example, see Wisdom 7:15 – 8:1.

[17] Cf. Zech. 4:1–6.

[18] Yes – one talent was worth six thousand denarii, and a denarius was a normal day's wage for a working man. How much does an ordinary worker earn in nineteen years? That's a talent! See Carson, 'Matthew', p. 516.

talents (28), or (more literally) 'the one who *has* the ten talents' – and who at that point gets an eleventh talent, taken from servant number 3.

Wow – in this throwaway line we discover that the master has actually given the money to his servants, not just what they earned but the original stake as well. This is the *joy* they enter – this sharing of the master's riches, along with the new responsibilities he now gives them.

This enormous generosity is vital to the meaning of this parable. It would be possible to reduce its meaning to a simple moral lesson: the Lord wants us to make the most of the opportunities he gives us and the 'talents' (in the other sense) he has entrusted to us. Yes, of course he does – and it is also true that 'From everyone to whom much has been given, much will be required.'[19] If God gives us gifts in the 1 Corinthians 12 sense – spiritual gifts and ministries – then he expects us to seize every chance to use them! We must multiply the spiritual capital they represent.

But that is not the core meaning of this parable. Rather than just being about the servants – and their use or non-use of the talents – the parable is more deeply about the master and their relationship with him. It all comes out in the words of servant number 3 when he makes excuses for burying his talent: *Master, I knew that you were a harsh man, reaping where you did not sow, and gathering where you did not scatter seed; so I was afraid, and I went and hid your talent in the ground* (24–25). And the master seems to concur with this evaluation of his character, as he responds:

> *You wicked and lazy slave! You knew, did you, that I reap where I did not sow, and gather where I did not scatter? Then you ought to have invested my money with the bankers, and on my return I would have received what was my own with interest.*
> (26–27)

But we know from the end of the parable that the master is not *a harsh man* who exploits others – he is incredibly generous, fantastically so. Servant 3 has got him quite wrong, and in verses 26–27 the master is simply playing back to him his own perception of his character. If he really believed that – and so didn't want to give his master yet another opportunity to profit from someone else's hard labour – then why didn't he at

---

[19] Luke 12:48.

least put the money in the bank? His failure to do this reveals his heart: he simply doesn't want to serve this master. He calls him *Master* (24; literally 'Lord'), but in reality he doesn't like him, doesn't want to be in relationship with him, wants to bury his connection with this 'Lord'.

Servants 1 and 2, on the other hand, relish their connection with him. Servant 1, on receiving the money, *went off at once* to put it to work (16) – and actually these words are front-loaded to the start of the sentence in the Greek, to emphasize that he got cracking with no delay. He can't wait to get working for his Lord. If we asked him for a character assessment of his master, we can bet that it would be very different from that of servant 3.

The point is this: even though the master is not present, and is away for *a long time* (19), all three servants are still in relationship with him. They respond to him as they know him to be, although their assessments are very different. It is as if he is still present with them as they handle his money (or decide not to). Which of them has rightly understood him? It's servants 1 and 2, of course, but we only know that for sure when he returns and acts with such huge generosity towards them.

So for us: the call is to prepare for his return by living in relationship with him, and serving him with everything we've got – passionately, unremittingly, creatively, delightedly, and appropriately in line with our gifts. If we manage to 'double up' what he's entrusted to us, that's great, but it seems that the amount is not the important thing. The vital thing is that *he is worth serving* in that kind of way. It's worth giving everything for him, because everything we have comes from him, anyway.

At the end of the parable we meet the principle of retribution, the basic principle underlying the judgment that follows, when Jesus returns. Paul puts it like this: 'All of us must appear before the judgement seat of Christ, so that each may receive recompense for what has been done in the body, whether good or evil.'[20] This parable makes clear that it's the quality of our relationship with our absent-but-coming Lord which is the vital thing: how we are with him *now* will determine how we are with him *then*. Servant 3 is called *worthless* (30), or (more exactly) 'useless', because he has proved of no 'use' to his master, and therefore lands up in the place that he has chosen, away from this Lord whom he sees as tyrannical and exploitative – in *the outer darkness, where there will be weeping and gnashing of teeth* (30).

---

[20] 2 Cor. 5:10. See also Rom. 2:6–10.

Here's the challenge: can we really love and serve a God who rules the world with apparent indifference to people's suffering? The third servant's 'fear' of him is not inappropriate (25). The 'master' who leaves and returns (a picture of the Son of Man) is modelled on a kind of autocratic, all-powerful and very wealthy overlord not unknown in the Ancient Near East – the kind of 'Lord' who was *really* as servant 3 pictures him: exploitative, tyrannical and completely unappreciative of those who serve him. The 'Lord' in this parable might well be *a harsh man* (24) – except that he is not. Servants 1 and 2 know better.

So the parable brings before us two sorts of fear, with the question: what sort of fear will we have before the Son of Man? The third servant's fear of his supposed capriciousness, injustice and unpredictability, or the other servants' fear which motivates them to love and serve him, however long he stays away – that 'fear of the LORD' which is 'the beginning of wisdom' (Prov. 9:10)?

The fourth parable in this sequence takes the ideas further: what kind of 'trading' will please the coming Lord? What exactly does he want us to do? What will lead him to call us *blessed by my Father*, and invite us to *inherit the kingdom prepared for you from the foundation of the world* (34)?

4. The Sheep and the Goats (25:31–46)

The answer to the question is clear: the coming Lord (described here as *the king*, 34) wants us to serve the poor, because he so identifies himself with them that, if we serve them, we will actually be serving him. So, although in one sense he is absent until he *comes in his glory, and all the angels with him* (31),[21] in another sense he has been present all along, in the persons of the poor: the hungry, the thirsty, the stranger, the naked, the sick, the prisoners. This list is given four times,[22] just to make sure we get the point! If we serve them, we are serving him. If we ignore them, we are ignoring him.

This could hardly be further from the image of the standard Middle Eastern despot who is the central figure in the last parable! This king is not just out and about among his people, but identifies with them to such

---

[21] Our old friends pop up here again – Dan. 7:13 and Zech. 14:5!

[22] Vv. 35–36, 37–39, 42–43, 44.

an extent that their pains are his, and so the *relief* of their pain is the relief of his, also.

This brings us to a vital point of interpretation. Who exactly are these poor in whom the absent Son of Man is already present? When *the right-eous* protest that they do not know how or when they cared for the king, his explanation is: *Truly I tell you, just as you did it to one of the least of these who are members of my family, you did it to me* (40). The Greek literally says 'one of the least of these my brothers', and undoubtedly this means those who belong to the circle of his disciples, pictured as his family. We have already met this picture in Matthew: for instance, when Jesus' mother and brothers come to find him, Jesus points at his disciples and roundly declares, 'Here are my mother and my brothers! For whoever does the will of my Father in heaven is my brother and sister and mother.'[23]

So as far as Matthew is concerned, it seems very clear that the poor in this parable are Jesus' impoverished disciples engaged in the mission to bring the gospel to all the nations before he comes again (24:14) – *all the nations* that are now *gathered before him* (25:32): and the criterion of judgment is whether they have been welcomed and served.

However, a wider meaning is often found here. As Paula Gooder says, this parable 'would, for many Christians, be the passage that motivates them into social action and care for the poor'[24] – seeing Jesus in the face of the poor, whoever they are. Is this wrong? It's not what Matthew had in mind, but Gooder comments,

> If pressed, I would say that while the popular interpretation is not what the parable originally meant, it is still valid. The abiding popularity of seeing this parable as motivation to care for those in need points to the fact that it sums up, in a convenient and vivid form, much of Jesus' teaching about serving and caring for others, particularly the poor and the outcast.[25]

I think this is wise. The parables are sometimes 'flexible friends' with meaning that stretches beyond their original. Caring for the poor and the rejected in Jesus' name – reaching out with practical compassion and

---

[23] Matt. 12:49–50.

[24] Paula Gooder, *The Parables* (Norwich: Canterbury Press, 2020), p. 73.

[25] Gooder, *Parables*, pp. 76–77.

provision – is a vital part of gospel ministry. It is deeply etched on his heart: so that, if and when we his servants are persecuted for doing this, *he suffers with us*. Similarly, all who support us in our mission, standing with us because they like what they see – giving us 'a cup of cold water', as Jesus puts it earlier in Matthew – 'will by no means lose their reward' when the Son of Man comes.[26] What does that mean – 'not lose their reward'? Will he welcome into his kingdom *all* whose heart for the poor has motivated them into sacrificial service, associating themselves with the needy, the shamed and the condemned, whether they have identified as Jesus' followers or not? I'm going to wait and see.

So Jesus tells us how to be ready for his return. It boils down to passionate service, motivated by deep love for him: get stuck in, organize the house, trim the lamps, exercise his gifts, serve the poor, and we'll be ready when suddenly the day dawns.

But here's a fascinating question. How *can* the Son of Man be so closely identified with the sufferings of his people while he is 'away'? Is this just very intense sympathy, felt from afar? Or is it more than that? Our next passage addresses precisely this point!

---

[26] See Matt. 10:40–42. My translation of v. 42.

John 14:1–31

9. At home with the Lord

John 14[1] begins with these famous and beautiful verses which I have frequently read at funeral services (one of the passages suggested by the Church of England):

> *Do not let your hearts be troubled. Believe in God, believe also in me.*
> *In my Father's house there are many dwelling-places. If it were not so,*
> *would I have told you that I go to prepare a place for you? And if I go and*
> *prepare a place for you, I will come again and will take you to myself,*
> *so that where I am, there you may be also.*
>
> (1–3)

When my wife died in 2018, I found huge comfort in the message these verses seem to convey: that at death, the Lord comes to us and takes us to be with him in his *Father's house*, where there is a *dwelling-place* prepared and waiting. 'Place' and 'house' go together, because both words connote the heavenly 'temple', where God dwells and where a 'place' is prepared for us among the many *dwelling-places* there. Glorious, wonderful, comforting . . . and true?

Possibly not. Some think that Jesus is talking here not about the moment of death but about his second coming – *I will come again.*[2] That seems

---

[1] In what follows I do not attempt to unpack the whole chapter. The chapter on John 14 in Motyer, *Come, Lord Jesus!* (pp. 144–164) is much fuller and attempts this.

[2] So e.g. D. A. Carson, *The Gospel according to John* (Leicester: Inter-Varsity Press; Grand Rapids, MI: Eerdmans, 1991), p. 488; and R. E. Brown, *The Gospel according to John*, Anchor Bible Commentary (London: Geoffrey Chapman, 1971), p. 626. 'Idiosyncratic' is Carson's word for the idea that it refers to Jesus coming to believers at their death.

very possible, and I might seem to be agreeing with it by including the passage in this book! Others think he is promising to return to the disciples in resurrection after his death,[3] or maybe through his Spirit at Pentecost.[4] These seem possible, too: at this point the disciples are feeling deeply distressed because Jesus has just told them that he is about to leave, and that they cannot come with him.[5] We could look ahead to 16:16, where he says, 'A little while, and you will no longer see me, and again a little while, and you will see me.'

What is Jesus promising here? I need to know if I have been wrongly applying his promise by using it at funeral services! – and indeed by finding encouragement here after my wife's death.

1. 'I am coming' in John 14

Verse 3 is actually the first of four times in this passage where Jesus promises to *come* to his disciples, and it seems likely that we should interpret them in connection with one another. Let's collect the other three:

> (1) *I will not leave you orphaned; I am coming to you. In a little while the world will no longer see me, but you will see me; because I live, you also will live. On that day you will know that I am in my Father, and you in me, and I in you.*
> (18–20)

This definitely seems to be about Jesus' coming to them in and through the Holy Spirit. He has just promised the Spirit to them – *the Spirit of truth, whom the world cannot receive, because it neither sees him nor knows him. You know him, because he abides with you, and he will be in you* (17). When the Spirit comes, Jesus comes, and the disciples will no longer be *orphans*.

> (2) *Judas (not Iscariot) said to him, 'Lord, how is it that you will reveal yourself to us, and not to the world?' Jesus answered him, 'Those who love me will keep my word, and my Father will love them, and we will come to them, and make our home with them.'*
> (22–23)

---

[3] So B. Lindars, *The Gospel of John*, New Century Bible (London: Oliphants, 1972), p. 471.

[4] So J. N. Sanders and B. A. Mastin, *The Gospel according to St John*, Black's New Testament Commentary (London: A&C Black, 1968), p. 321.

[5] John 13:33.

Jesus' answer to Judas' question seems to be that he will be revealed to the world through the church being transformed by God's love, because together he and the Father have 'made their home' there. So again, this seems to be about Jesus 'coming' to them through the Spirit, this time bringing his Father with him!

Remarkably, the Greek word translated *home* here (23, Greek *monē*) appears also in verse 2 where NRSV translates it *dwelling-places*. NIV has 'home' in verse 23 but 'rooms' in verse 2. Neither version helps us by using different translations when there must be a connection between these two appearances of the same word.[6] Jesus and his Father create a 'home' for themselves with us (23), matching the 'home' which Jesus is preparing for us with him in the heavenly temple (2). Does this hint that the 'coming' in verse 3 is the same – Jesus coming back to the disciples at Pentecost?

> (3) *Peace I leave with you; my peace I give to you. I do not give to you as the world gives. Do not let your hearts be troubled, and do not let them be afraid. You heard me say to you, 'I am going away, and I am coming to you.' If you loved me, you would rejoice that I am going to the Father, because the Father is greater than I.*
> (27–28)

Again, this 'coming' seems to be closely tied to the gift of the Spirit, *whom the Father will send in my name* to teach the disciples *and remind you of all that I have said to you* (26). Because the Spirit comes in the *name* of Jesus, the Spirit's coming is a coming of Jesus himself to them.

Famously, the Johannine expert R. E. Brown (mentioned in a footnote above) described the Holy Spirit in John as 'the presence of Jesus when Jesus is absent'[7] – and this seems an apt description of the way in which the Spirit is presented in these three other 'coming' passages. Behind this is some amazing theology, of course. The Holy Spirit *of God* has become the Spirit *of Jesus*: so when the Holy Spirit comes, he brings with him both the Father and the Son to be present to Jesus' followers. Wow! We can illustrate this mind-bending truth by comparing the four verses in which the gift of the Spirit is progressively described in this part of John:

---

[6] These are the only two occasions where *monē* appears in the New Testament. It is related to the verb *menein*, 'abide' or 'remain', which will be used prominently in the next chapter of 'abiding' in Jesus, in his word and in his love, like branches in the vine (John 15:4–10).

[7] Brown, *John*, p. 1141.

- 14:16: '*I will ask* the Father, and *he will give* you another Advocate, to be with you for ever.'
- 14:26: 'But the Advocate, the Holy Spirit, whom *the Father will send in my name,* will teach you everything.'
- 15:26: 'When the Advocate comes, whom *I will send* to you *from the Father,* the Spirit of truth who *comes from the Father,* he will testify on my behalf.'
- 16:7: 'I tell you the truth: it is to your advantage that I go away, for if I do not go away, the Advocate will not come to you; but if I go, *I will send him* to you.'

The sequence here is striking. The Father's agency in bestowing his own Spirit on whomever he will is *supplemented* by the agency of the Son, who also becomes a Giver of the Spirit – even in his own right, in the last verse. The Spirit is already with the disciples, because Jesus is with them (14:17), and when the Spirit comes, he will confirm Jesus' teaching to them (14:26), 'testify' on Jesus' behalf (15:26), and 'take what is mine and declare it to you' (16:14). This is because 'all that the Father has is mine' (16:15) – *including the Holy Spirit!*

The theologically minded will want to say to themselves at this point that the doctrine of the Trinity is lurking behind all this, even though it will take the church three hundred years fully to articulate what this might mean for the relationship between Father, Son and Holy Spirit – and the discussion is going on still![8]

2. The 'sheep and goats' puzzle

We have discovered the answer to that question left unanswered by Matthew! How can the Son of Man be so closely present to 'the least of these who are members of my family', intimately sharing their pains, while he is still away and not yet sitting 'on the throne of his glory'?[9] The answer is that the Holy Spirit, who is the Spirit of Christ and who therefore brings Christ's presence wherever he goes, lives in all who belong to Christ. As Paul puts it, 'Anyone who does not have the Spirit of Christ does not belong to him.'[10] But if we do have the Spirit, then it's not just a matter

---

[8] See Brian Edgar, *The Message of the Trinity*, The Bible Speaks Today (Leicester: Inter-Varsity Press, 2004).

[9] Matt. 25:31, 40.

[10] Rom. 8:9b.

of 'belonging' to Jesus in some distant sense. We are intimately connected to him: Paul goes so far as to describe our bodies as 'limbs of Christ'.[11] Our connection with Jesus, by his Spirit, *includes* our physical identity and realities. So he shares not only all our pains, but also our relief when others reach out to us and minister to us. He is fully part of our experience, just as we, being 'in' him, are wrapped into his – his death and resurrection.[12]

This is a glorious truth worth dwelling on! And we will return to it when we look at 1 Corinthians 15.[13] But let's get back to our starting question:

3. Does 'I will come again' (14:3) refer to the second coming?

It seems that the other three references to his 'coming' in John 14 all refer solidly, and wonderfully, to his coming in the person of the Holy Spirit – so is this what it means in 14:3 as well?

No! The other three 'comings' all relate to the disciples' continuing life in the world. His coming in the Holy Spirit will mean that they will *see* him, even though *the world will no longer see* him (19). It will mean that they begin to display the life, love and words of God himself to the world around them (23–24). And it will mean that they have the *greater* presence of God himself to fortify them as they face the power of *the ruler of this world*, the devil (28–30). But in 14:3 Jesus' coming is about taking them out of this world to be with him *in my Father's house* (2), in the special *place* prepared for them there.

As in Acts, the second coming is not a prominent theme in John. But it surely appears here! The earthly temple, the physical place of God's presence on earth, was believed to be the earthly counterpart of his heavenly dwelling, and that belief lies behind Jesus' words in 14:2–3. At the heart of his second coming lies the promise to *take you to myself*, so that all of us who, as Jesus' followers, have struggled and agonized our way through earthly life – struggling for the staples of food and drink ('hungry'), alienated from the norms of society around us ('strangers'), shamed in our lack of all that gives status and approval ('naked'), labouring under physical weakness ('sick'),[14] and condemned as useless and harmful ('in prison') – are

---

[11] 1 Cor. 6:15, literal translation.
[12] See especially Rom. 6:1–5.
[13] See below, ch. 12.
[14] Sickness or disability was regarded as evidence of being under the curse of God (or the gods).

brought by him into his glorious heavenly home, to a place prepared for us there. As in Matthew 24, his coming means the gathering of the elect from the four corners of the earth,[15] but now we discover what happens to them, once gathered!

This is truly a prospect to calm troubled hearts and to strengthen faith (14:1), and to give peace and courage in the face of all that we must bear (27).

In a moment we will ask how the second coming relates to the other 'comings' in John 14. But first let's come back to the important question we began with:

4. Is it OK to read 14:1–3 at funerals? Thoughts on time and eternity

If *I will come again* refers to the second coming, we might conclude that it's a bit of a stretch to apply it to the individual deaths of believers. Perhaps it is even quite wrong to do so.

Assessing this question raises another thorny one – the question of what has been called the 'intermediate state'. Where do believers go when they die? A long-standing and traditional view has been that they 'sleep' in Christ until the day of resurrection, which we may identify with the day of the second coming. Paul calls the dead 'those who have fallen asleep' in 1 Thessalonians 4:13 (literal translation) – and it seems that the question bothering the Thessalonians is precisely what has happened to brothers and sisters in Christ who have died before the second coming. Paul tells them that, at the second coming, 'the dead in Christ will rise first', and then 'we who are alive, who are left, will be caught up in the clouds together with them to meet the Lord in the air; and so we will be with the Lord for ever'.[16]

We look at this passage in our next chapter. At first sight the thought that the dead 'sleep' until Christ returns seems pretty clearly what Paul means – in which case applying John 14:1–3 to the death of individual believers is not really appropriate: the dead *rest*, and *wait*, until the morning dawns. But elsewhere Paul writes of being 'with' Christ after death, which he describes as 'far better' than his present life 'in the flesh'[17] – and this seems to imply that the 'sleep' of the dead is a conscious

---

[15] Matt. 24:31.

[16] 1 Thess. 4:16–17.

[17] Phil. 1:22–23.

existence in fellowship with Christ, rather than an unconscious suspension of awareness. Maybe 'sleeping' is a description of their state from *our* point of view, rather than from theirs or Christ's.

In another fascinating but complex passage Paul uses the same imagery of the 'house' that we meet in John 14:

> For we know that if the earthly tent we live in is destroyed, we have a building from God, a house not made with hands, eternal in the heavens. For in this tent we groan, longing to be clothed with our heavenly dwelling – hoping that[18] when we have taken it off we will not be found naked . . . We wish not to be unclothed but to be further clothed, so that what is mortal may be swallowed up by life.[19]

Clearly the 'earthly tent' is our present physical body, and Paul is reaching towards the idea of the resurrection body which he develops in 1 Corinthians 15. God has a new 'building' already prepared for us – the parallel with John 14 is striking. And Paul seems to imply that our 'longing' to 'put on' this new building (like a new suit of clothes) straight after death is not unrealistic. We are not going to have to be naked or 'unclothed', without any kind of 'dwelling'!

How can we put all this together? All I can do is to share the conviction to which I have come after much mulling of these passages and of the theological issues they raise.

One of the problems caused by the traditional view (of sleeping in Christ) is that it presumes that the dead still exist within *chronos*, like us. The calendar is ticking along for them, as for us. So they are waiting for the second coming too, and the longer Jesus delays, the longer they must 'sleep'. But Christ is the Lord of time. As we know, space and time are bound up with each other inseparably, so to create the universe is to create time and space together.[20] The risen Jesus is not bound by time as we are, and it makes sense therefore to imagine that the 'dead in Christ' are not bound by time, either. 'In him' they enter another continuum entirely.

If this is so, then we can certainly imagine that *the moment of our death is the moment when Christ comes again* to take us to be with himself. The

---

[18] I have adjusted the NRSV translation, 'if indeed', slightly here.

[19] 2 Cor. 5:1–4.

[20] See e.g. Carlo Rovelli, *Reality Is Not What It Seems: The Journey to Quantum Gravity* (London: Allen Lane, 2016).

kairos-moment which is our death – the only sure thing we know about our future, which we can pray about and offer up to God – is the moment at which we 'move' straight to that great *kairos*, the final Day, the day of judgment and resurrection when Christ comes again, and we are 'clothed' with our new heavenly dwelling and are ushered into the *dwelling-place* prepared for us!

So it could be OK, after all, to read John 14:1–3 at funerals and to take comfort from it, as I did when my wife died.

There is an interesting consequence of taking this view. If the dead in Christ pass out of time and enter straight into the new creation, then they – we – are all there, already. In fact, words like 'already' cease to be appropriate. Those who have died do not have to hang around in the new creation waiting for the rest of us to join them. Sharing this conviction with my wife before she died, I said to her that I thought I would be separated from her by death, but she would not be separated from me. The new creation to which we pass, on death, is the perfected world in which we are all 'already' sanctified and glorified (including our grandchildren and generations yet to be!). Maybe this is how Paul is able to use the past tense of being 'glorified' in Romans 8:30, and how he is able to say that we have not only been 'raised up' with Christ but also 'seated . . . with him in the heavenly places'[21] – again, past tense. It's almost as though we exist in two places – both here (within time, in the flesh) and 'in the heavenly places' (outside time, in Christ).[22]

Finally, coming back from ethereal realms to John 14, let's ask . . .

5. How do all these 'comings' fit together?

It is remarkable how the Greek word *mone* is used of two 'dwelling-places' in John 14: of the 'dwelling-place' in *my Father's house* prepared for us (2) – which we are definitely understanding to be that heavenly 'building' ready for us after death – and of the 'dwelling-place' which the Father and the Son together make for themselves in the church (23). That's a signal of the connection between the 'coming again' of the Lord in verse 3 (his final coming to 'take his power and reign') and his prior coming to the church in and through his Spirit.

---

[21] Eph. 2:6.

[22] See also Col. 3:3. An excellent book on all this (though without this final speculation) is Paula Gooder, *Body: Biblical Spirituality for the Whole Person* (London: SPCK, 2016).

In both cases, home-making is involved. And that's about *relational connection*. To be 'at home' with others means, in essence, four things:

- Experiencing and enjoying one another's presence,
- Talking – engaging in conversation,
- Setting goals – planning shared activity, and
- Undertaking shared 'doing'.

These four cover just about everything that a well-functioning family will experience together. We just have to wait and see how they might look in the 14:3 'home' prepared for us with Jesus! But it is not difficult to see how John develops all four ideas in relation to the life we share with God (Father, Son and Holy Spirit) *here and now*, as he comes to us and makes his 'home' with us. Looking beyond John 14, and taking these points in the same order, we can point to:

- The gift of shared peace, joy and love, Jesus' calling his disciples his 'friends', and the language of being 'in' each other;[23]
- The sharing of God's 'word' and 'words' with us (which are of course also the words of Jesus), the Holy Spirit as our teacher, and our responsive prayer;[24]
- Jesus' purpose that we should do 'greater works', 'bear fruit' for him, and bear the opprobrium of the world as he has done;[25]
- Jesus' call to live out his love before the world, and to testify about him as the Spirit does.[26]

These 'comings' are closely related to one another. We saw this first in Psalm 18,[27] where David uses the wonderful language of theophany to describe the deliverances he had experienced in his life. We saw it again in Acts 3, where the 'times of refreshing' anticipate the 'time of universal restoration'.[28] God's rescue of us involves *him coming* to us: supremely of

---

[23] John 14:27; 15:9–11, 14–15; 14:20; 15:4; 17:21–23.

[24] John 14:10, 13, 15, 21, 24, 26, etc.!

[25] John 14:12; 15:16, 18–19; 16:2.

[26] John 14:23–24 (cf. 13:34–35); 15:10; 16:26–28; 15:26–27; 16:8–11.

[27] Our second chapter, above.

[28] Acts 3:20–21.

course in the incarnation of his Son, but now also in all the 'comings' of his Spirit to share our life and enable us to walk with him, until that final Coming which will raise us and the whole world to the glory he intends.

Part 3
The second coming in the letters of Paul

1 Thessalonians 4:13 – 5:11

10. The coming of the Lord: Part 1

We jump into Paul, to look at five passages on the second coming full of rich and vital teaching.

Our first passage picks up where we have just been, in John 14. We can't separate the second coming from all the vital questions that concern our future, because we as Christians have a unique perspective. Uniquely among all world religions and philosophies, we believe that we humans cannot know fully who we are, right now, because our identity – our true nature – will only be fully known at the End. As John puts it:

> Beloved, we are God's children now, but what we will be has not
> yet been made clear. All we know is that, whenever he is made clear
> [at his coming], we will be like him, because we will see him as he
> truly is.[1]

This is all about being gradually 'conformed to the image of his Son', as Paul puts it in Romans 8:29. So when we see *Jesus* 'as he truly is', we will then for the first time truly know ourselves. This applies both on an individual level and on a macro, global level (as we will see especially when we look at 1 Corinthians 15).[2] God's final purpose for us is to be fully and wholly who he created us to be *in union with his Son*, who is both the Beginning and the End of creation.[3]

---

[1] 1 John 3:2, my translation. See chapter 20, section 2, below (pp. 255–257).
[2] Below, chapter 12.
[3] See Col. 1:15–20.

One of the questions that arises, therefore, is how our death fits into that plan and purpose of God. We've already thought about this a little, in the last chapter. Now we come to a passage in Paul that raises the same issues. The Thessalonians were deeply worried that some of their number had died *before* the coming of the Lord. Since Paul had so emphasized to them the vital importance of the second coming and the challenge of being ready for it (see his summary of his message to them in 1 Thess. 1:9–10), what happens to those who die before he comes?

1. A little bit of background

Paul wrote 1 and 2 Thessalonians not long after founding the church there on his second missionary journey, probably in AD 51.[4] He had given them teaching about the second coming while with them,[5] but two things then happened:

- The Thessalonians sent Paul some questions about the coming of the Lord, probably through Timothy,[6] and Paul responds to these questions in the passage we look at in this chapter; and
- After sending 1 Thessalonians to them, he got word that they (or some of them) had got into a state of eschatological super-excitement, believing that 'the day of the Lord is right upon us',[7] and giving up work as a result.[8] Paul responds to this in 2 Thessalonians, our focus for the next chapter.

One fascinating feature of Paul's writing in both letters is his close relationship with the teaching of Jesus. Many details reveal that, even though the Gospels had not been written at this point, Paul was aware of the teaching that we now have in Matthew 24 (paralleled in Mark 13 and Luke 21).[9] He probably refers to this background in 1 Thessalonians 4:15: 'this we declare to you by the word of the Lord'. He is conscious of drawing directly on Jesus' teaching, although it is clear that he handles it freely with apostolic authority, as we will see.

---

[4] See Acts 17:1–10.
[5] 2 Thess. 2:5; 1 Thess. 1:10.
[6] See 1 Thess. 3:6.
[7] 2 Thess. 2:2 (my translation).
[8] See 2 Thess. 3:6–13 (also 1 Thess. 4:10–12).
[9] I set out the many detailed echoes of Jesus' teaching in *Come, Lord Jesus!*, pp. 100–102.

2. An overview of 1 Thessalonians 4:13 – 5:11

Paul has a special way of introducing answers to questions that have been sent to him, and we meet this special introduction both in 4:13 and in 5:1, where he picks up two questions the Thessalonians have asked about the second coming. This introduction is often translated 'now concerning . . .', although it has disappeared from the NRSV in 4:13. A better rendering would be: 'Now concerning those who have fallen asleep, brothers and sisters, we do not want you to be ignorant, so that you may not grieve like the others who have no hope . . .'[10] The 'others who have no hope' are the Thessalonians' pagan neighbours – whom they were once like.[11] Ancient paganism gave very little assurance about an afterlife: it simply prescribed festivals and sacrifices demanded by gods whose favour was essential for day-by-day prosperity. People were left deeply uncertain about life after death. Then along came the gospel, which made resurrected life not just an expectation but the centrepiece of God's action towards us in Christ! To be saved from death and sin, and to live with him for all eternity – this is the very heart of God's plan for us in Jesus. It's not surprising that the gospel truly was 'good news' in Thessaloniki, as throughout the ancient world. No wonder, too, that the Thessalonians were keen to understand as clearly as they could what Jesus gives us after death.

This passage falls into two parts – marked by the 'now concernings . . .' in 4:13 and 5:1 – which relate to each other just as Matthew 24 and 25 do: Paul addresses first 'what happens?' and then 'how should we get ready for it?' Both his answers end with the exhortation to *encourage one another* (4:18; 5:11). This seems to be Paul's purpose in writing, and he wants the Thessalonians to use his *words* (4:18) to carry on a process of mutual encouragement. In addition, the passage begins and ends with reference to the possibility of 'falling asleep' before Jesus comes, and to our sharing in Jesus' death and resurrection.[12]

Interestingly, Paul uses 'sleep' not just as a metaphor for dying, but also for not staying alert, 'dropping off' on the job (5:6–7). Using 'sleep' in this second sense arises undoubtedly from the influence of Jesus' teaching.[13]

---

[10] My translation. NRSV uses 'die' for 'fall asleep'.

[11] Cf. 1 Thess. 1:9.

[12] Compare 4:13–14 and 5:10.

[13] See Matt. 24:42.

We can analyse the passage around the two questions it addresses:

4:13–18 Question 1: 'Paul, what happens to our loved ones who have died before Jesus' return? Do they miss out on his coming kingdom?' (4:13). Paul's response:

(a) v. 14: Everything depends on our connection to Jesus' death and resurrection. This means that, when he comes, *God will bring with him those who have* [*fallen asleep*].

(b) vv. 15–17: On the Lord's own authority I can say three things to you:

(i) v. 15: Those alive when he comes will have no advantage over those who have already died.

(ii) v. 16: For when the trumpet sounds, the dead in Christ will rise first.

(iii) v. 17: Then we will all be caught up together to meet the Lord in the clouds.

(c) v. 18: So encourage one another by saying this to each other!

5:1–11 Question 2: 'Paul, when exactly is he coming? What exactly are the vital moments in God's plan?' (5:1). Paul's response:

(a) vv. 2–3: The 'exact' timing is that he's coming like a thief in the night, and like labour pains to a pregnant woman! No escape. How can we be ready? Three things to do:

(i) vv. 4–5: Know who you are! You already have 'the Day' within you – you are *children of light* and *children of the day*; you don't belong to night and darkness.

(ii) vv. 6–7: So keep focused! Let's stay awake in daytime sobriety, and not doze in night-time inebriation!

(iii) vv. 8–9a: Arm yourselves! Put on faith, love and hope as the armour we need to protect ourselves and keep ourselves living in line with God's salvation purpose for us.

(b) vv. 9b–10: It doesn't matter if we die before he comes, because the vital thing is sharing Jesus' resurrection life.

(c) v. 11: So keep on encouraging one another, as you are doing!

One fascinating thing to notice immediately is the extent to which Paul uses picture language here. Image piles upon image – not just 'sleep' as a metaphor both for dying and for forgetting about his coming, but also drunkenness, the armour, the metaphors of day and night and of pregnancy and thieves . . . piling on top of the great pictures in 4:16–17 of the archangel's voice and the trumpet of God and the clouds and meeting Jesus there. Even the innocuous word *meet* (4:17) carries a delightful metaphor: it's a special word that connotes a local delegation greeting a visiting monarch in order to welcome him into their city.[14] So we will 'meet and greet' the Lord as we welcome him back to his earth.

The plethora of images raises the vital question of the extent to which, if at all, they are to be understood *literally*. Some of them obviously not, like the armour in 15:8 and the labour pains in 15:3. But what about the clouds and the trumpet call and the meeting in the air (14:16–17)? Are these 'just' symbols, or did Paul expect it to be literally like this? This is such an important question that we'll keep it on ice and come back to it at the end of the chapter, after we take a closer look at each of the two parts of our passage in turn.

3. With the Lord! (4:13–18)

We have to imagine our way into the 'feel' of the question Paul is tackling here. The Thessalonians had been led to believe that the Lord Jesus would be coming very soon. So when several of their number died, they naturally wondered whether these now departed brothers and sisters would be deprived in some way – would they miss out on Jesus' glorious return? What happens to them?

The modern version of this is to wonder where we go when we die – what happens to *us*? What will it be like – what can we expect? I developed a few thoughts around this in the last chapter, but noted at the time that 1 Thessalonians 4:13 and 16 are a problem for the view I expressed.[15] Here Paul says that the dead are 'asleep', and that when Jesus comes *the dead in Christ will rise first*. This suggests that the dead go into a state of suspension which could be called 'sleep' until the Lord's *cry of command* summons them dramatically to life. I'm thinking of Sir Stanley Spencer's famous painting *The Resurrection, Cookham* in the Tate Gallery in London: a very powerful imagining of what this might look like when the Day dawns and the graves burst open and the dead (many of them known to

---

[14] Cf. Matt. 25:6; Acts 28:15. The use of this image especially underlines the 'imperial' flavour here: Paul's readers would think of the pomp and circumstance surrounding a visitation by the emperor. But this is no mere Roman potentate: the true King of all is arriving!

[15] See above, pp. 113–115.

Spencer, who grew up in Cookham) emerge joyfully to life in the church-yard, as flowers bloom around them.

It's a very literal imagining of 1 Thessalonians 4:16 – with quite a splash of resuscitation thrown in. It could be a problem for this view of resurrection that so many of us have been cremated, our bodies completely dispersed. On these grounds many have objected to cremation: how can we rise to life if there is nothing of our bodies left? As a country vicar in the Church of England I buried many elderly parishioners in the church-yard surrounding the church, and there was something very moving about 'laying to rest' someone who had lived his or her whole life in the village and was now 'sleeping' in the churchyard, overlooking the fields where he or she had worked, waiting for Resurrection Morning to dawn.

There are two separate (but connected) questions for us here: whether this view of the dead 'sleeping' is right, and whether burial is essential, so that there is at least something of our bodies left for resurrection to work on! Paul helps us with both. Let's tackle them in turn.

a. Do the dead 'sleep' until resurrection?

There's a fascinating tension in Paul's teaching here. On the one hand, he says *the dead in Christ will rise first* (16) because he wants to assure the Thessalonians that *we who are alive, who are left until the coming of the Lord, will by no means precede those who have [fallen asleep]* (15). That's the issue that worries the Thessalonians: will their deceased loved ones miss out in some way, when the Lord comes? No, says Paul, they will *rise first*, and *then* (important word) *we who are alive, who are left, will be caught up in the clouds together with them to meet the Lord in the air* (17). This seems to match Spencer's picture: the living are onlookers as the dead rise at the Lord's command. And *then* we all rise to meet him, like a local delegation greeting a visiting monarch.

But on the other hand, verse 14 holds a different comforting thought for the Thessalonians: *since we believe that Jesus died and rose again, even so God will bring* with him *those who have [fallen asleep] through Jesus.*[16] You can see what Paul is thinking: the dead are *in Christ* (16), so it follows that, when he comes, they will be *with him*. This is all because *we believe that Jesus died and rose again* (14), and (unspoken thought) we who believe

---

[16] I have adjusted the NRSV translation here, attaching the phrase *through Jesus* to 'fall asleep' (as in NIV and NKJV). This is a much more natural translation, and a vivid thought: to die 'through Jesus', as through a door, is to die into a place of life and safety.

have died and risen with Christ.[17] So how could the dead be anywhere else, when he comes again? They are already *with him*, and therefore accompany him when he comes.

How do verses 14 and 16 fit together? I have to say that the commentaries on 1 Thessalonians tend to bypass this question. If they address it, the answer is to make verse 14 say the same as verse 16. For instance, Charles Wanamaker suggests that *God will bring* the dead not to earth but to heaven with Jesus when he comes (i.e. by raising them from the dead),[18] and John Stott suggests that the resurrection in verse 16 precedes the 'coming' with Jesus in verse 14. Having been raised (16), they will then come with him (14).[19]

Neither suggestion seems right. Verse 14 seems clearly to say that God will bring the dead with Jesus when he comes again to earth, because when they died, they died 'through' him so that they are now 'in' and 'with' him. And verse 16 seems clearly to say that, when he descends from heaven, the dead in Christ will rise, and *then* (17) the living will join them to *meet* the returning Christ and welcome him to earth. How can both be true? A couple of thoughts will help us.

i. Little words with a big message

Paul loves piling up prepositions to express our relationship with the Lord – we die 'through', 'with' and 'in' him. In Romans 14:7–9 we meet another two:

> We do not live to ourselves, and we do not die to ourselves. If we live, we live *to* the Lord, and if we die, we die *to* the Lord; so then, whether we live or whether we die, we are the Lord's [literally, we are '*of* the Lord']. For to this end Christ died and lived again, so that he might be Lord of both the dead and the living.[20]

So it's through, with, in, to and of – all the ways in which we are *connected* to Jesus Christ, whether we are living or dead. In Romans 14 Paul

---

[17] See Rom. 6:3–5; 2 Cor. 4:10–11; Gal. 2:19–20; Phil. 3:10–11; Col. 2:12–13; etc.

[18] Charles A. Wanamaker, *The Epistles to the Thessalonians*, New International Greek Testament Commentary (Grand Rapids, MI: Eerdmans; Exeter: Paternoster, 1990), p. 170. A consequence is that he has to deny the special meaning of *meet* in v. 17 (p. 175).

[19] John Stott, *The Message of 1 & 2 Thessalonians: Preparing for the Coming King*, The Bible Speaks Today (London: Inter-Varsity Press, 2021), p. 79.

[20] Emphasis added.

emphasizes that the relationship we have with him before death carries on through death, because he is the same Lord. So whatever it means to 'sleep' in Christ, it surely cannot mean *less* than it means for us now to be 'in', 'to', 'of' (etc.) him. According to Philippians 1:23, it is 'far better' to be 'with' Christ after death than before. However we interpret the rising of *the dead in Christ*, it cannot be that they are suddenly going to start being 'with' him at that point.

ii. The 'overlap of the ages'

Our old friends *chronos* and *kairos* can help us here, because the same story can be told differently from the perspective of each. *Chronos* tells a story of 'sleeping in Christ' until the appointed time of resurrection finally arrives. *Kairos* tells how God has wonderfully intervened to make features of the age-to-come real in our experience now. In the second half of our passage, Paul is going to tell the Thessalonians that they are already *children of light and children of the day* (5:5), even though the *salvation* for which *God has destined us* (9) has not yet fully arrived. This is actually the basis of his encouragement: *since we belong to the day, let us be sober, and put on the breastplate of faith and love* (8). On this basis the dead are fully included in this advance entry into the blessings of the age-to-come!

Famously, Paul attaches this thought to the Holy Spirit, whom he calls a 'first instalment', 'guarantee' and 'pledge' of what is yet to come,[21] and the 'first fruits' of our coming inheritance.[22]

So it's all a matter of perspective. From the perspective of the old age, the dead are dead, awaiting resurrection when Christ comes again and the old age ends. But from the perspective of the new age which has already arrived with Jesus, the dead are alive 'in Christ' and enjoying what that means even more than we do now.

In 4:14 and 16 we meet these perspectives rubbing against each other, and we simply have to hold them both to be true, because of the different time perspectives in which we live. We live in both the old age and the new! We will come back to this, especially when we look at 1 Corinthians 15:20–28.[23]

---

[21] These are the NRSV translations of the Greek word *arrabon*, used of the Spirit in 2 Cor. 1:22; 5:5; and Eph. 1:14.

[22] Rom. 8:23.

[23] Chapter 12 below.

b. Are bodies essential for resurrection?

Short answer – Yes and No! It's a firm 'No' to Sir Stanley Spencer: resurrection is not resuscitation. This is the view that Paul argues against in 1 Corinthians 15:35ff., where he develops an analogy which helps us here. He compares our bodies to seeds which, when sown, give rise to plants completely different from them. So our bodies, 'sown' in death, give rise (under the hand of God) to 'resurrection' bodies which are imperishable, glorious, powerful, spiritual, very different from our present poor specimens![24] But seeds disappear completely when they germinate. Our old bodies don't need to be present, because God is in charge of this process – he 'gives it [us] a body as he has chosen'.[25] It's no problem for God if for some reason our physical bodies are lost completely. But on the other hand, we definitely need those new 'spiritual' bodies in order to 'inherit the kingdom of God' and live with him there.[26]

In any case – if my musings on John 14:3 are right – he gives us our resurrection bodies at the moment of our death, because then *chronos* collapses for us and we are whisked away to the day of resurrection and the second coming of the Lord.

4. Be prepared! (5:1–11)

In the second half of the passage we see Paul's pastoral heart beating and glowing: he wants his beloved Thessalonians to be prepared! First (1–5), picking up several of the words and metaphors we met in Jesus' teaching in Matthew 24 – 25, Paul underlines:

- The unpredictability of *the day of the Lord* – it could come at any time, like a thief in the night (2).
- Its inevitability: precise date unknown, but it's as inevitable as labour follows pregnancy (3)!
- Its dismissability: people can easily fail to prepare for it by ignoring what's at stake. It could mean *sudden destruction* if we are not ready (3)!

---

[24] 1 Cor. 15:35–49.

[25] 1 Cor. 15:38.

[26] 1 Cor. 15:50.

- Its familiarity: we already belong to it as *children of the day*, and so we can embrace it as something completely in line with our nature. It won't burst upon us as something alien to who we are (4–5).

Paul's initial reply to their question is fascinating: 'You yourselves know *exactly* that the day of the Lord comes like a thief in the night' (2, my translation). But – as Jesus points out when he uses this simile in Matthew 24:43 – we can't know 'exactly' when a thief might break in! Probably Paul's use of the word 'exactly' is ironic, and he's picking it up from their use of it in their question to him. They ask for an 'exact' time, but neither they nor we can know that. The only *exact* thing we can say about the timing of the Lord's coming is that it's unpredictable!

Then (6–11) Paul issues three appeals to the Thessalonians (and to us):

- *For alertness* (6–8a). Keep awake, keep sober! We have seen what Paul means illustrated vividly in Matthew 24:42 – 25:13.
- *For preparedness* (8b). Paul loves military metaphors, and he will later develop this one greatly in Ephesians.[27] Faith, love and hope pop up as a threesome at the start of the letter,[28] and here they are again at the end. If they are alive and active, they will protect us from slipping into dozy unawareness. Especially *hope* . . .
- *For focus* (9–10). Hope is *the hope of salvation* (8), which in this context has a double meaning: 'real' soldiers can hope for 'safety' as they go into battle, but it is by no means guaranteed! But our hope for 'safety' now, and for 'salvation' from death, is solid and assured *because of Jesus*. His death for us means that *whether we are awake or asleep* – that is, on both sides of our death – *we may live with him* (10). This is what *salvation* means. How glorious!

5. The trumpet shall sound! (4:16)

Let's finish with a look at Paul's great second-coming description in 4:16, which is unique in his letters: *For the Lord himself, with a cry of command, with the archangel's call and with the sound of God's trumpet, will descend from heaven, and the dead in Christ will rise first.*

---

[27] Eph. 6:10–17.
[28] 1 Thess. 1:3. See also 1 Cor. 13:13; Eph. 1:15–18; Col. 1:4–5.

Earlier we raised the question whether we should understand these images literally or not. When Jesus comes, will we literally hear a cry, a call and a trumpet blast? David Williams comments that they are all 'different ways – figurative ways – of expressing the one thought that Jesus' coming will be with irresistible authority and indescribable grandeur'[29] – and of course, if this is what they mean, then irresistible authority and indescribable grandeur will be there in spades, whether or not we literally hear an archangel's voice and a trumpet call. It's what they symbolize that matters. That's the vital thought.

Once again the Bible itself helps us unpack the symbolism. Three of Paul's images – the cry of command, the trumpet and the cloud – come together in Numbers 9:15 – 10:16, where the Israelites are being told how to travel through the Sinai desert. They are to be led by the cloud that indicates God's presence: when it stays put over the tabernacle, they must stay put, and when it moves, they must break camp and set off. When it stops, they must do the same. This moving and stopping of the cloud is called 'the command of the LORD'.[30]

But of course not everyone would notice that the cloud had moved off, and so Moses is told to 'make two silver trumpets . . . for summoning the congregation, and for breaking camp'.[31] The trumpets were a summons for the people to gather 'at the entrance of the tent of meeting'.[32] 'When the assembly is to be gathered, you shall blow',[33] and different signals were envisaged including an alarm which not only summoned the people into battle[34] but also called on the Lord: 'so that you may be remembered before the LORD your God and be saved from your enemies'.[35] There were also trumpet calls to summon people to worship at the great festivals or when sacrifices were offered at the tabernacle.[36]

This is so rich as background to the symbols in 1 Thessalonians 4:16! When the Lord comes in the clouds, as we saw in Matthew, he will 'send out his angels with a loud trumpet call, and they will gather his elect from the

---

[29] David J. Williams, *1 and 2 Thessalonians*, New International Biblical Commentary (Peabody, MA: Hendrickson; Carlisle: Paternoster, 1995), p. 84.

[30] Num. 9:23.

[31] Num. 10:1–2.

[32] Num. 10:3.

[33] Num. 10:7.

[34] Cf. 1 Sam. 13:3–4.

[35] Num. 10:9.

[36] Num. 10:10.

four winds, from one end of heaven to the other'.[37] All three images – the Lord's *cry of command*, the *archangel's call* and the *sound of God's trumpet* – point to the same thing: that vast worldwide gathering of God's people, assembling them at his door, so that they may be ready to move as he wills and join in worship in his sanctuary. The first to be gathered in this way, says Paul, are *the dead in Christ.* In fact, they are already in him, and therefore already gathered, present and correct and ready to spring to life and serve him.

So will we literally hear a trumpet? I don't know, but we will certainly be summoned to stand before him, 'gathered' like Israel before the tent of meeting, and – whether from the grave or from the earth – we shall rise to greet him as he claims his throne.

---

[37] Matt. 24:31.

2 Thessalonians 2:1–12

11. The coming of the Lord: Part 2

1. In a mess . . .

Yes, the Thessalonians were in a mess, over the second coming – and what a blessing for us! If they hadn't got so messed up, Paul would never have written 2 Thessalonians, and how much we would have missed! We meet unique teaching here, which Paul had given them in person (*Do you not remember that I told you these things when I was still with you?*),[1] but which he now needs to repeat and underline.

But . . . what he says here is so different from his teaching in 1 Thessalonians! So different, in fact, that some have wondered if 2 Thessalonians could really be by Paul. In 1 Thessalonians the emphasis falls on the *immediacy* and *unexpectedness* of the coming of the Lord – like a 'thief in the night' for whom they have to watch without falling asleep,[2] coming (it seems) within Paul's own lifetime.[3] But now, in 2 Thessalonians, the emphasis falls on things that have to happen first, before the Lord comes: so he can't be coming either immediately or without warning. Something called *the rebellion* has to happen (3), and someone called 'the man of lawlessness, the son of destruction'[4] has to appear, whom Paul describes in verses 3–4 and 8–10. Right now, something or someone called 'the restrainer' is holding back the 'man of lawlessness' from appearing (6–7) – and only when he finally appears will the Lord Jesus himself appear and

---

[1] 2 Thess. 2:5; cf. 1 Thess. 5:2.

[2] 1 Thess. 5:2–6.

[3] 'We who are alive, who are left' seems to imply this: 1 Thess. 4:15, 17; cf. 1 Cor. 15:52.

[4] This is a literal translation: nrsv has *the lawless one . . . the one destined for destruction*.

destroy [him] with the breath of his mouth, annihilating him by the manifestation of his coming (8).

Paul didn't mention any of this in 1 Thessalonians! Personally, I'm not too worried about these differences, because in 1 Thessalonians 4 – 5 he was specifically tackling the questions the Thessalonians had asked, and – as we'll see in this chapter – it is perfectly possible for Paul *both* to expect Jesus to come imminently *and* to believe that certain things have to happen first.

The key to understanding this difficult passage is to realize that Paul is interpreting and passing on *Jesus' teaching*. He's interpreting it particularly in the light of Daniel's prophecy of 'the abomination of desolation', to which Jesus refers.[5] None of the Gospels had been written at this time, but it could well be that something like what we now have in Matthew 24, Mark 13 and Luke 21 was already circulating in written form (in Greek) when Paul was still Saul, a newly converted ex-Pharisee just discovering the calling that the risen Jesus Christ was laying on him. He certainly knows it, anyway! – and clearly it has shaped his sense of his call as an apostle.

So we have some quite hard work here, to get to the heart of Paul's teaching. Once again, I'm simply going to present the understanding of it to which I've come after much wrestling and debating, and not bother you (the reader) with too much 'some say this, some say that'![6]

2. The problem, and Paul's strategy

Paul starts in chapter 1 with a vivid presentation of the coming of the Lord, emphasizing two things: when he comes, he will (1) deliver those who are clinging to him (and to one another) in faith and love through 'persecutions and . . . afflictions',[7] and (2) pass 'just judgment' on their persecutors 'who do not know God and . . . do not obey the gospel of our Lord Jesus'.[8] Thus he directly connects the coming of the Lord to the *present* situation and experience of the Thessalonians, facing persecution for their new-found faith in Christ.[9]

---

[5] Matt. 24:15; Mark 13:14 (nrsv 'desolating sacrilege').

[6] There are two much fuller chapters on 1 and 2 Thessalonians in Motyer, *Come, Lord Jesus!*, pp. 226–269.

[7] 2 Thess. 1:4.

[8] 2 Thess. 1:8.

[9] See also 1 Thess. 1:6; 2:14–15; 3:2–3.

Then in chapter 2 he gets to the issue that concerns him:

As to the coming of our Lord Jesus Christ and our being gathered together to him, we beg you, brothers and sisters, not to be quickly shaken in mind or alarmed, either by spirit or by word or by letter, as though from us, to the effect that the day of the Lord is already here.
(1–2)

Paul doesn't know where they got the idea from (though he is aware that some are ascribing it to him – *as though from us*), but he wants to scotch completely the notion that *the day of the Lord is already here*. What does this mean? Does *is already here* mean 'has already come', the NIV translation?[10] Or does it mean 'is just at hand', the ASV translation – that is to say, not here but *very nearly* here?[11] The Greek could mean either, but there is a big difference between the two. This is one instance where it can't mean both!

In 1 Corinthians 7:26 Paul uses the same verb to refer to an 'impending' crisis, and this meaning seems much more likely here. They think that the coming of the Lord is literally around the corner – a matter of days?[12] Some hints in Paul's language here suggest that he is thinking of the words of warning with which Jesus begins his reply to the disciples' question in Matthew 24: 'Beware that no one leads you astray. For many will come in my name, saying, "I am the Messiah!" and they will lead many astray.'[13] Similarly Paul begins his response to this crazy idea about the day of the Lord with *Let no one deceive you in any way* (3), using different Greek words but expressing exactly the same thought. He has just told them not to be *alarmed*, using a rare Greek word which occurs in the New Testament only here (2) and in Matthew 24:6.[14] And in his opening line the word translated *gathered together* is the same as the one we meet in Matthew 24:31, used of the angels 'gathering together' the elect when the Son of Man comes.[15]

---

[10] So also other mainstream translations, e.g. CEV, ESV, GNT, NKJV.

[11] Also KJV – 'is at hand'.

[12] We gather later (2 Thess. 3:6–12) that some have given up work and are sponging off other church members. This would fit with a case of hyper-eschatological excitement about the coming of the Lord – maybe next week! Paul does his best to calm them down.

[13] Matt. 24:4–5; cf. Mark 13:5–6; Luke 21:8.

[14] Also in the parallel in Mark, 13:7.

[15] Also in Mark 13:27.

These hints that Jesus' teaching lies in the background do two things for us:

- They confirm that the problem is the one Jesus warned about – people saying that the Messiah is at the door, but it's not true; and
- We will understand Paul best if we seek to read his teaching through the 'lens' provided by Matthew 24. He is taking them back to Jesus.

One particular problem for us is that, because he is reminding them of what he told them before, he doesn't elaborate but assumes they will know what he is talking about. This applies particularly to the mysterious 'restrainer' in verse 6: he says *you know what is now restraining him* [the 'man of lawlessness'] – well, they might, but we don't. I have counted no fewer than twelve different interpretations of 'the restrainer'![16]

I receive puzzles like this with a sense of God's providence. God could so easily have prodded Paul to remind the Thessalonians who and what the restrainer is. But he didn't. Therefore not knowing for sure, and debating the possible meanings, is actually part of God's intended meaning for us.

We'll look at the stages of Paul's response to the problem, and then ask how we should interpret him for today.

3. The rebellion, the 'man of lawlessness' and the temple (2:3–4, 8–11)

Paul is very clear about the series of events that must take place before the coming of the Lord Jesus:

> Let no one deceive you in any way; for that day will not come unless the rebellion comes first and the lawless one is revealed, the one destined for destruction. He opposes and exalts himself above every so-called god or object of worship, so that he takes his seat in the temple of God, declaring himself to be God.
> (3–4)

---

[16] Details in *Come, Lord Jesus!*, pp. 264–265.

Then, after talking about the 'restrainer' (5–7), Paul goes on,

> *And then the lawless one will be revealed, whom the Lord Jesus*
> *will destroy with the breath of his mouth, annihilating him by the*
> *manifestation of his coming. The coming of the lawless one is apparent*
> *in the working of Satan, who uses all power, signs, lying wonders, and*
> *every kind of wicked deception for those who are perishing, because they*
> *refused to love the truth and so be saved. For this reason God sends them*
> *a powerful delusion, leading them to believe what is false.*
> (8–11)

You'll notice how the passage begins and ends with warning about being deceived (see how 10–11 balance 3a). And then these two sections about *the lawless one* (3b–4 and 8–9a) bracket the section in the middle about the restrainer. So the passage has a broadly chiastic structure, which in this case serves greatly to highlight the danger of being deceived. This is no passing thought for Paul. In fact, he shares it with Jesus, who warns his disciples, 'False messiahs and false prophets will appear and produce great signs and omens, to lead astray, if possible, even the elect. Take note, I have told you beforehand.'[17] Here 'lead astray' is the same word that Paul uses in verse 11 (translated *delusion* above).[18] So his reference in verse 2 to a *spirit* or a *word* as the possible source of this *powerful delusion* is explained: he expects that false prophets, maybe even performing deceptive *signs* ascribed to the power of the Spirit, may have led the Thessalonians astray.

So what must they not be deceived about? Verses 3–4 list three things that must happen first, before the Lord comes:

- The *rebellion*.
- The revelation of *the lawless one* ('the man of lawlessness').
- The self-exaltation of *the lawless one* in *the temple of God*, *declaring himself to be God*.

These seem to be closely connected in Paul's mind. Key to understanding him is to realize that he is doing what Jesus encourages 'the

---

17 Matt. 24:24–25.
18 Used also in Matt. 24:4, 11.

reader' to do in Matthew 24:15: 'So when you see the desolating sacrilege standing in the holy place, as was spoken of by the prophet Daniel (let the reader understand) . . .' As a faithful 'reader', Paul has gone back to Daniel and is understanding Jesus' teaching in the light of Daniel's prophecy about the 'abomination of desolation' or 'desolating sacrilege'. We need to go there, too!

Daniel refers to this 'abomination' three times – in 8:13; 9:27; and 11:31. It's worth looking at all three. On the first occasion it is connected to his vision of the 'little horn' which wars against God's 'holy ones' and 'speaks words against the Most High'.[19] Daniel sees this horn making war on Israel, abolishing the sacrifices and taking over the temple.[20] He then hears two of the angelic 'attendants' talking. One asks the other, 'How long will it take for the vision to be fulfilled – the vision concerning the daily sacrifice, the rebellion that causes desolation, the surrender of the sanctuary and the trampling underfoot of the LORD's people?'[21] The answer is a coded number ('2,300 evenings and mornings', i.e. the number of times the sacrifices do not take place!),[22] looking back to the 'time, two times, and half a time' during which the 'little horn' will rule over God's people.[23] The time of suffering is strictly determined, and restricted.

The word translated 'rebellion' in the attendant's words is one of the range of words for 'sin' in Hebrew, and this one has the particular meaning 'sin as revolt against authority'. Paul's word for *rebellion* means any kind of revolt or uprising, not necessarily just against God. Later this 'horn' is described as 'a fierce-looking king, a master of intrigue',[24] and Daniel is told, 'He will cause deceit to prosper, and he will consider himself superior . . . He will destroy many and take his stand against the Prince of princes.'[25] Paul twice uses the same word 'deceit' (used in the Greek version of Daniel) in describing the 'man of lawlessness' (9, 11).

As Daniel's vision develops we then hear that 'the people of the ruler who will come will destroy the city and the sanctuary', and 'at the temple

---

[19] Dan. 7:21, 25.
[20] Dan. 8:9–12.
[21] Dan. 8:13, NIV.
[22] Dan. 8:14.
[23] Dan. 7:25.
[24] Dan. 8:23, NIV.
[25] Dan. 8:25, NIV.

he will set up an abomination that causes desolation, until the end that is decreed is poured out on him'.[26]

Third, in Daniel 11 the predictions about the abolition of the daily sacrifices and the 'abomination that makes desolate' are repeated,[27] and the figure behind it is called a 'king': 'The king shall act as he pleases. He shall exalt himself and consider himself greater than any god, and shall speak horrendous things against the God of gods.'[28] But his fate is sealed: 'He shall prosper until the period of wrath is completed, for what is determined shall be done.'[29]

So we see five basic features of this prophecy:

- There will be war in which God's people are defeated
- by a powerful 'ruler' or 'king'
- who deceives the people and speaks arrogantly against God, regarding himself as a god
- and abolishing the sacrifices in the temple, setting up an 'abomination' there that makes it desolate of God's presence,
- until his time comes and he too is defeated – 'until the decreed end is poured out upon the desolator'.[30]

Daniel's prophecies were initially fulfilled in the period 167–164 BC, when the Greek Syrian king Antiochus IV 'Epiphanes' captured Jerusalem, abolished the worship of Israel's God and set up an altar to the Greek god Zeus in the temple. The name he gave himself (Epiphanes) expressed his belief that he was an 'epiphany' of Zeus on earth. In this act he was supported by some leading Jews, not least by the high priest Menelaus whom Antiochus had appointed. He was eventually defeated by the Maccabees, and temple worship was re-established. But Jesus clearly felt that Daniel's prophecy would be fulfilled again, when his own prophecy of the destruction of the temple came to pass.

This is the raw material out of which Paul's teaching grows, as he meditates on Jesus! He himself comes up with the title 'the man of lawlessness', and adds this figure to Jesus' prophecy, along with the notion of

---

[26] Dan. 9:26, 27, NIV.
[27] Dan. 11:31.
[28] Dan. 11:36a.
[29] Dan. 11:36b.
[30] Dan. 9:27.

the 'restrainer' (on which see below). Against this background we can understand the main elements of Paul's expectation:

- The *rebellion* (the war setting, prophesied so vividly by Jesus in Matt. 24:15–22);
- The arrogant self-exaltation, *declaring himself to be God*;
- The temple location of this rebellious self-assertion – that is, the Jerusalem temple;
- The use of signs and wonders to deceive (Paul has focused Jesus' words about 'false messiahs and false prophets' onto the single 'man of lawlessness');[31]
- The fulfilling of God's purpose and timetable, even through the deception; and
- The final destruction of this 'man of lawlessness' by the coming of the Son of Man.

But doesn't this leave us with a huge problem? It didn't happen! Charles Wanamaker roundly declares: 'The passage [i.e. this section of 2 Thess. 2] can no longer be understood as valid, since the temple was destroyed in AD 70 without the manifestation of the person of lawlessness or the return of Christ occurring.'[32]

This is indeed a big challenge. We will return to it shortly, after a brief look at . . .

4. The restrainer (2:6–7)

How fascinating this is. Paul backs up his case that *the day of the Lord* cannot be imminent by reminding the Thessalonians that something or someone is holding up the *lawless one* from appearing – and therefore also delaying the coming of the Lord:

> *And you know what is now restraining him, so that he may be revealed when his time comes. For the mystery of lawlessness is already at work, but only until the one who now restrains it is removed. And then the lawless one will be revealed, whom the Lord Jesus will destroy with the*

---

[31] See Matt. 24:24.
[32] Wanamaker, *Thessalonians*, p. 248.

breath of his mouth, annihilating him by the manifestation of his
coming.
(6–8)

In verse 6 the restrainer is a thing, in verse 7 a person. What could Paul be thinking of? Many suggestions have been made, including the obvious political ones: lawlessness is restrained by the rule of law, is it not? Maybe specifically by the rule of the Roman emperor?[33] Both in Daniel and in Jesus there is an emphasis on the fulfilment of *God's* purposes: things happen on *his* timetable. So maybe God's *plan* is the restrainer, enforced by God himself? It's hard to think of God being *removed*, however (7b).

Within Jesus' teaching the preaching of the gospel to all the nations is the limiting factor: the end cannot come until this has been achieved.[34] And in Mark and Luke's versions, an emphasis falls on the Holy Spirit as the enabler of this proclamation.[35] In Matthew Jesus talks about 'the increase of lawlessness' through this period of proclamation.[36] So maybe these are the best candidates: the preaching of the gospel, enabled by the Holy Spirit, goes ahead in the face of the lawlessness – the rebellion against God's rule – that threatens to engulf it but never succeeds. There will come a point when the job is done, and the Holy Spirit will withdraw from that ministry, and then *the lawless one will be revealed*.[37]

Whatever the answer – maybe a combination of these? – Paul knows that something is restraining the end from coming, so that he can pursue his God-given ministry with all zeal.

5. But was Paul wrong?

And indeed Jesus? At the climax of Jesus' teaching he makes the emphatic statement, 'Truly I tell you, this generation will not pass away until all these things have taken place.'[38] At first sight 'all these things' covers all the events Jesus has just described, including both the 'abomination of desolation' and the coming of the Son of Man in glory. So we have to face

---

[33] So John Stott, *Message of 1 & 2 Thessalonians*, pp. 138–141.

[34] Matt. 24:14.

[35] See Mark 13:11; Luke 21:14–15.

[36] Matt. 24:12.

[37] So A. L. Moore, *1 and 2 Thessalonians*, New Century Bible (London: Nelson, 1969), p. 103.

[38] Matt. 24:34.

the fact that part of his prophecy was fulfilled (the destruction of the temple), but the more vital and compelling part – the coming of the Son of Man – was not: even though Jesus ties the two closely together with the words 'immediately after the suffering of those days'.[39]

In Paul's case the problem is even greater, because he has expanded the 'abomination of desolation' prophecy into this expectation of the 'revelation' (3, 8) of 'the man of lawlessness'. If – as seems clear – he is building on Jesus' teaching, then he will certainly have expected all this to happen within one generation. Indeed, it seems as though Matthew 24:14 may have motivated his pressing missionary zeal: he knew that spreading the gospel through the whole world was the essential precondition for the coming of the Lord – within one generation! Having evangelized all around the eastern Mediterranean, he tells the Romans that he wants to press on to Spain, after visiting them[40] – and at the time of writing Colossians (probably during his imprisonment in Rome, about ten years after writing 2 Thessalonians) he could say that the gospel was 'bearing fruit and growing in the whole world'.[41] He may have thought that the job was nearly done!

However, I do not think that (had he lived to see it) Paul would have been greatly fazed by the non-appearance of the Son of Man when the Jerusalem temple was destroyed. He would have had to reread 'all these things' in Matthew 24:34 as we did above – to mean 'all these things that *presage* the end' (but not including the end itself, the coming of the Son of Man).[42] And the theological space for an adjustment of expectation is clearly provided within the requirement that the gospel must be preached first to all nations: obviously, more time is needed! All must have a chance to repent. The Lord will not come until they have.[43] And that is the space we still inhabit, nearly two thousand years after Paul's ministry.

But what about the non-appearance of a specific 'man of lawlessness' in AD 70? Events both prior to and following the capture of the city certainly included the desecration of the temple, but no specific *lawless one* emerged. Let's think about this as we broaden the question:

---

[39] Matt. 24:29.

[40] Rom. 15:19, 23–24.

[41] Col. 1:6.

[42] See above, pp. 93–94.

[43] See Acts 17:30–31; Rom. 9:22–24. We will come back to this in ch. 16 when we look at 2 Pet. 3:9.

6. What about us, reading Paul today?

We have a problem, too. How should we 'receive' Paul's teaching for ourselves today, granted that he himself would certainly have had to adjust it in the light of events as they turned out, just a few years after his death? Is Paul's teaching no longer 'valid' for us, as Charles Wanamaker says? We can say three things:

a. We can warmly affirm the notion of 'the restrainer'!

It's very clear that something is holding back the end. And the unfinished task of world evangelization rests on our shoulders, as it did on Paul's.

b. We too must do as Paul did, responding to Jesus' invitation to 'let the reader understand'[44]

This is an invitation to go back to Scripture and to reread it in the light of events. Jesus gave the New Testament writers, *and us*, permission to think that the significance of Daniel's prophecy of 'the abomination of desolation' was not exhausted in 167 BC, nor in AD 70. When might we see it – what would qualify? John too reflects on Daniel as he develops the notion of the coming 'Antichrist' whose 'spirit' is 'already in the world' – manifest in 'many antichrists' who 'have [already] come'.[45] This parallels Paul's distinction between the *mystery of lawlessness* which is *already at work* (7), and 'the man of lawlessness' who is to be revealed. It seems that significant evil figures are 'trailed' by the evils we see around us all the time.

Through the centuries Christians have debated this, identifying a range of different things and people as 'the man of lawlessness', 'the Antichrist', the 'Beast' or 'the whore of Babylon'. John Stott helpfully surveys the range of views,[46] and comments, 'This process of reinterpretation and reapplication within Scripture itself, from Daniel through Jesus to Paul and John, gives an important flexibility to our understanding.'[47] In other words, we are invited to continue the same process as we look at the world today and ask where we see either the *mystery* or the 'man' of lawlessness.

---

[44] Matt. 24:15.

[45] 1 John 4:3; 2:18.

[46] Stott, *Message of 1 & 2 Thessalonians*, pp. 130–138.

[47] Stott, *Message of 1 & 2 Thessalonians*, p. 136.

The Jerusalem temple has gone, but there are many processes, people or movements that seek to undermine or oppose anything that represents God's presence in the world, as the temple did. 'Lawlessness' is what refuses to recognize and love his authority and rule.

c. In rereading Paul for today, we should reflect particularly on his use of the word 'reveal' in verses 3 and 8

The Greek word means 'unveiling' or 'unmasking': it's the word from which we get 'Apocalypse', the proper name for the book of Revelation. That book is about 'unveiling' what is really there but normally hidden from view. For instance, it 'unmasks' the true reality of the Roman Empire by showing its 'bestial' quality hidden behind the mask of benevolent power bringing peace to the world. The imperial cult, for instance – the practice of worshipping Roman emperors or the goddess 'Roma' – was very popular across the eastern Mediterranean, especially in the area covered by the letters to the seven churches.[48] They *loved* Rome! It had brought peace and prosperity to the whole region. But John (the author of Revelation) sees it very differently indeed, and unmasks not only the totalitarian use of power and war, but also the injustice and idolatry inherent in the Roman trade system – as well as the sporadic persecution of the church, either directly by Rome or indirectly allowed by Rome.[49]

Perhaps this kind of 'unmasking' is what Paul has in mind for 'the man of lawlessness'. Or, if Paul doesn't have it in mind, maybe we should read it that way. Everyone thinks 'the man of lawlessness' is wonderful, until Jesus comes and he is truly *revealed*. Maybe, when Jesus comes, 'the man of lawlessness' won't be a 'he' but a 'they', made up of all who exercise power unjustly and cruelly behind closed doors, displaying a benevolent face to the world. This seems more likely: Jesus himself envisaged many 'false prophets'. Or maybe there will be a huge concentration of systemic evil in one power or person before Christ comes. Whatever its shape, evil power in all its forms will be unmasked and overthrown by our coming Lord, and that's the vital expectation Paul gives us here.

Reading Paul in this way would have two consequences for our interpretation of verses 8–9:

---

[48] Rev. 2 – 3.

[49] See J. Nelson Kraybill, *Imperial Cult and Commerce in John's Apocalypse*, JSNTSup 132 (Sheffield: Sheffield Academic Press, 1996).

i. Everything in verse 8 happens at the same time
. . . That is, the coming of the Lord, and the unmasking and 'annihilation' of *the lawless one*. The 'revelation' of the lawless one has not preceded the Lord's coming. These are not successive events, because the unmasking and destruction are paired consequences of the Lord's coming! As far as Paul's Greek is concerned, this is a perfectly possible reading.

ii. The coming of the lawless one (9) is not the same as his 'revealing' or 'unmasking'
He comes first, with deceptive signs and wonders, admired by all who cannot see the truth (10) and don't know that they are locked into delusion and falsehood (11) and are heading for God's judgment for 'delighting in injustice'[50] (12). But then he – they, all the power-brokers, war-mongers and despots (those Revelation calls 'the kings of the earth and the magnates and the generals and the rich and the powerful')[51] – will flee before the coming of the Lord, unmasked and disempowered by *the breath of his mouth* (8).

I think Paul would be happy if we reread him in this way. Interestingly, I think that Charles Wanamaker would also be happy with this approach (although he doesn't interpret the revealing as 'unmasking', as I do). He sees clearly that Paul was expecting something that did not happen as expected, and suggests that as a result we need to broaden out the interpretation:

> Political figures and nation states arrogate to themselves Christian symbols to legitimate their unjust and oppressive practices such as apartheid, militarism, and imperialism . . . Contemporary Christians must recognize in this a manifestation of the pervasive and arrogant evil described by Paul in 2 Thes. 2:4.[52]

We see evil all around us, in so many forms, many of them buttressed by political power conferring a spurious legitimacy. And sometimes the evil becomes gross and overwhelming, and this is when we most long for the Son of Man to come and 'reveal' evil's true colours and 'annihilate' it

---

[50] NRSV: *took pleasure in unrighteousness.*

[51] Rev. 6:15.

[52] Wanamaker, *Thessalonians*, pp. 248–249.

from his beautiful world. The word 'annihilate' (8) means 'disqualify' or 'nullify', and fits well with the idea of removing from office, depriving of power. When the Son of Man comes, all other powers will be shown for what they are and will cast their crowns before him.

This word 'annihilate' is at the heart of the next passage to which we turn in Paul, where we will explore further this overthrow of the 'powers' and the profound *political* implications of the coming of the Lord.

1 Corinthians 15:20–28

12. 'He must reign until . . .'

We turn to one of the most famous passages in Paul. Everyone knows of 1 Corinthians 15 as 'the resurrection chapter', and at its heart there sits this highly significant paragraph about the connection between the resurrection and the second coming.

These verses form the chapter's theological core. They begin with one of Paul's famous 'But in fact . . .' phrases. This is a specific Greek expression which Paul uses some eighteen times in his letters to introduce a significant shift or counter-argument, usually an emphatic 'But!' introducing some new gospel fact that changes everything.[1] Here it heralds the biggest imaginable gospel reversal: *But in fact Christ has been raised from the dead, the first fruits of those who have* died (20). The Corinthians' faith is not futile (14) and based on a lie (15), and human life does not end in total loss after pitiful deception (17–19), *because* Christ has been raised from the dead.

This emphatic assertion of the resurrection is needed because 'some' in the Corinthian church have misunderstood what it means, and how it affects us (12). This lies behind Paul's opening insistence that the resurrection is a solid, historical fact attested by many witnesses, including himself.[2] He wants the Corinthians to know that their faith is based on thoroughly reliable testimony, undergirded by the Scriptures which enable us to understand what resurrection actually means. His repeated 'in accordance with the scriptures' in verses 3–4 is especially important for our paragraph, as we'll see.

---

[1] See e.g. Rom. 3:21; 6:22; Eph. 2:13.
[2] 1 Cor. 15:1–8.

For us, the remarkable message of verses 20–28 is that *resurrection and second coming belong together as evening belongs to morning*. They define each other, and form a single 'package', so that we can only know what Jesus' resurrection truly means when we view it from the perspective of the end – and the Corinthians badly need to understand this. Here's a little trailer of what's to come:

The resurrection of Jesus means . . .

- a whole new humanity (20–23), living in
- a whole new world (24–27a), based on
- a whole new order (27b–28).

We'll set the scene, and then plunge in to look at each of these mini sections in turn.

1. So what's the problem in Corinth?

Paul states it succinctly in 15:12: 'Now if Christ is proclaimed as raised from the dead, how can some of you say there is no resurrection of the dead?'

What were the 'some of you' actually saying? It's important to bear in mind that they were not denying life after death, nor the possibility of a spiritual relationship with God that transcends death. Far from it. The issue was whether the resurrection *of the body* is part of our expectation.

We need a little Greek philosophy in order to understand the issues here. The 'some of you' were denying the resurrection of the body because they were wedded to a Greek 'dualistic' anthropology which emphasized the 'soul' or the 'spirit' at the expense of the body: not a million miles from some forms of spirituality in the church today! In fact, it has often been suggested that Christianity has a 'down' on the body, and wants us to live as if we were not the embodied creatures we are. This body–spirit 'dualism' goes back to the philosopher Plato, and had become thoroughly embedded in Graeco-Roman culture by the first century. Indeed, it is still the dominant assumption in Western culture today – that the real 'I', the essential person, is a *disembodied* 'Self' who lives within our bodily experience but is distinct from it. Our instinct is not to say 'I *am* a body' but 'I *have* a body.' We objectify our bodies, making them just the vehicles of the person – so that it is easier then to believe (if we want to) that the 'person' has immortality built in and therefore survives death.

It looks as though the 'some of you' in Corinth thought that they had already entered the full heavenly, spiritual experience, essentially leaving their bodies behind as they enjoyed total communion with God. So 'no resurrection' means 'we've got it already – there's nothing left to be had!' They had completely collapsed *chronos* in favour of *kairos*. The *kairos* of their present relationship with God – especially as mediated by their vivid experience of the Spirit – had swamped all sense of their need to wait for (indeed to *long for*) 'the redemption of our bodies'.[3]

In response Paul insists that *resurrection means resurrection of the body*, both for Jesus and for us. This is why he emphasizes the stages of Jesus' resurrection journey in 15:3–5:

- Christ died . . .
- was buried . . .
- was raised . . .
- and appeared!

'Was buried' is not a throwaway add-in between 'died' and 'was raised'. The Christ who 'appeared to Cephas, then to the twelve . . [then] to more than five hundred brothers and sisters at one time', then to James and all the apostles and finally to Paul himself (5–8), is the *same* as the Christ who died and was buried: that is, the same embodied human being is the subject of this whole story. The body that was buried is the body that 'was raised'. If this did not happen, then for Paul Christ did not rise. Paul does not buy that Greek dualism which allows human life to continue away from the body, as 'immortal soul'. We need to *be raised* from death, just as Jesus was, by the direct intervention of God.[4]

That's why Paul insists that *chronos* cannot simply be expunged in this way. In our paragraph he adds two further bullet points to the sequence of Jesus' story:

- he will come again . . .
- and will hand the kingdom back to God the Father!

Jesus' story is not yet complete.

---

[3] See Rom. 8:23.
[4] For further discussion of this, see Gooder, *Body*.

There's another vital aspect of their misunderstanding of the resurrection which we need to grasp. The 'some of you' were thinking entirely individualistically about it. Each individual must enter the resurrected experience of full life in Christ. Sounds great. But Paul has already addressed the way in which this separates those who have it (those who've got the 'knowledge') from those who haven't.[5] The fact is, our embodied reality is actually much bigger than the little bit of flesh-and-blood that each of us is. We belong to one another, and in particular we are 'the body of Christ' together. The Spirit doesn't just give us new life individually, but joins us into a collective 'body' which is a shared experience of union with the risen Christ:

> For just as the body is one and has many members, and all the members of the body, though many, are one body, so it is with Christ. For in the one Spirit we were all baptized into one body – Jews or Greeks, slaves or free – and we were all made to drink of one Spirit.[6]

Our embodiment, for Paul, is *shared* – and not just with one another, but also with Christ. In fact, it is shared with one another *because* it is shared with Christ. We are *his* body. In chapter 6, arguing against the random use of prostitutes by Christians, Paul even tells the Corinthians that their bodies are 'limbs of Christ'.[7] He uses a very 'physical' word to emphasize that we are connected to Christ as whole entities. We don't connect to him with the 'spirit' apart from the body. Our *bodies* are 'spiritual', and are connected to Christ as body-soul-spirit entities which exist in connection with the others who are also joined to Christ by the Spirit. This is wonderful, is it not?

But of course, as bodies, we already exist in multiple connections – in marriage, family, friendship, locality, groups of various kinds, relationships of commerce and profession, religions, cultures, nations – and these collectives often involve struggle and conflict as well as harmony and cooperation. Harmony within one group can entail conflict with another. War arises from our division into nations, along with the pursuit of wealth, power and status. Graeco-Roman culture was clear about how

---

[5] See 1 Cor. 8:1–13.

[6] 1 Cor. 12:12–13.

[7] 1 Cor. 6:15, literal translation.

societal relations were supposed to work, with a strong sense of the 'order' of things, with the gods at the top, then the rulers, the rich, the powerful and the respected in various layers of honour, until you got to slaves at the bottom. People did their best to rise up the order by seeking greater influence and honour, but this was difficult, especially for slaves. These power structures in society, and between societies, were solidly entrenched and maintained by force if necessary.

Our collective belonging in Christ is entwined with all these other belongings – but it's completely different. Christ turns all these 'normal' relations upside down. In the church, slaves can be prophets, and the whole church (including their masters) must listen. 'Jews or Greeks, slaves or free':[8] in Christ, all these basic ethnic, economic and 'class' distinctions are overcome, transcended, wound up – what's the best expression to use? We will meet Paul's favourite expression for it in verses 24 and 26. He has already underlined to the Corinthians how God is up-ending the 'orders' of society, because of the cross. Crucifixion was the ultimate shaming, the fate of rebellious slaves – but the gospel of Jesus Christ proclaims a *crucified man* as God incarnate, come among us. This changes everything![9]

In our passage we learn, in a nutshell, where this revolutionary message of the cross is heading. Enter the good news: *the whole of our embodied reality, including all these wider communities and powers, is being judged and redeemed because of the bodily death and resurrection of Jesus Christ.* That's what our passage is about! Let's get into it.

2. A whole new humanity (15:20–23)

One writer calls these verses 'the high point of the whole epistle'.[10] I think they must be some of the most glorious in all of Scripture!

> *But in fact Christ has been raised from the dead, the first fruits of those who have fallen asleep.*[11] *For since death came through a human being, the resurrection of the dead has also come through a human being;*

---

[8] See 1 Cor. 12:13 quoted above.

[9] See especially 1 Cor. 1:18–31, and Tom Holland, *Dominion: How the Christian Revolution Remade the World* (New York: Basic, 2021), pp. 1–17.

[10] Gerhard Barth, quoted in Anthony C. Thiselton, *The First Epistle to the Corinthians: A Commentary on the Greek Text* (Grand Rapids, MI: Eerdmans, 2000), p. 1226.

[11] NRSV has *those who have died.*

for as all die in Adam, so all will be made alive in Christ. But each in his
own order: Christ the first fruits, then at his coming[12] those who belong
to Christ.

Physical death – the 'end' of our bodies – is the universal fate of all humankind, from kings to slaves and all in between. None can avoid it. Until now! The resurrection of Christ marks the beginning of a whole new era for us humans. There are three things to rejoice in here.

a. The fact of the resurrection

Jesus' resurrection is past, but provides the pledge and assurance of our resurrection still to come – because he is *the first fruits* (20, 23). The 'first fruits' were the first part of the harvest given as an offering to God, in thankfulness for the rest of the harvest which was about to be reaped[13] – a sign and promise of the full harvest to come. So Paul wants to insist, to the 'some of you' who think they've got the resurrection already, that it is still to come, that we are in the *interim* between the offering of *the first fruits* and the harvest they herald. Not there yet, but not long to wait!

b. The 'how' of the resurrection

The obvious question is, *how* does Jesus' resurrection provide the assurance of ours yet to come? What 'mechanism' lies behind the 'first fruits' image? And the answer is that we are back into Paul's prepositions.[14] Here we have two of them: the key is to be 'in' Christ (22), and 'of' him (23). *Those who belong to Christ* are literally 'those who are of Christ'. To be 'in' and 'of' him means that his resurrection is also ours – in due course, when the full harvest is brought in.

For Paul, being 'in' Christ is like being 'in' Adam (22). The Hebrew name 'Adam' given to the first human actually means 'humankind',[15] so to be *in Adam* is simply to be human: to belong to this extraordinary race of *Homo sapiens*, who alone of all species on earth are conscious of our own mortality. We know what it means that we die. We can hold the future moment of our death in imagination, and know that it is a 'bringing to

---

[12] Greek *parousia*, which Paul also uses in 1 Thess. 4:15 and 2 Thess. 2:1, 8, and which seems to have been used first in the Greek version of Jesus' apocalyptic teaching (see above, ch. 8, n. 10).

[13] Deut. 26:1–11; Neh. 10:35–39.

[14] See above, ch. 10, section 3a (i) (pp. 127–128).

[15] See Gen. 2:7, 20, 25.

nothing' – literally an 'annihilation' – of all that we are and have longed to be: a truly horrifying fate, when we allow ourselves to feel it. Psalm 90 comes to mind again![16] We might struggle through to seventy or even eighty years, but then

> our years come to an end like a sigh . . .
> they are soon gone, and we fly away.[17]

Like the psalmist, we need to find the Lord as a 'dwelling-place' in the face of our mortality,[18] and to be *in Christ* is to do just that. For all who *belong to* him, there is solid expectation of resurrection to new life.

c. The timing of the resurrection

It takes place *at his coming* (23)! Paul is really underlining the 1 Thessalonians 4:16 perspective here, rather than the 1 Thessalonians 4:14 perspective.[19] The needs of the 'some of you' are motivating him: they need to know that the resurrection has not yet taken place. As far as the *chronos*-process of our world is concerned, the clock just keeps ticking until the day comes which will include – at the appointed hour, minute and second – the *kairos* of Christ's *coming* and the moment of resurrection. Of course, as we have seen, there is more to be said about the dead, and about why Paul describes them as 'those who have fallen asleep', as he does here (20). But the 'some of you' do not need that. They need to hear about 'the last trumpet' which will sound at that 'twinkling of an eye' moment when Jesus comes again and 'we will be changed' *physically*, so that we no longer bear Adam's image but the image of 'the man of heaven', the risen Christ.[20]

3. A whole new world (15:24–27a)

The thoughts we developed above about the groups and authorities under which we live as embodied human beings are vital here. Resurrection deals with all that, too!

---

[16] See above, pp. 15–16.
[17] Ps. 90:9–10.
[18] Ps. 90:1.
[19] See above, ch. 10, section 3a (pp. 126–127).
[20] See 1 Cor. 15:49–53.

> *Then comes the end, when he hands over the kingdom to God the Father,*
> *after he has destroyed every ruler and every authority and power. For he*
> *must reign until he has put all his enemies under his feet. The last enemy*
> *to be destroyed is death. For 'God has put all things in subjection under*
> *his feet.'*[21]

There are five vital points to draw out here:

a. The timing of 'then'

First, *then* in verse 24 does not imply that there is a gap between Jesus'
coming (23) and *the end*! Some have read it this way, and thus have sought
to construct a kind of timetable of end-time events which only begin with
the coming of Jesus. Paul makes it clear in 1 Corinthians 1:8 that for him
there is no distinction between *the end* and Jesus' coming: 'He will also
strengthen you to the end, so that you may be blameless on the day of our
Lord Jesus Christ.'

Here in 15:24 *then* expresses consequence, not subsequence! The
coming of Jesus *means* 'the end'.

b. Destroying the 'powers' – now and then

The second even more vital point: Jesus' coming is the 'end' of a process of
'destroying' *every ruler and every authority and power.* These 'rulers' and
'powers' are the 'political, social and spiritual structures that overwhelm
the powers of mere individuals', says Anthony Thiselton.[22] I think he
is right: Paul has in mind all the structures, influences and authorities
under which we live, including demonic forces. All these are in process of
being overthrown: notice *after he has . . .* (24). A literal translation would
be 'when he shall have destroyed . . .': in other words, this process of
'destroying' is going on now, and his coming will mark the moment when
that process is completed. Back in 2:6 Paul used the same word in a 'present
continuous' tense: 'Yet among the mature we do speak wisdom, though it
is not a wisdom of this age or of the rulers of this age, who are being
destroyed.'[23] The 'rulers of this age' are already being destroyed by the
'wisdom' Paul preaches – and this is of course the gospel message that

---

[21] NRSV puts these words in quotation marks, because Paul draws them from Ps. 8:6. There could also be
quotation marks around *he has put all his enemies under his feet* (25), because this comes from Ps. 110:1.

[22] Anthony C. Thiselton, *First Corinthians: A Shorter Exegetical and Pastoral Commentary* (Grand Rapids,
MI: Eerdmans, 2011), p. 55.

[23] NRSV has 'who are doomed to perish'. This paraphrase misses the 'present continuous' sense of the verb.

God chose what is foolish in the world to shame the wise; God chose what is weak in the world to shame the strong; God chose what is low and despised in the world, things that are not, to reduce to nothing things that are.[24]

This is the good news of the cross! – the news that a shamed and crucified figure, the lowest of the low, is God's means of salvation for the world, so that the socially enforced structures of rich and poor, slave and free, weak and strong (etc.!), are being 'reduced to nothing' in the church. Here 'reduce to nothing' is the same Greek word as the one translated 'destroy' in 2:6 and in our passage (24, 26).

'Reduce to nothing' is actually a better translation than 'destroy': the word means 'disempower', 'decommission', 'render useless'. Thiselton prefers 'annihilate' in the sense of 'render non-operative' or 'bring to nothing' (the word 'annihilate' is based on the Latin *nihil*, nothing).[25] Think of a US president after leaving office: all that power has gone; he's been shrunk back down to human size.

In this sense Jesus 'destroys' every power, influence, structure and system which does not submit to the rule and kingdom of God – in two ways: at his coming, when finally all powers will hand their crowns to him and he will hand them back to God; and right now, as the gospel creates a people among whom these powers are already being dethroned.

A marvellous passage in Ephesians draws out this 'present tense' undermining of the powers. Paul talks about God's plan behind the present preaching of the gospel: it is 'so that through the church the wisdom of God in its rich variety might now be made known to the rulers and author-ities in the heavenly places'[26] – and there in Ephesians Paul is emphasizing the 'new thing' that the church is, composed of Jews and Gentiles together: its multi-ethnic nature displays how the 'powers' that divide people into hostile groups, and keep them separate, are being 'annihilated' in Christ. The book mentioned in a footnote above (Tom Holland, *Dominion*)[27] is a powerful analysis of the way in which the gospel of the crucified Christ has deeply influenced world culture, way beyond the specific reach of the

---

[24] 1 Cor. 1:27–28.

[25] Thiselton, *Commentary on the Greek Text*, pp. 1222, 1231.

[26] Eph. 3:10.

[27] See n. 9 above.

church. The powers are being 'reduced to nothing'.[28] How vital it is that we, the church, make this as real and clear as we can in our life together as Jesus' followers! National, racial and economic barriers must tumble in him as we foreshadow the new world coming.

One particularly potent way in which the church can – *should* – work to defuse the powers right now is in the area of ecology and climate change. Whole systems of international trade, finance and culture lock us into agricultural and industrial processes which are destroying the delicate ecosphere God has made for us. The powers are at work. One day they will be overthrown – but what about now? What are we doing to preserve and rescue the planet, in the name of the loving God who made it and the beautiful Saviour who is redeeming it?

c. Powers earthly and spiritual

Behind the obvious 'powers' that dominate life on earth – political, ideological, national, religious, ethnic, economic, military, social – the Bible discerns spiritual forces, what Paul later in Ephesians calls 'cosmic powers of this present darkness'.[29] The double *every* here in 1 Corinthians 15:24 underlines Jesus' comprehensive victory: whether spiritual or earthly or some combination of the two, *all* powers will be dethroned, and a massive, cosmic transfer of power will take place. All 'kingdoms' will belong to the one who is his 'God and Father'. *It will be resurrection for the whole cosmos.*

Amazingly, in Colossians 1:16–20 Paul includes the powers themselves in the cosmic 'reconciliation' that God is working through the cross of Christ. They were created 'through' him, they finally exist 'for' him, and they will be brought back by him. However, this reconciliation can't include . . .

d. The last enemy . . . The last enemy to be disempowered is death

Paul probably means *last* in the sense of 'ultimate', the greatest of all the powers ranged against us. In our culture we tend to suppress the fact of our death, because in many countries there is a developed health service that can give a feeling of protection. But other cultures know what it is like to live with the constant imminent possibility of sudden death – as indeed

---

[28] A similar case is developed by David Bentley Hart, *Atheist Delusions: The Christian Revolution and Its Fashionable Enemies* (New Haven, CT: Yale University Press, 2009).

[29] Eph. 6:12. See Clinton E. Arnold, *Powers of Darkness* (Leicester: Inter-Varsity Press, 1992).

all cultures did before the advent of modern medicine. And many of the other 'powers' use the fact and the fear of death as their main leverage – threatening it, promising deliverance from it, or even inviting people to give their lives willingly as an expression of devotion.

Anyone who has lived through the death of a close friend or relative knows what an awful 'enemy' it is. And maybe it is the *last* enemy also because there's no deliverance from it at all, until Jesus comes again. Until then, we have to 'sleep' – there's no way round it.

e. Scriptural vision fulfilled

But when he comes, at last there will be victory over death! And this will mean the realization of the vision of Psalm 8:6. At last we will be a human race who are not victims in our environment, slaves to forces beyond our control (again, both earthly and spiritual), but who rule in the world over which God set us at the start,[30] with *all things in subjection under [our] feet* (27). The vision of the psalm has never been fully realized in practice, not until that moment when Jesus comes again and *as man, resurrected and ruling*, establishes his kingdom over all powers – and we are raised to rule with him.[31]

But because he as *first fruits* has already risen, he is already ruling, presiding over the process of *anticipatory submission* of the powers within the church. Paul sees this indicated in another psalm – Psalm 110:1, quoted in verse 25. He is reigning *until* the final moment when all his enemies submit to him: and under his present rule, they are losing their grip, as we learn to love one another as he has loved us.

4. A whole new order (15:27b–28)

At first sight these words are a little strange, and unexpected:

> But when it says, 'All things are put in subjection', it is plain that this does not include the one who put all things in subjection under him. When all things are subjected to him, then the Son himself will also be subjected to the one who put all things in subjection under him, so that God may be all in all.

---

[30] Gen. 1:28.
[31] See also Heb. 2:5–9.

Paul has already talked about the 'order' of things – *But each in his own order: Christ the first fruits, then at his coming those who belong to Christ* (23). The word translated 'subject' or *subjection* here comes from the same Greek root, based on the word 'order': in other words, this is all about things finding their proper place – first under Christ the *first fruits*, and then under God who will become *all in all* when Christ comes again and gives his newly won kingdom back to God the Father (24).

What will this look like? We live in a world of rival powers and ideas, many of which do not acknowledge God as Creator, Ruler and Judge. The powers assert their own right to control and direct our lives – and in many ways we cannot help being subject to 'systems' that manage us. We all depend on international trade, for instance, which exerts huge control over poorer economies around the world, and can exercise this power with injustice, or with mercy and generosity. But the world is being redeemed from this slavery to random powers whose *essence* is not to submit to God's rule – and one day he will be *all in all*.

It's hard to unpack what this will look like, except to say: let's imagine a world in which all are able to flourish completely, in relationship with a heavenly Father who fully provides for all. A world in which we live in harmony with the substance of the earth, as children of its soil. A world in which the *history of Jesus Christ* – incarnate among us, sharing and bearing our death, buried in our soil then rising again, bringing his new life to the world and restoring all things to their 'proper' place under God – is written into the shape and story of 'all things'. 'All things' go the same way as he does, dying and rising again in him. What a glorious vision!

But here is a vital question. What precisely does Paul mean by this 'all' – both here in verse 28, and in verse 22 where he says *all will be made alive in Christ*? Does he literally mean every single thing, every single person? We turn now to a vital passage in Romans where some other famous 'alls' appear and which will help us to answer this question.

Romans 11:25–36

13. Mercy on all

We turn to a glorious passage at the heart of Romans: it concludes Paul's long argument about 'Israel and the nations' in Romans 9 – 11, and some believe that it concludes the whole of his argument so far in Romans. For our purposes, it contains the only specific reference to the second coming in Romans, phrased in language drawn from Isaiah 59:20, quoted in verse 26:

> *Out of Zion will come the Deliverer;*
>   *he will banish ungodliness from Jacob.*

Paul will have understood 'Zion' here as God's heavenly residence, the place from which the returning Christ will come.[1]

In fairness we must note that not all see a reference to the second coming here. Some (most notably N. T. Wright)[2] think that Paul saw this prophecy fulfilled in the going out of the gospel from Jerusalem. I used to hold this view myself.[3] But it seems clear actually – as we will see – that Paul is looking forward to end-time events ushered in by Christ's return. This is the view of most commentators.

Let's structure our overview of the passage around a vital theological question:

---

[1] As for instance in Ps. 14:7.

[2] N. T. Wright, *Paul and the Faithfulness of God* (London: SPCK, 2013), pp. 1248–1251.

[3] S. Motyer, *Israel in the Plan of God* (Leicester: Inter-Varsity Press, 1989), pp. 153–154.

1. Does 'all' mean 'all'?

We ended the last chapter by asking: when Paul says, in 1 Corinthians 15:22, that 'all will be made alive in Christ', does he mean this literally? In other words, is he telling us that the whole non-Christian world will be turned around – that our non-Christian friends and relatives, for whom we long and pray, will certainly be saved through Christ even though they don't currently believe in him? Indeed, that the *enemies* of the gospel, of whatever stamp, will finally turn to Christ and be saved?

Here in Romans 11 we meet some very similar 'alls'. First Paul says that there is a *mystery* to be understood:

> So that you may not claim to be wiser than you are, brothers and sisters,
> I want you to understand this mystery: a hardening has come upon part
> of Israel, until the full number of the Gentiles has come in. And so all
> Israel will be saved.
> (25–26)

The full number of the Gentiles . . . all Israel: does this mean every single Gentile, every single Jew? Then Paul broadens out this 'all' in verses 30–32, giving it a fascinating twist, and apparently suggesting that he does indeed mean every single human being:

> *Just as you* [Paul is addressing the Gentile believers in Rome] *were
> once disobedient to God but have now received mercy because of their*
> [i.e. the Jews'] *disobedience, so they have now been disobedient in order
> that, by the mercy shown to you, they too may now receive mercy. For
> God has imprisoned all in disobedience so that he may be merciful to all.*

Paul is thinking of a massive, all-humanity swing or switch between disobedience and mercy, with the two great 'masses' of humankind – Jews and Gentiles – interacting with each other in the process, and resulting in the salvation of 'all'. This is actually the substance of his argument in Romans 9 – 11, which he is here bringing to a conclusion: basing his thoughts on a principle drawn from Deuteronomy 32:21 (quoted in Rom. 10:19), he has argued that Israel's rejection of the Christ has meant that the gospel has gone out to the Gentile world – but God's purpose behind this, all along, was not to replace Israel with a new Gentile people of God, but to call Israel back to himself.

Paul sees this happening through his own ministry: 'Inasmuch then as I am an apostle to the Gentiles, I glorify my ministry in order to make my own people jealous, and thus save some of them.'[4] 'Glorify my ministry' means something like 'I make sure that the Jews know how much their God is blessing the socks off Gentile believers in Jesus!' But Paul's hope for the salvation of 'some of them' in Romans 11:14 is rather different from the emphatic *all* which we meet in Romans 11:26 and 32! It seems that Paul is looking ahead to the end, in our passage – to a moment when the 'some of them' saved through his ministry will expand into the salvation of *all Israel*, a moment when *out of Zion will come the Deliverer* to *banish ungodliness from Jacob* and *take away their sins* (26–27), and bring this to-and-fro process between Israel and the Gentiles to a glorious conclusion with mercy for all humankind.

Is that right? Is the whole messy confusion of our present world, with rival atheisms and religions and ideologies and materialisms capturing people's hearts and making it so difficult for the gospel truly to be heard – is all this going to be transformed into universal submission to Christ when he comes again?

To judge from our passage, it seems as if Paul would answer a resounding Yes to this. Focusing on Israel, he argues that, even though they are currently *enemies of God*, this is *for your sake* (28). Their current alienation from God has a purpose in God's plan, and is not the end of the story. *They are beloved, for the sake of their ancestors; for the gifts and the calling of God are irrevocable* (28–29). God cannot go back on his covenant commitment to Abraham, to 'be God to you and to your offspring after you',[5] and for Paul this clearly means that they will surely be saved. He finds this promised in Scripture:

> And this is my covenant with them,
>> when I take away their sins.
> (27)[6]

The salvation of Israel, for Paul, is bound into God's universal plan, the core feature of a universal mercy touching 'all' (32).

---

[4] Rom. 11:13–14.

[5] Gen. 17:7.

[6] This is a combined quotation of Jer. 31:33 and Isa. 27:9, attached to his main quotation of Isa. 59:20 in v. 26.

2. To him be the glory for ever . . . Amen

Before we dig further into the identity of this 'all' and the questions this raises for us – especially around evangelism and the doctrine of hell – let's complete our overview of the passage by noticing where Paul goes in response to this vision of universal mercy:

> *O the depth of the riches and wisdom and knowledge of God! How unsearchable are his judgements and how inscrutable his ways!*
> *'For who has known the mind of the Lord?*
> *Or who has been his counsellor?'*
> *'Or who has given a gift to him,*
> *to receive a gift in return?'*
> *For from him and through him and to him are all things. To him be the glory for ever. Amen.*

Paul falls into beautiful praise, overwhelmed by the grandeur of God's plan, which he understands in part but which at the same time transcends understanding. His *judgements* are *unsearchable*: in other words, we can never completely understand why he acts as he does. His *ways* are *inscrutable* – in fact, 'unmappable' would be a better translation, keeping the underlying image within the word: we can never draw a map of his ways. This is remarkable, seeing that Paul has just been attempting to do exactly this – to provide an overview enabling us to see the pattern of God's overall plan leading to 'mercy for all'. But it's not the full story. What he knows, he knows – but he knows enough to know that he doesn't know the whole, and his not-knowing bursts into adoration.

It's a carefully structured outburst of praise. The three qualities of God which Paul celebrates – his *riches and wisdom and knowledge* – are each picked up and unpacked by the Old Testament quotations in verses 34–35, in reverse order. Each quotation asks a question expecting the answer 'No-one!'

- Knowledge: *For who has known the mind of the Lord?* (34a).[7]
  No-one can fully plumb the depths of God's understanding of his world and his plan for it.

---

[7] Paul quotes Isa. 40:13a.

- Wisdom: *Or who has been his counsellor?* (34b).[8] No-one can offer God any advice about how to act! Well – we can of course *offer* him advice, but our wisdom is no match for his.
- Riches: *Or who has given a gift to him, to receive a gift in return?* (35).[9] No-one can put God in his or her debt: we are always and only dependent on his grace.

The result: a vision of a God who is the *source, means* and *goal* of all that is, and the only worthy object of our worship: *For from him and through him and to him are all things. To him be the glory for ever. Amen* (36).

Paul is back with his theological prepositions again. He loves them. All things are 'to' God, because all things originate 'from' God, and reach their goal 'through' God. This is an even broader vision, involving *all things* rather than just all people. For Paul, of course, the cross is at the heart of this vision: so he is not saying that both evil and good originate from and cohere in God, in some kind of Buddhist way. The evil that arises within God's creation, including our sin and all the 'powers' that dispute God's rule, passes *through* the cross and is dissipated, its power defused, so that (as Paul puts it in 1 Cor 15:28) God can be 'all in all'.

As Paul puts it in Colossians 2:14–15, God has nailed the record of all our sins to the cross, and at the same time 'disarmed the rulers and authorities and made a public example of them, triumphing over them in it' (that is, in the cross). Because of the cross, *all things,* even sin, injustice and all the cruelty that the powers can inflict on the world, can pass 'through' God and ultimately be 'to' him.

What a vision! But let's face it: it raises huge questions for us, as well as inspiring worship. Two huge questions, to be precise:

a. Universal salvation?

Within this vision of universal restoration, does Paul believe that all humans without exception will be saved? Traditional evangelical teaching has been that those who die without Christ are lost, that is, that there is no eternal life for those who die outside Christ, but instead 'the punishment of eternal destruction'.[10] Hell has been understood as a place

---

[8] Paul quotes Isa. 40:13b.

[9] This is a complicated quotation in which Paul seems to be giving his own translation of either Job 35:7 or Job 41:11.

[10] This is Paul's expression – see 2 Thess. 1:9.

163

of everlasting conscious torment in separation from God. Indeed, earlier in Romans Paul has been clear about the real possibility of 'wrath and fury . . . anguish and distress' on 'the day of wrath, when God's righteous judgment will be revealed'.[11] There, he seems to think that eternal consequences hang on our response to the preaching of the gospel.

How can we square this with our passage here? Will there actually be no 'wrath' on 'the day of wrath', because God's mercy will prevail? Does it finally not matter whether we preach the gospel round the world or not, because in any case God intends to show mercy to all when the Deliverer comes from Zion? This seems to make a nonsense of Jesus' firm words about the sheep and the goats,[12] and his insistence that the Son of Man will not come until the gospel has been 'proclaimed throughout the world, as a testimony to all the nations'[13] – why is this necessary, if all the goats are going to be sheep anyway? Jesus himself uses the expression 'eternal punishment' for the final destination of the goats.[14] How do we square all this up?

And what if there's no answer? What if these questions are so deeply twisted into the 'unmappability' of God's ways that we can never know? Here's our second huge issue . . .

b. Living with uncertainty?

Who has been his counsellor? Paul asks, echoing Isaiah (34). It's important to recognize *how much* and *how often* we want to be God's counsellors – that is, to have a seat at the table when the shape of the world is decided. Every time we long for the innocent not to suffer, for there to be equity and peace and freedom from pain, every time we pray for healing or deliverance or an end to war – or the salvation of our friends – our very prayer and longing is expressing this desire to advise him. We want him to act! Usually, our longing is at heart a desire to bring the world back into order, to sort it out, to set things straight(er). Paul himself expresses just such a longing and prayer, for Israel's salvation, in Romans 10:1.

We are facing an epidemic of anxiety and associated poor mental health at the moment. Global issues such as the coronavirus pandemic (now approaching its third year as I write) and the growing climate crisis crowd

---

[11] See Rom. 2:5, 8–9.
[12] Matt. 25:31–46; see above, ch. 8.
[13] Matt. 24:14.
[14] Matt. 25:46.

in on top of the host of other issues that cause anxiety today. Anxiety grows when we feel out of control, when we face an uncertain future that feels like a threat to our safety, and we feel that we don't have the resources to cope – and it can become completely disabling, paralysing people's lives through panic disorders and post-traumatic stress. How much uncertainty can we live with, before life becomes unbearable?

The trouble is, anxiety is built into human life anyway. It comes with the package. Irvin Yalom, the great American psychotherapist, suggests that every issue that leads people to seek counselling arises from one of the four great anxieties we face as humans, caused by death, meaninglessness, isolation and freedom – with the first underlying the other three.[15] We desperately need our lives to make sense, but death finally makes nonsense of us all.

By 'freedom' Yalom means the terrible responsibility to take decisions and act, in spite of the other three anxieties. We can't avoid waking up in the morning. Of course, we often blank out these anxieties, smothering them under business (or addictions), latching onto *something* to give our lives meaning, and living as if we will never die – so these basic anxieties transfer themselves onto other troubling issues which become our conscious focus.

And here is Paul actually *celebrating* God's 'inscrutability'! He is not plunged into anxiety by this uncertainty, but worships God *for* the unmappability of his ways. What's the secret?

We'll tackle each of these questions in turn, starting with this second one:

3. The need for meaning

The longing for order and meaning goes very deep in us humans. We saw it in Psalm 89![16] Ethan the Ezrahite's world was knocked over by the destruction of Jerusalem in 586 BC. He didn't turn to atheism – he kept praying – but suddenly God was different: God became the author of 'vanity, nothingness' for all mortals,[17] rather than the secure provider of 'steadfast love' towards David and his house. As we saw, Ethan needed

---

[15] Irvin D. Yalom, *Existential Psychotherapy* (New York: Basic, 1980). We will engage more fully with Yalom below, in ch. 19.

[16] See above, ch. 1.

[17] Ps. 89:47.

a bigger perspective: but Psalm 90 simply makes the same lack of meaning a *universal* experience, inviting us to take refuge in a God *beyond* all the local, comfortable meanings with which we might seek to find purpose and reason for our lives.

The German-American theologian and philosopher Paul Tillich tackles this in his great and famous book *The Courage to Be*.[18] Courage is the capacity, he says, to stand tall, to affirm our existence in the face of the threat of death, of meaninglessness, and of all that says we are useless and worthless. We see this courage supremely in Jesus facing the cross, as he puts his trust in 'the God beyond God' (as Tillich puts it) – that is, the God who really is, beyond the god shaped to address our own fears and needs. That's what Paul is doing here! Through Romans 9 – 11 he has sought to develop a view of God's grand historical purpose which makes sense of Israel's rejection of her Christ. But finally his celebration of the *depths* of God's plan focuses on his unknowability: and he is not made anxious by this, because this God is the God and Father of our Lord Jesus Christ, the God whose grace is always greater,[19] and who in amazing love has made atonement for our sin and death in Christ.[20] Knowing that, he can *rest* in God's unknowability.

It's fascinating that Paul's third question (35) comes from Job. Like Ethan, Job was questioning God out of the depths of an agony which could not find *meaning* in God's actions. Eventually he was able to accept God's unknowable freedom and grace, like Paul: *who has given a gift to him, to receive a gift in return?* We cannot put God under debt, to act as we would like him to. But in spite of our struggles – and all appearances to the contrary – we can *trust* him to act in grace towards us.

This struggle to find meaning takes us into the other issue we face here:

4. Evangelical universalism?

Can we believe that all will be saved, without exception? It's not surprising that the doctrine of hell causes anxiety – and not just that we might end up there, but that our God (the God and Father of Jesus Christ) could truly enact the unceasing torment of his enemies. As from Job's questions, good theology can emerge from questions like these.

---

[18] New Haven, CT/London: Yale University Press, 2000 (first published 1952).

[19] Rom. 5:17.

[20] Rom. 5:8–9.

An important book has challenged our assumptions about final judgment in recent years. Gregory MacDonald's book *The Evangelical Universalist*[21] argues with passion that we should take very seriously, indeed literally, the 'all' in Romans 11:32 and elsewhere.[22] It was first published under a pseudonym, because the author knew that he was arguing for a position greatly at odds with traditional evangelical orthodoxy. Later in an expanded second edition[23] he reveals his identity: he is Robin Parry, who has worked for many years as a senior editor in Christian theological publishing.

As a book it is an instance of theology at its best – drawing on philosophy and systematic theology as well as biblical studies, in a tone both eirenic and deeply engaged. I don't agree with his universalism, but he opens up the debate helpfully, and anyone wanting to look more deeply into this issue must read his book![24]

The debate continues. A recent book by David Bentley Hart argues passionately for universalism and against the traditional hell,[25] while a magnificent treatment of the theme has been published by Michael McClymond.[26] In two volumes and 1,200 pages he surveys the history of the debate throughout church history, illustrating the many dimensions of the discussion, and engaging with about 150 writers from all eras of the church.

Christian universalism argues that God is working towards nothing less than *a saved world*, from which none will be excluded, and finds this precisely reflected in Paul's 'all' language, as here in Romans 11. Because many die in a state of unbelief, this view argues that post-mortem judgment is a stage in the process of salvation: the offer of salvation through Christ is never withdrawn, even after death, and will eventually be accepted by all – because, over time, we cannot imagine that any would finally refuse it.[27] And so even though there are biblical texts which seem

---

[21] Eugene, OR: Wipf & Stock, 2006; London: SPCK, 2008.

[22] Other important Pauline texts (in addition to Rom. 11:25–36 and 1 Cor. 15:22) are Rom. 5:18; Eph. 1:8–10; Phil. 2:9–11; Col. 1:15–20.

[23] Eugene, OR: Wipf & Stock, 2012.

[24] See also Nigel M. de S. Cameron (ed.), *Universalism and the Doctrine of Hell* (Grand Rapids: Baker, 1992).

[25] David Bentley Hart, *That All Shall Be Saved: Heaven, Hell and Universal Salvation* (New Haven, CT/London: Yale University Press, 2019).

[26] Michael J. McClymond, *The Devil's Redemption: A New History and Interpretation of Christian Universalism* (Grand Rapids, MI: Baker Academic, 2020).

[27] On this see David J. Powys, 'The Nineteenth and Twentieth Century Debates about Hell and Universalism', in Cameron, *Universalism*, pp. 93–138.

to speak of eternal punishment, universalism reinterprets these in the light of this wider vision of none-left-out salvation.

This universalism thus generally depends on the assumption of the continuation of *chronos* after death, which does not seem to chime with the texts we have looked at already. McClymond's view is that it is 'a well-meaning but unfortunate form of false hope – overshooting the mark, going too far, and thus subverting the biblical optimism of grace'[28] – because biblical grace takes very seriously both the power of evil and the significance of human choice, as we will see below. Having said this, however, Paul's 'all' is very powerful and should not be drained of its significance! We can't tackle all the details of the arguments here (we will pick up more of the issues in the next chapter and in ch. 18), but there are four features of our passage which speak into this debate.

a. All Israel . . . merciful to all

In weighing up the extent of the salvation Paul is expecting, we have to bear in mind that 'all' is quite a fluid word. It doesn't necessarily mean 'every single person without exception'. For instance, within a few chapters in 1 Samuel, 'all Israel' means 'everyone living in Israel',[29] 'the whole Israelite army',[30] 'all the representatives of Israel'[31] and 'the whole nation as an ethnic entity'.[32] Paul himself switches between 'all' and 'many' in the closely related passage in Romans 5:

> For if the many died through the one man's trespass, much more surely have the grace of God and the free gift in the grace of the one man, Jesus Christ, abounded for the many . . . Therefore just as one man's trespass led to condemnation for all, so one man's act of righteousness leads to justification and life for all.[33]

It seems as though 'all', for Paul, means something like 'in total', without presuming the inclusion of any particular individual. And this is especially important because of the argumentative purpose of our passage, which gives it its particular thrust:

---

[28] McClymond, *Devil's Redemption*, p. 1063.

[29] 1 Sam. 3:20 – a *geographical* 'all'.

[30] 1 Sam. 4:5 – a *military* 'all'.

[31] 1 Sam. 7:5 – a *political* 'all'.

[32] 1 Sam. 11:2 – a *racial* 'all'. The 'all' of 'all Israel' in Rom. 11:26 could be called a *covenantal* all.

[33] Rom. 5:15, 18.

b. Watch out – don't be arrogant!

The first words in verse 25, *So that you may not claim to be wiser than you are*, look back to a strongly worded warning in the preceding verses. Paul is actually addressing the Gentile Christians in the Roman church, who (it seems) were congratulating themselves on believing in the Messiah in whom Israel failed to believe. Paul says, 'Do not vaunt yourselves over the branches',[34] and goes on,

> If God did not spare the natural branches, neither will he spare you.[35] Note then the kindness and the severity of God: severity towards those who have fallen, but God's kindness towards you, provided you continue in his kindness; otherwise you also will be cut off.[36]

This is a strange warning to meet in the very context in which Paul will say that all will be saved for sure – if that is really what he says! The fact is that Paul lays enormous emphasis on our personal responsibility before God, and any interpretation of his 'universal' statements which undermines this must be wrong. In Paul's view of the life of faith, we must be led by the Spirit and 'put to death the deeds of the body', for 'if you live according to the flesh, you will die'![37] It's easy to overlook this moral urgency in Paul – but it goes with his insistence that 'the Lord knows those who are his',[38] so none of us can presume on some automatic ticket to his grace. We all need to 'continue in [God's] kindness' (22), or we may lose our place.

So to say definitely, with Gregory MacDonald and other universalists, that all will be saved, is to prejudge something which, from our perspective within *chronos*, has to be left open. We cannot deliver ourselves from the anxiety caused by our freedom! Within God's ordering of our lives, we have the freedom not to be his, and *we cannot predict* what the outcome of that freedom might be. Universalism tries to predict the unpredictable.

c. He will banish ungodliness . . . take away their sins

Paul's view of what happens at the second coming is truly thought-provoking. Jesus will not just come as a judge, giving rewards or

---

[34] Rom. 11:18.
[35] This is the NRSV marginal translation, which I think is in line with the more likely Greek text at this point.
[36] Rom. 11:21–22.
[37] Rom. 8:13.
[38] 2 Tim. 2:19.

condemnation in response to the state people are already in. Here in Romans 11, he will also come as a *Deliverer*, bringing an end to *ungodliness* and dispensing forgiveness (26–27). This seems to support the view that judgment includes the possibility of people responding in repentance and faith to the vision of the returning Christ, and receiving salvation at that point. In particular, it will be in fulfilment of the covenant with Israel that this opportunity will be given: *this is my covenant with them, when I take away their sins* (27) – the moment of Israel's 'acceptance' which (Paul has already said) will mean 'life from the dead' for the rest of the world.[39]

This makes a lot of sense when we consider the ways in which we, the church, have managed to obscure, distort and dishonour the gospel, so that people have not had a clear view of Christ even though officially they have 'heard' of him. When he comes again, he will be clearly seen and the blessing of true faith will be unmistakeable, and people will be able to step out of their *ungodliness* and have their sin 'taken away' – praise him! – although we must preserve the possibility that not all will want him, even then.

d. Yes – a saved world!

Even though some may finally refuse, the whole thrust of Paul's argument has been that God's purpose of grace and salvation will certainly be achieved – in spite of the topsy-turvy way in which it gets there. God's covenant with Israel has not failed because of their rejection of the Messiah, even though Paul knows how desperately serious their disobedience is. God will turn it around, even through the stratagem of Paul's own ministry. The very unbelief he encounters serves its purpose en route to the saved world for which he longs and works – *for God has imprisoned all in disobedience so that he may be merciful to all* (32)!

I am not persuaded by the arguments for an evangelical universalism. My concern is simply that Paul should be clearly heard, within this debate. There are three vital points to be made, to preserve Paul's emphases:

1. Yes, God's plan of salvation will issue in a *saved world*, nothing less.
2. But nothing about the certainty of this outcome undermines the pressing challenge of preaching the gospel throughout the world, because

---

[39] Rom. 11:15.

3. God holds people completely responsible for the decisions they take in their lives, and nothing about point 1 undermines this truth either! Judgment will justly reflect our responses to Christ.

Point 3 in particular means that we cannot make any predictions about the outcome of the salvation process – except point 1! Points 1 and 3 exist in theological tension with each other, for sure, but Paul holds both, with passion, at the heart of his vision for the gospel and for our obedience to it.

Now we turn to another wonderful passage which likewise ends with an 'all' statement about the outcome we are heading towards.

Philippians 3:1–21

14. The Saviour from heaven

1. An off-the-cuff mini theology of the Christian life?

Our next port of call is this glorious chapter in Philippians, justly famous for what Paul writes about his own life, conversion to Christ and ambitions in verses 3–14, and ending with a fascinating reference to the second coming in verses 20–21:

> But our citizenship is in heaven, and it is from there that we are expecting a Saviour, the Lord Jesus Christ. He will transform the body of our humiliation so that it may be conformed to the body of his glory, by the power that also enables him to make all things subject to himself.

NRSV uses some cumbersome literal translations here, in *body of our humiliation* and *body of his glory*, because (I think) it wants to bring out the connection with Philippians 2:8–9, which we will explore later. We are talking about *bodies* here – ours and his! So some of our thoughts about bodies above[1] will help us as we unpack this passage.

Amazingly, the whole chapter seems to be an afterthought. Verse 1 apparently sets out to round off the letter and introduce the final greetings: *Finally, my brothers and sisters, rejoice in the Lord! To write the same things to you is not troublesome to me, and for you it is a safeguard.*

'Finally' normally introduces the concluding paragraph(s) in Paul's letters.[2] But here, we have two chapters yet to run! *The same things*

---

[1] Ch. 12, section 1 (pp. 148–151).

[2] See 2 Cor. 13:11; Eph. 6:10; 1 Thess. 4:1; 2 Thess. 3:1; and Phil. 4:8.

probably refers to Paul's repeated encouragement to 'rejoice': references to joy (both Paul's and the Philippians') abound in the first two chapters.[3] The letter is about living Christ-shaped lives in love and unity, embracing sacrifice willingly and gladly as Christ did. The joyful hymn in 2:5–11, celebrating Christ's sacrifice and exaltation, sits at the theological heart of the letter. So the encouragement to *rejoice in the Lord* in 3:1 nicely sums it up: joy will *safeguard* the Philippians into the future.

But then, after beginning to wind up, Paul suddenly plunges in again in 3:2: *Beware of the dogs, beware of the evil workers, beware of those who mutilate the flesh! For it is we who are the circumcision . . .*

He instinctively knows there is more to say, and this wonderful chapter simply unfolds from this warning in verse 2 – probably without conscious planning on Paul's part – until he reaches a climax with the words about the second coming quoted above.

So this chapter seems to have a 'last will and testament' flavour to it. Paul is in prison as he writes (probably in Rome),[4] and doesn't know how his imprisonment will turn out.[5] He thinks that he will see the Philippians again,[6] but he can't be sure. What does he *really* want to say to them – his above-all *Finally . . .* words to them? He gives an off-the-cuff mini theology of the Christian life, aimed at the believers in Philippi, but relevant for us all. If we want to live confidently, joyfully and hopefully, coping with whatever life throws at us, this chapter holds the key to fit all locks!

2. All things subject to Christ!

Let's start with the last words of verse 21, because they connect us to Romans 11. We are still in the realm of *all things*! The power that enables Christ to transform our bodies is far more than just the power to transform bodies. It's a supreme power, over *all* things – but here *all things* has a slightly different flavour, because of the special Roman background important in Philippians.

Philippi had been turned into a Roman colony by the emperor Augustus in 31 BC, and was proud of this special status and relationship with the

---

[3] See 1:4, 18, 25; 2:2, 17–18, 28–29.

[4] See Markus Bockmuehl, *The Epistle to the Philippians*, Black's New Testament Commentary (London: A&C Black, 1997), pp. 25–32.

[5] See 1:12–14, 20–24.

[6] 1:26; 2:24.

imperial capital. The official language in Philippi was Latin, and many of its residents were Roman citizens. Roman power secured its safety, Roman law and customs shaped its public life, Roman officials ran its local government. Archaeologists have noticed that all the surviving inscriptions on public buildings or monuments in Philippi from this time are in Latin. Rome was its saviour, and the term 'saviour' was often used either of Rome or of Rome's emperors, who were worshipped as gods in the Roman imperial cult. For instance, one famous inscription (not in Philippi) praises Augustus as the bringer of peace, order and prosperity to the world, and calls him 'the father-god and saviour of the common race of humans'.[7]

Three features of Paul's words about the second coming relate to this political background:

- *Our citizenship is in heaven* (20): like the residents of Philippi, we too belong elsewhere! Here *citizenship* means more than just an on-paper belonging, as with a passport. Just as Philippi lived the life of Rome in Macedonia, so the roots and rules of our shared life are not here but *in heaven*, from where . . .
- *we are expecting a Saviour, the Lord Jesus Christ*: he is a *true* Saviour! The emperor in far-off Rome claimed the name, but could not deliver Rome's citizens from *death*. But Jesus can – and finally will, when he comes again.
- He truly has the power *to make all things subject to himself*. The empire claimed it, and many loyal Romans in Philippi affirmed it, but only Jesus has it.

It is significant that Paul wrote this letter in Greek, not in Latin. Greek was the language of all the 'others' in Philippi – the locals, the traders and the slaves, who could not claim Roman citizenship. But they too are citizens of another place: and what a place, so much more amazing than Rome! Paul is putting the Roman Empire on notice, and with it all other megapowers that claim authority over human bodies: your days are numbered! There is coming a Saviour – a real one, one with real power over all things, and who therefore is really able to transform things for us. And the power that he will exercise universally, to bring the whole created

---

[7] The 'inscription of Halicarnassus', quoted by W. Foerster in Gerhard Kittel and Gerhard Friedrich (eds.), tr. Geoffrey W. Bromiley, *Theological Dictionary of the New Testament*, vol. 7 (Grand Rapids, MI: Eerdmans, 1971), p. 1012.

order under his glorious rule when he appears from heaven, will in particular transform our *bodies*: no longer weak and mortal, short-lived and 'humiliated', but conforming instead to *the body of his glory*, his glorious resurrected body, victorious over death and all powers.

Paul is drawing on the ideas he expresses more fully in 1 Corinthians 15 – particularly about our resurrection bodies which will bear Christ's 'image',[8] and about Christ's victory over the 'powers' including the 'last enemy', death.[9] The *all things* which he subjects to himself are not just the physical stuff of the world, but more particularly all the powers of the world which (like Rome) either ignore or dispute his rule at the moment.

One interesting difference, comparing Philippians 3:21 with 1 Corinthians 15:28, is that in 1 Corinthians it is *God* who subjects all things to Jesus: whereas here in Philippians, Jesus subjects everything to himself. Jesus Christ takes up and exercises God's own agency. Something similar happens in the lovely little 'hymn' in Philippians 2:5–11, to which Paul looks back in these verses: it alludes to Isaiah 45, where God issues an appeal to 'all the ends of the earth' to 'turn to me and be saved',[10] and then declares,

By myself I have sworn,
     from my mouth has gone forth in righteousness
     a word that shall not return:
'To me every knee shall bow,
     every tongue shall swear.'[11]

But of course for Paul (and for the author of this hymn, if different),

at the name of Jesus
     every knee [shall] bend,
     in heaven and on earth and under the earth,
and every tongue [shall] confess
     that Jesus Christ is Lord,
     to the glory of God the Father.[12]

---

8 1 Cor. 15:49.
9 1 Cor. 15:24–26.
10 Isa. 45:22.
11 Isa. 45:23.
12 Phil. 2:10–11.

Isaiah's expectation of universal worship is to be fulfilled when knees bend to *Jesus*, and all tongues confess *his* Lordship. Through the worship of Jesus, God (who is now 'the Father') will be glorified. This speaks so loudly of the way in which the New Testament (as Richard Bauckham puts it) 'include[s] Jesus in the unique divine identity' as Creator and Ruler of the universe.[13] This is what 'all things subjected to Jesus' (3:21) looks like: all knees bowing to him, including all heavenly and hellish powers, above and below the earth as well as on it. Some knees may bow reluctantly, and some may do it gladly but for the first time[14] – but all will bend to his rule.

There's a lovely 'other way round' quality here. Two different Greek words for 'form' are used in both places (2:7–8 and 3:21), as well as the same word translated 'humble' or 'humiliation'. In his incarnation, Jesus took the 'form' of a slave, adopting human 'form', and 'humbled himself' to share our death. Now, in his glory, he 'transforms' our 'humble' bodies so that they 'conform' to his. He took our form, and when he comes again, we will take his. That's what it means that he is the Saviour!

For Paul, this second-coming prospect is totally life-transforming. It is not just a matter of waiting for that moment to come, but of living *now* in a transformed way that *anticipates* 'the day of Jesus Christ'.[15] This is the great burden of Philippians 3, leading up to this concluding vision of the Day. So we will now look back over the passage that leads up to this point. How must we live now, in the light of the coming Day?

3. Overview of Philippians 3

The chapter falls into four paragraphs, which we can helpfully analyse under the leading notion of *the pursuit of safety*. A sense of safety, or security, is vital for us human beings, a need felt as deeply in the first century as it is today. I'm reflecting on Yalom's four anxieties and the way in which they weave themselves through our whole human experience:[16] where can safety and security be found by creatures threatened by death, undermined by meaninglessness, condemned finally to isolation in spite of our need for relationship (we die alone) and – on top of all that! – faced

---

[13] Richard Bauckham, *God Crucified: Monotheism and Christology in the New Testament* (Carlisle: Paternoster, 1998), p. 26.

[14] See our thoughts above on Rom. 11:26–27 (pp. 169–70).

[15] Paul's name for the day of the second coming in Phil. 1:6.

[16] See above, p. 165.

with the need to take decisions every moment, sometimes of life-changing significance? Paul's presentation develops in stages:

- 3:2–7 Safety and security are not found through 'trusting in the flesh' but . . .
- 3:8–11 . . . through 'knowing' Jesus Christ.
- 3:12–16 We cannot know him fully now – it's a prize to be reached for;
- 3:17–21 . . . and we need the encouragement of the right people as we wait for the security of the heavenly city!

4. Finding security – not through the flesh! (3:2–7)

How powerful Paul's words are! First he issues a warning:

> *Beware of the dogs, beware of the evil workers, beware of those who mutilate the flesh! For it is we who are the circumcision, who worship in the Spirit of God and boast in Christ Jesus and have no confidence in the flesh.*

There is a trap into which we may fall, illustrated by those he calls *the dogs*, a rude expression indeed. It seems these people are 'the circumcision faction',[17] those who argued and campaigned for the acceptance of circumcision and all the signs of Jewishness by Gentile converts to Christ. Paul rejects all of this, because he thinks it is a mistaken search for *confidence* in the wrong place. So, second, he illustrates the *temptation* into which these 'dogs' had fallen – and which we all feel:

> . . . *even though I, too, have reason for confidence in the flesh.*
> *If anyone has reason to be confident in the flesh, I have more: circumcised on the eighth day, a member of the people of Israel, of the tribe of Benjamin, a Hebrew born of Hebrews; as to the law, a Pharisee; as to zeal, a persecutor of the church; as to righteousness under the law, blameless.*

Like Paul, we seek security through status and belonging, looking for significance and meaning through the labels we can apply to ourselves.

---

[17] See Gal. 2:12.

And how far Paul went! In the eyes of his contemporaries, he was *blameless* in his adherence to the law. He could have lived all his life basking in the sense of status and achievement provided by his Jewish success story. Markus Bockmuehl perceptively comments that Paul's mention of his pride in belonging to *the tribe of Benjamin* would have connected to the Philippians' pride in belonging to the ancient Roman 'tribus Voltinia', the family line on the basis of which their citizenship was assigned to them.[18]

We need to ask ourselves what labels and achievements fit the bill for us, too. What gives us that sense of meaning and status? It will be different for each of us. Hold your own list in mind, and then feel how *shocking* it is that, third, Paul throws it all away: *Yet whatever gains I had, these I have come to regard as loss because of Christ.*

Paul uses financial, marketplace language here: profit and loss. But the currency is turned upside down. What looked like a huge profit is actually a stonking loss, he says, *because of Christ*: Christ has enabled him to see things completely differently, as he now explains.

5. Finding security – through knowing Jesus Christ (3:8–11)

Paul unpacks this completely revolutionary change of perspective in verse 8:

> More than that, I regard everything as loss because of the surpassing value of knowing Christ Jesus my Lord. For his sake I have suffered the loss of all things, and I regard them as rubbish, in order that I may gain Christ.

He is thinking, of course, of his experience on the Damascus road which turned his life inside out.[19] But he's not simply saying that, as a result of that experience, he lost all he had before. True though that is, his point is much more profound: Jesus showed him that *everything* is *loss*, compared with the *surpassing value* of knowing him. Compared with that, *everything* is really *rubbish*, in fact 'refuse' or 'dung'. Excrement! The word Paul uses is very strong, used only here in the New Testament.

---

[18] Bockmuehl, *Philippians*, pp. 4, 196.
[19] Acts 9:1–9.

This reminds us of Jesus' parables of the treasure in the field and the pearl of great price: the 'kingdom of heaven' is something of such huge beauty and value that it's worth sacrificing everything else in order simply to possess it.[20] Graham Kendrick beautifully expresses this in his hymn 'Knowing You (All I Once Held Dear)'.[21] It's not that all these other things *are* completely worthless: in Romans Paul agrees that being a Jew has great value attached,[22] and that the law is 'the embodiment of knowledge and truth'.[23] It's a matter of comparison: these other things (possessions, status, reputation, achievement) are complete rubbish *compared with* the *surpassing value* of knowing Jesus.

So what, precisely, is the value of knowing Christ? In the next three verses (9–11) Paul unpacks this, specifying four ways in which he longs to connect with Jesus through knowing him. To 'know' him is to connect with him in such a way that his life becomes ours: we begin to share in his story, so that it becomes ours, also. These four features of Jesus' story begin to move us towards that glorious vision of the second coming at the end of the chapter.

a. Righteousness based on faith

> . . . *And be found in him, not having a righteousness of my own that comes from the law, but one that comes through faith in Christ,*[24] *the righteousness from God based on faith.*
> (9)

'Righteousness' is a key term in Paul's theology. Much has been written about its meaning, and it is easily misunderstood because in English it sounds as though it's about morality: as though the *righteousness from God* that Paul seeks to have from Christ is some kind of transformation of his character – he becomes a 'righteous' person. That is what he was striving to have through the law, and what he was so successful at – *blameless*, in fact (6)! He is *not* saying that Christ has enabled him to be even more *blameless* in his character and behaviour than he was as a Pharisee.

---

[20] Matt. 13:44–46.

[21] Published in 1993 and now one of the most popular hymns in UK churches. The song, performances of it and the story of its composition are available at <www.grahamkendrick.co.uk>.

[22] Rom. 3:1–2.

[23] Rom. 2:20.

[24] Or (NRSV margin) 'through the faith of Christ'. I comment on this shortly.

Rather – connected here to *knowing* Christ – righteousness is about *intimate relational connection*, with all that this implies. Imagine two friends who are completely involved in each other's company – maybe they've been married to each other for forty years! Their knowledge of each other is more than just that they can list each other's likes and dislikes. There's a soul connection, based on a 100% acceptance of each other, warts and all, and on a commitment which means that their friendship is rock-solid. Nothing can shake it. In Pauline terms, they stand in righteousness towards each other.

Paul has given up seeking to win that kind of relationship with God through his 'blameless' adherence to the law. Instead, he has discovered that God simply gives it to us through Christ – it is *righteousness from God*. All we need to receive it is a responsive *faith*: that is, a readiness to receive the gift of the relationship, and to live in it. Of course it's one-sided to start with – he knows us far better than we know him. That's why Paul emphasizes his *desire* to know Christ, to press on deeper into the relationship, whatever it might mean – starting with the conscious rejection of all the *rubbish* that gets in the way.

Because it is so deeply relational, the experience of this *righteousness from God* is about entering into 'the faith of Christ'. This is a possible translation of the phrase usually rendered *faith in Christ*. Technically, it is about whether the genitive ('of Christ') should be understood as 'objective' (that is, Christ is the 'object' of the faith: it is faith *in* him exercised by us) or 'subjective' (that is, Christ is the subject of the faith: it is the faith that he himself exercises, his personal faith in God or faithfulness to him). Opinions are divided among experts.[25]

There's actually a middle way: to take the genitive as a 'genitive of origin', and to understand it as 'faith from Christ', that is, 'the faith that Christ brings into the world', the unique way of relating to God which Jesus both lived in and communicates to us. He related to his Father uniquely as *father*! And he trod a unique path of obedience and trust, a path beautifully painted in the hymn of 2:5–11. But now he invites us into the same 'faith', so that it is not uniquely his, but ours also. Knowing him, we step into his story and make it ours. And that leads to . . .

---

[25] Bockmuehl has an excellent summary of the issues, the evidence and the debate: *Philippians*, pp. 210–212.

b. Sharing his resurrection power

I want to know Christ and the power of his resurrection . . .
(10a)

The NRSV begins a new sentence here, by inserting *I want*. Actually Paul just carries on, with a 'so that': the whole purpose of being *found in him* (9) is 'so that I may know Christ'. And then Paul specifies exactly what knowing Christ entails – the *and* that follows is explanatory: 'so that I may know Christ, that is, . . .' *the power of his resurrection and the sharing of his sufferings* (10). Knowing Jesus entails sharing his story in two particular respects – resurrection and suffering. How fascinating that Paul puts them this way round. In Jesus' case they were the other way round, as in 2:5–11: resurrection was the glorious consequence of, and reward for, his obedient suffering and submission to death. But for Paul, as he presses in to know Christ, resurrection is the first goal, because his life within us gives us the power to cope with the sufferings we face. The *power of his resurrection* is the power we know now, within our present lives.

And how we need it! Because we can't know Christ without also . . .

c. Sharing in his sufferings

. . . And the sharing of his sufferings by becoming like him in his death . . .
(10b)

Once again the hymn in 2:5–11 gives us the essential background. Christ 'emptied himself' of his divine position in order to take 'the form of a slave', because we humans are enslaved under the power of death. Jesus stepped into that place, becoming 'obedient to the point of death – even death on a cross' (the most shameful form of death).[26] Our body, our death, our shame – he became 'like' us. So we don't have to do anything to be 'like' him, except to open ourselves to God's gift, so that his faith becomes ours. Our sufferings just come with the package of being human – although, as Paul illustrates in verses 5–7, accepting God's gift by faith may then mean *more* suffering as we lose our reliance on the illusory security we have found for ourselves, and launch out into discipleship. But, as the American missionary martyr

---

[26] Phil. 2:7–8.

Jim Elliot said, 'He is no fool who gives what he cannot keep to gain that which he cannot lose'![27]

d. Sharing in the final resurrection

> . . . *If somehow I may attain the resurrection from the dead.*
> (11)

Sharing in the *power* of his resurrection now, in the midst of all our struggles, is but a stage on the way to final resurrection. The last chapter of Jesus' story – his second coming, when he makes our bodies like his, glorious and powerful (21) – will be the last chapter of our story too! There's no doubt in Paul's *if somehow*. This is not a vain struggle to reach the unreachable. He's expressing the way in which *everything* in his life is shaped around achieving this glorious goal – through knowing Jesus, that is, through living in intimate fellowship with him, sharing his sufferings and experiencing his power.

6. Finding security – through being 'grasped' by Jesus (3:12–14)

Now that focus on the goal becomes Paul's leading thought: *Not that I have already obtained this or have already reached the goal; but I press on to make it my own, because Christ Jesus has made me his own* (12).

It is extraordinary to reflect that Paul is in prison as he writes this. Twice he uses the word 'pursue' (12, 14), translated *press on* by NRSV. He uses the image of racing athletes fixing their eyes on the marker (*the goal*, 14) at the end of the race track as they power towards the finishing line. Paul may be stuck indoors, unable to go anywhere, but in his mind and heart he is straining every sinew to get to that line! The prize on the line is worth every effort: *the prize of the upward*[28] *call of God in Christ Jesus* (14). In all likelihood, the prize is precisely what he then goes on to describe

---

[27] Elliot wrote this in his journal in 1949, before going to Ecuador as a missionary. He was killed by a group of indigenous warriors in January 1956. Elliot's journal is held in the archive of the Billy Graham Center at Wheaton College, Illinois, and a photograph of the journal page including this famous saying can be seen at 'Jim Elliott's Journal Entry', *Anchored in Christ* (blog), 28 October 2013, <https://www.kevinhalloran.net/jim-elliot-quote-he-is-no-fool/>, accessed 22 June 2022.

[28] NRSV has *heavenly*. But the Greek is simply 'upward' – Paul doesn't mention heaven here.

at the end of the chapter: the glorious transformation of our bodies when Jesus comes again. That's an 'upward call' indeed!

Paul is so focused on this goal that he describes himself as *forgetting what lies behind and straining forward to what lies ahead* (13). He has illustrated what this means in his words about his own past, in verses 4–7. He doesn't mean, of course, that he has literally forgotten his early history. He means that he refuses to be *determined* by his past, so that his past irrevocably shapes his present and his future. He has been 'grasped' by Christ Jesus (12; a better translation than *made me his own*): Jesus has 'gripped' him and called him away, and so his past as a brilliant Pharisee loses its power over him.

Our present sense of safety and security is so often threatened by our history. Traumatic experiences in the past can deeply disturb our present and make the world feel very unsafe. Working through such experiences can take a long time, but to fix our eyes on Christ's 'upward call' can be a wonderful help. *Right now* he calls us to let go of all that binds and restricts us, and to live in a new story – his story – in which he shares all our suffering, and gives us his resurrection power to respond to God's call. He has *grasped* us! And in his grip we are secure, however tough the way.[29]

7. Finding security – through connecting with the right people (3:15–21)

This is not an easy calling! We need the encouragement of others to keep us going. This is about finding security not in a cosy safe place, hidden away from the terrible challenges of life, but out there in the unpredictable rough and tumble. Paul's encouragement here has four elements:

a. Be strong in the face of disagreement (3:15–16)
Paul encourages the Philippians to hold on to the convictions they already have (16) – not to be unduly swayed by the differing views of others. We're all on the same journey: God will change our views if they're wrong, and we can trust him to do that both for us and for those around us (15). But what can give us confidence when opinions differ?

---

[29] A very good book which looks at the psychological and emotional elements of making this kind of 'shift' is André Radmall, *Get Unstuck: Change the Script, Change Your Life* ([UK]: Rethink Press, 2021).

b. Have reliable role models (3:17)

Paul is an apostle! He knows that people will not go wrong if they imitate him. The background to this is the argument he reports in 1:12–18. Some Christians were ashamed of Paul, because imprisonment carried such stigma with it. But actually it is completely in line with the gospel that a *shamed, imprisoned Jew* is a chief spokesperson for Christ.

c. Avoid lifestyles that don't centre on the cross of Christ (3:18–19)

Paul's words are very strong here. He could be thinking of the *dogs* of verse 2, or the rivals of 1:17 who use Christ as a way of opposing Paul. Or he could have in mind people like the members of the Corinthian church who thought that freedom in Christ was freedom to indulge physical appetites of all sorts.[30] Whoever they are, they have lost that sense of an 'upward call', and *their minds are set on earthly things* (19b).

It's worth noting the strength of Paul's language about these enemies of the cross: *Their end is destruction*, he says (19a), which most naturally suggests that the end point of all who resist the message of the cross is finally to cease to exist. The ultimate destiny of 'the lost' is a fiercely debated aspect of the discussion surrounding the extent of salvation – universal or not?[31] Fortunately we don't need to decide the answer to this in order to appreciate Paul's teaching about the second coming.

And so finally . . .

d. Look forward to safety through the Saviour! (3:20–21)

We are back where we started. Finally, we connect with Jesus Christ the coming Saviour, whose power secures our safety for all eternity. A focus on the second coming of Christ is absolutely essential for authentic, biblical Christian believing, because at its heart is the twofold conviction that (1) we belong in an *eternal* relationship with Jesus Christ (*our citizenship is in heaven*), and (2) so far as that relationship is concerned (to steal the words of Ronald Reagan's 1984 campaign slogan), 'we ain't seen nothin' yet!'

---

[30] 1 Cor. 6:12–20.

[31] In the essays collected in Cameron, *Universalism*, John Wenham defends the view that the lost cease to exist ('The Case for Conditional Immortality', pp. 161–191), a view opposed by Kendall S. Harmon (pp. 193–224) and Henri Blocher (pp. 283–312).

Part 4

The second coming in the later New Testament

Hebrews 9:23–28

15. The high priest reappears

1. Three appearings

We turn to the letter to the Hebrews, and to a passage which at first sight sends us rocking back on our theological heels – very different from anything we've looked at before, and containing some stiff challenges to understanding. But it's important: it contains the only reference to the second coming in Hebrews, and in fact is the only passage in the New Testament that calls it the 'second' coming. It gives us a unique perspective on what it means for us to *live by faith* now, in the interim between the first and second 'comings' of Christ: what can keep us going, in the face of the sheer toughness of our lives and all that tells us faith is an illusion?

As you read the passage, notice the *three* 'appearings' of Christ around which these verses are structured (24, 26, 28). In fact, three different Greek verbs are used, with a different shade of meaning, as we will see. And if you're familiar with the ritual of the Day of Atonement in the Jerusalem temple, see if you can spot how the imagery and theology of that annual festival is feeding into the presentation here.

> *Thus it was necessary for the sketches of the heavenly things to be purified with these rites, but the heavenly things themselves need better sacrifices than these. For Christ did not enter a sanctuary made by human hands, a mere copy of the true one, but he entered into heaven itself, now to appear in the presence of God on our behalf.*
>
> *Nor was it to offer himself again and again, as the high priest enters the Holy Place year after year with blood that is not his own; for then he*

would have had to suffer again and again since the foundation of the world. But as it is, he has appeared once for all at the end of the age to remove sin by the sacrifice of himself.

And just as it is appointed for mortals to die once, and after that the judgement, so Christ, having been offered once to bear the sins of many, will appear a second time, not to deal with sin, but to save those who are eagerly waiting for him.

I've divided the passage into the three mini paragraphs into which it falls, each of which ends with a reference to Christ's 'appearing'. The third, of course (28), is his second coming – which is called the second, rather than the third, because the first one (24) is a new, extra 'appearing', happening *now*, as Jesus *appear[s] in the presence of God on our behalf.* The 'appearing' in verse 26 is his incarnation, because it is on the cross that he sacrifices himself.

We will tour through the passage paragraph by paragraph, unpacking its remarkable imagery and theology. Even though the imagery is based around the rituals of the Day of Atonement, we can helpfully use legal metaphors to get into its meaning.

2. Into court! (9:23–24)

In general, the UK does not permit cameras inside courtrooms, so UK viewers see two kinds of reports when legal cases feature in the TV news: we might see the defendant and his or her legal team arriving at the court and going through the doors while the voiceover explains the issues; or we might see the defendant emerging from the court after the case, to stand on the steps while his or her lawyer gives an impromptu press conference, expressing jubilation over winning or regret over losing. There are no photographs or film of proceedings within the court.

Something similar is happening in this passage!

- Our great Advocate enters the heavenly Court, *to appear in the presence of God on our behalf* (24).
- Then the evidence for our acquittal is presented, away from the cameras, out of our sight (25–26).
- And finally Christ our Advocate reappears, to announce our salvation (27–28).

To get into the marrow of all this, we need to fill in the ceremonial background on which Hebrews is drawing.

a. The Day of Atonement

This was the one day in the year when the high priest (and he only) entered the Most Holy Place in the tabernacle or the temple.[1] This was the central sanctuary, where the ark of God was kept during the time of the tabernacle and Solomon's temple. The high priest had to start by offering sacrifice for his own sins, so that he would not die when entering the direct presence of God. An interesting little note in Exodus reveals that he had bells sewn along the bottom of his robe so that he could be 'heard when he goes into the holy place before the Lord, and when he comes out, so that he may not die'.[2] We can imagine the nervousness of the crowd waiting outside, in case the bells suddenly stopped tinkling.

Once inside, the high priest sprinkled the blood of a sacrificed goat (one of two used in the Day of Atonement rituals) onto the 'mercy seat' on top of the ark. Leviticus explains the purpose of this:

> Thus he shall make atonement for the sanctuary, because of the uncleannesses of the people of Israel, and because of their transgressions, all their sins; and so he shall do for the tent of meeting, which remains with them in the midst of their uncleannesses.[3]

When he came out again, the high priest recited the sins of Israel over the second goat (which was then expelled into the desert, symbolizing the carrying away of all Israel's sins), and pronounced God's blessing on the people, actually using the divine name on this one occasion in the year. The Day of Atonement was truly the high point in the worship calendar.

b. Making atonement for the sanctuary?

The focus on making atonement *for the sanctuary* is puzzling. But it is clearly vital in the mind of the author of Hebrews, for this is what he underlines in verse 23, extending the idea to the *heavenly* sanctuary which Jesus has entered *on our behalf*. This is peculiar; why would heaven need to be *purified*?

---

[1] The description is in Lev. 16. Hebrews always refers to the tabernacle, rather than the temple.

[2] Exod. 28:35.

[3] Lev. 16:16. See also the summary statement in Lev. 16:33.

The background idea is that the heavenly 'holy place', where God truly lives, is mirrored on earth by the physical sanctuary where he comes to 'dwell' among his people. Moses was told to build and furnish the tabernacle 'according to the pattern that was shown you on the mountain'[4] – and this was interpreted to mean not just that God drew up the plans, but that the tabernacle on earth matched his dwelling in heaven. Hebrews uses several words to express this relationship: the heavenly tabernacle is the 'true' one,[5] of which the earthly 'tent' is a 'sketch and shadow'[6] or a *mere copy*, as here in verse 24.[7]

The author of Hebrews is following through the logic of this when he writes verse 23. If the earthly 'copies' need purification by ritual sacrifice, that need in itself must reflect something about the heavenly original. What sacrifice could be required to purify *the heavenly things themselves*? Surely something even greater.

To understand this, we need to bear in mind the purpose of the tabernacle. One of its names was 'the tent of meeting',[8] because it was the place where the God of Israel and his people could meet. But it stood 'in the midst of their uncleannesses',[9] right in the middle of the camp. We need to imagine muck splashed onto the tabernacle by passing traffic – that's the 'uncleannesses' of the people surrounding it, defined further as 'their transgressions, all their sins'. Mud sticks, and stains. If God kept his distance, there wouldn't be a problem. But because he wants to go with his people[10] and dwell 'in their midst',[11] something has to be done to wash the muck off, to keep the 'impurity' away from him.

So here is a huge paradox: on the one hand, God wants to be with his people – in fact, this is the whole purpose of his covenant relationship with them. But on the other hand, he can't, because of their sin. The answer is a compromise: the 'tent of meeting' will be pitched right in the centre of the camp, but will contain a 'Most Holy Place' where God will dwell in splendid isolation, actually 'meeting' only one man once a year, the high priest on the Day of Atonement. The high priest represents the

---

[4] Exod. 25:40, quoted in Heb. 8:5.

[5] Heb. 8:2.

[6] Heb. 8:5; cf. 10:1.

[7] *Mere* has been added by NRSV. The word *copy* is the counterpart of the word 'pattern' in 8:5.

[8] E.g. Exod. 28:43; 39:32.

[9] Lev. 16:16, quoted above.

[10] See Exod. 33:14–17; Deut. 1:32–33.

[11] E.g. Deut. 7:21; 10:8; 12:5–7, 18.

whole people as he enters – but he can do so only because of the elaborate means provided to 'make atonement' for the sins of the people, the muck staining the tabernacle.

c. Drawing near . . .

What a picture! The author of Hebrews uses these Day of Atonement rituals to understand Jesus' death, resurrection and *ascension* as providing similar atonement: *Christ did not enter a sanctuary made by human hands, a mere copy of the true one, but he entered into heaven itself, now to appear in the presence of God on our behalf* (24).

We instinctively think of *heaven* as 'up there', or at least away from here, not where we are – a different place. But that is not how the author of Hebrews thinks of it. Heaven is right here, in our midst, and we can 'draw near' – a favourite word in Hebrews, as for instance in Hebrews 4:16: 'Let us therefore approach [draw near to] the throne of grace with boldness, so that we may receive mercy and find grace to help in time of need.'[12]

The Greek verb translated 'approach' was a kind of technical term in the Old Testament to describe 'approaching' God to worship.[13] Because Christ appears *now* in the heavenly sanctuary, we can 'approach' *now*, too, whenever we have need. 'Appear' has the flavour of entering the stage or bursting onto the scene, an appearance that changes the action. And if his appearance enables *us* to draw near too, it certainly does change things. Like the high priest on the Day of Atonement, he appears *on our behalf* – that is, representing us, standing in for us, so that it is as though we appear there too, with him.

So the purification of *the heavenly things* is not such an odd idea after all: it's about enabling the closeness to God that we feel every time we pray. It's about opening the door into his presence for *us*, too, in all our sinfulness and uncleanness. We can come! *None too impure to enter.* This is a beautiful message to encourage sinners of all shapes and sizes.

3. Presenting the evidence (9:25–26)

In these two verses we peek behind the scenes, into the heavenly courtroom, to savour the evidence presented by the ascended Christ. It would

---

[12] See also Heb. 7:25; 10:22; 11:6; 12:22.

[13] E.g. Exod. 16:9; Lev. 9:5, 8; 21:17–18; Num. 16:40; Heb. 10:1; 12:18.

be helpful if the translation began (as it certainly could), 'Nor is it . . .' rather than *was it*, because this is about how Christ presents himself *now* in heaven. Let's make that change:

> *Nor is it to offer himself again and again, as the high priest enters the Holy Place year after year with blood that is not his own; for then he would have had to suffer again and again since the foundation of the world. But as it is, he has appeared once for all at the end of the age to remove sin by the sacrifice of himself.*

The author of Hebrews has a 'down' on the sacrifices offered in the tabernacle (and, in his day, in the temple in Jerusalem). Because he thinks of the tabernacle just as a sketch or shadow of the heavenly sanctuary which is the real deal, the sacrifices offered there were not effective, but also only functioned as pale foreshadowings of the real sacrifice, which is that of Jesus on the cross. If asked whether the worshippers really experienced forgiveness and cleansing in the tabernacle/temple, his answer would be 'Yes, of course – but only because the death of Christ was effective for them, too.'[14] Let's unpack this a little more.

a. Sacrifices that don't work . . . and one that does

The author thinks that 'it is impossible for the blood of bulls and goats to take away sins'.[15] And he thinks that this impossibility was signalled within the Old Testament itself by the fact that the sacrifices had to be repeated constantly:

> Since the law has only a shadow of the good things to come and not the true form of these realities, it can never, by the same sacrifices that are continually offered year after year, make perfect those who approach. Otherwise, would they not have ceased being offered, since the worshippers, cleansed once for all, would no longer have any consciousness of sin? But in these sacrifices there is a reminder of sin year after year.[16]

---

[14] He says this in 9:15.

[15] Heb. 10:4. Bulls and goats were the two animals sacrificed on the Day of Atonement.

[16] Heb. 10:1–3.

The annual repetition of the Day of Atonement, he says, simply underlined its ineffectiveness. But Jesus' sacrifice of himself is effective *once for all*, as he puts it a few verses later: 'It is by God's will that we have been sanctified through the offering of the body of Jesus Christ once for all.'[17]

So in the heavenly sanctuary Jesus presents not *blood that is not his own* (like the high priest on the Day of Atonement), but his own blood, the evidence of his self-giving sacrifice on the cross for us. He 'appears' in the sanctuary *as* the crucified and resurrected Lamb of God. This self-presentation is sufficient *to remove sin* once and for all. But this doesn't happen automatically apart from our participation, even though (like the worshippers on the Day of Atonement) we are not 'in there' where the action is centred. Our participation is vital. Craig Koester perceptively comments:

> Sin emerges from unfaith, and for sin to be abolished means that it must be displaced by faith, which is its opposite. When the proclamation of Christ's once-for-all death awakens faith, sin is set aside, making the conscience complete (9:14).[18]

So that's another paradox: Jesus presents before God the evidence of his once-for-all effective sacrifice which enables us and God to 'meet', but it doesn't become effective until we embrace it by faith, and confess that this is what Jesus was doing on the cross. Shortly, Hebrews will underline and illustrate the significance of faith in the glorious gallery of faithful heroes he calls us to imitate, climaxing with the faith of Jesus himself, 'the pioneer and perfecter of our faith'.[19]

b. 'Interceding' for us

This is all *on our behalf* (24), and Hebrews has already given us a steer on how to understand this heavenly *on our behalf* ministry of the risen Christ: he is 'interceding' for us. An amazing thought! The important passage is 7:25, where the author says that because of his 'permanent priesthood' (not dying and needing to be replaced, like all other priests),

---

17 Heb. 10:10.

18 Craig R. Koester, *Hebrews: A New Translation with Introduction and Commentary*, The Anchor Bible 36 (New York: Doubleday, 2001), p. 429.

19 Heb. 11:1 – 12:3. The description of Jesus is in 12:2.

Jesus 'is able for all time to save those who approach God through him, since he always lives to make intercession for them'.

'For all time' could be better translated 'completely': the idea is that nothing is *left out of*, and nothing *hinders*, the salvation Jesus gives. His continual 'intercession' for us in the heavenly sanctuary is about his constant presentation of his death as effective to save us. According to Craig Koester, Karl Barth described Christ's intercession as 'extending the benefits of his death'.[20] That seems right. It's not that he tracks our lives from heaven, sees what we need at each moment, and asks God for that. His 'intercession' is much bigger than this, because he is outside time. He sees the end from the beginning, and his life in eternity is directed towards presenting to God the *basis* and the *certainty* of our salvation. He is there, our 'great high priest who has passed through the heavens',[21] our forerunner into the sanctuary,[22] bearing the evidence of his once-for-all sacrifice to deal with our sins and 'perfect' us for God's presence.[23]

c. At the end of the age . . .

This 'outside time' aspect of Christ's ministry in the heavenly sanctuary is signalled here by the fascinating statement that Christ's 'appearance' among us took place *at the end of the age*. Actually, the author writes 'at the end of the ages', plural. The NRSV has (unhelpfully) reduced the plural to the singular. This is a kind of stock phrase: this word 'end' appears elsewhere only in Matthew 24:3 and in four other places in Matthew,[24] always in the phrase 'the end of the age' (singular), and always looking forward to 'the end', the wrapping up of all things when Jesus comes again. So its striking use here to refer to Christ's *first* coming must be connected to the use of the plural: this is something different. Time is running differently: all ages of earth converge on the 'moment' when Christ *remove[d] sin by the sacrifice of himself.* This is God's ultimate *kairos*-moment, so important within the sweep of *chronos* that it is as if all time bends towards this point, the 'appearing' of God's Son to deal with sin.

This Greek word 'appear' has the flavour 'reveal, make plain something previously hidden'. Just as every great detective novel ends with 'the

---

[20] Koester, *Hebrews*, p. 428, n. 310.

[21] Heb. 4:14.

[22] See Heb. 6:19–20.

[23] See Heb. 10:14. Cf. Rom. 8:33–34.

[24] Matt. 13:39–40, 49; 28:20.

reveal', the moment when the disparate clues come together and all is explained, so Christ's 'appearance' to deal with sin on the cross reveals what is most deeply true and significant for all ages of our world: sin has been 'removed' (that is, annulled, disallowed, set aside) and therefore *will not be* the defining focus of the human story. How glorious is that?

4. On the steps! (9:27–28)

It turns out that the adjusting of time implied by the use of the plural 'ages' in verse 26 is important for understanding these verses, too:

> *And just as it is appointed for mortals to die once, and after that the judgement, so Christ, having been offered once to bear the sins of many, will appear a second time, not to deal with sin, but to save those who are eagerly waiting for him.*

The author ties Jesus' second coming into the story of the cosmic Day of Atonement which he has been developing, and draws a parallel between that and our experience of death and judgment. We need to take care unpacking it – it's a subtle argument, and (like so much else in Hebrews) full of suggestive and encouraging theology.

a. The reappearance of the high priest

As we noted above, the ritual of the Day of Atonement involved the high priest 'disappearing' into the Most Holy Place, where only he was allowed to go once a year. The worshippers waited outside for him to emerge, signalling that atonement had once again been made. For those alert to the theology of the Day of Atonement, much hung on God's acceptance of the sacrifice within the Most Holy Place, signalled by his acceptance of the high priest. As Leviticus underlines and Hebrews reaffirms, this was meant to cover *all* Israel's sins, including all their unknown sins, 'sins of ignorance' for which no specific atonement could be made.[25]

The high priest was thus a very important figure. There is a fascinating passage near the end of the Apocryphal book of Ecclesiasticus (also called Ben Sirach) praising Simon son of Onias who was high priest around 220–195 BC. After summarizing his general contributions to extending

---

[25] See Heb. 9:7.

and repairing the temple, the praise focuses on the Day of Atonement, celebrating the moment when Simon appeared out of the Most Holy Place to offer the final sacrifice and pronounce the blessing:

> How glorious he was, surrounded by the people,
>   as he came out of the house of the curtain.
> Like the morning star among the clouds,
>   like the full moon at the festal season;
> like the sun shining on the temple of the Most High,
>   like the rainbow gleaming in splendid clouds . . .[26]

. . . and so on! There are eleven 'likes' in all, celebrating how

> when he put on his glorious robe,
>   and clothed himself in perfect splendour,
> when he went up to the holy altar,
>   he made the court of the sanctuary glorious.[27]

The author of Hebrews will certainly have known this passage, though there is no evidence that he is alluding to it. What we can gain from this parallel is a strong sense of the central importance of the high priest and of the Day of Atonement, and especially of that moment when the high priest emerged from the sanctuary, the work of atonement complete. It is that moment which Hebrews captures as picturing the moment of the second coming of Christ. The sacrifice has been presented to God and accepted, and now he 'appears' again to proclaim and enact 'salvation' to *those who are eagerly waiting for him.*

The word 'appear' here – again a different Greek verb – carries the particular flavour of *being seen*: he will come into view, and those who are expecting him will actually *see* him. And the purpose of his appearing is *not to deal with sin*: that's all in the past now. Sin has been completely dealt with. Rather, his appearing is *to save those who are eagerly waiting* – that is, to complete the salvation process, to tie up the loose ends and establish 'salvation' once and for all. The Greek says simply 'unto salvation' and places this phrase in an emphatic position at the end of the sentence.

---

[26] Sirach 50:5–7.
[27] Sirach 50:11.

This is the key message of Hebrews: salvation comes *not* through the yearly repetition of the same ineffective sacrifices at the hands of successive high priests, but *only* through the once-for-all sacrifice of himself by Christ our High Priest and his entry into the heavenly sanctuary, where his blood testifies that the sin of many has been permanently dealt with. And his second coming will be the *proof* and *public demonstration* of this effective salvation.

So Hebrews teaches us that the second coming is the essential, final element in the *single* 'act' of salvation performed by Jesus Christ. It is not complete until the high priest emerges to be cheered by the waiting crowds. No wonder the author uses language that suggests the collapsing of time, with all 'ages' converging on the cross (26). The *sacrifice of himself* is not complete until it has been presented in the Most Holy Place, and Christ has *appeared a second time* in glorious victory. It's a single act, a single *kairos*-event which spans the whole *chronos*-period between ascension and second coming, and turns us into that waiting crowd – waiting for salvation to be complete.

The *faith* of those waiting, as we saw above, is vital to the whole story, for we are one with him, *already* attached to him as our High Priest, and *already* depending on the effectiveness of his sacrifice to enable us to be where we are – standing at heaven's door, right on the doorstep. This is how the author pictures us in 10:19–22: we are like priests ourselves, standing right outside the Most Holy Place, and knowing that, because of him, we will have 'confidence to enter' when the moment comes. Heaven could not be this close if his sacrifice was not effective – but the story isn't over until the curtain parts and he appears!

b. The collapse of *chronos*

The overall structure of these verses (*just as . . . so . . .*) develops a striking parallel between our experience of death and judgment (27) and Jesus' experience of the cross and the second coming (28). What's going on here? The point the author is making is that these two tightly connected pairs – death/judgment and cross/second coming – are analogies of each other. This fits with the view I developed earlier, that the moment of our death *is* the moment when we shoot straight to the final day, the day of the second coming and the final judgment.[28] In fact, the *just as . . . so . . .*

---

[28] See above, ch. 9, section 4 (pp. 113–115).

parallel doesn't really work unless that is the case! The point is, *in relation to both, time (chronos) is collapsed.* Just as we move straight from death to judgment, so Christ moves straight from the cross (via resurrection and ascension) to the second coming, like the high priest entering and leaving the sanctuary on the Day of Atonement.

We're talking about divine time, of course – that 'reckoning' of a thousand years as 'like yesterday when it is past, or like a watch in the night' (Ps. 90:4): the point is that yesterday occupies no time span at all once it is past, and we usually sleep right through 'a watch in the night' with no awareness of time passing. God sees *chronos*-time like that.

We are *eagerly waiting* now, but God is not. However tough our present experience is, our faith jumps the gap between our present *chronos*-based experience of *waiting* and the *kairos*-event of the Cosmic Day of Atonement into which we are caught up as 'brothers and sisters' of Jesus Christ, 'the apostle and high priest of our confession'.[29] Hence Hebrews' wonderful encouragement to 'hold on' in faith,[30] to keep going with our eyes on the goal,[31] or – in the author's words – to 'consider how to provoke one another to love and good deeds, not neglecting to meet together . . . but encouraging one another, and all the more as you see the Day approaching'![32] This will sustain faith within us, standing on the threshold of heaven.

That reminder of Psalm 90 and of God's experience of a thousand years takes us forward into our next passage.

---

29 See Heb. 3:1; 2:11.
30 E.g. 3:6; 4:14; 10:23.
31 E.g. 6:11–12; 12:18–24; 13:13–15.
32 Heb. 10:24–25.

2 Peter 3:1–18

16. The day of the Lord

The 'agenda' for this book would be huge if we were including all eschatological passages (that is, all passages that touch on God's future for the world). We've been focusing strictly on 'second-coming' passages, plus some Old Testament background. This chapter's passage, 2 Peter 3, only just squeezes onto the list!

Peter is writing to Christians in conflict with people who deny and mock their faith, and he quotes the words of the mockers in verse 4: *Where is the promise of his coming? For ever since our ancestors died, all things continue as they were from the beginning of creation!* These Christians were being ridiculed for their belief in the second coming, it seems. The word for *coming* is our old friend *parousia*, which we have met frequently before.[1] It's almost a technical term for the second coming in the New Testament, and Peter has already used it in the letter: 'We did not follow cleverly devised myths when we made known to you the power and coming of our Lord Jesus Christ.'[2]

So the *coming* in verse 4 must be that of the Lord Jesus. And so when Peter refers later to *the coming of the day of God* (12), using *parousia* again, he must be talking about the same coming, of the Lord Jesus, and describing it as *the day of God*. How fascinating! In verse 10, it's *the day of the Lord*, which we must understand as 'the day of the Lord *Jesus*'. Once again we see how Jesus steps into the role of God in New Testament

---

[1] In Matt. 24; and in 1 Cor. 15:23; 1 Thess. 4:15; and 2 Thess. 2:1, 8. Also in 1 Thess. 2:19; 3:13; 5:23; Jas 5:7, 8; 1 John 2:28.

[2] 2 Pet. 1:16.

eschatology. Undoubtedly these 'comings' and 'days' are all the same day as *the day of judgement and destruction of the godless* (7) and *the day of eternity* (18). This last one (the only appearance of this expression in the New Testament) means 'the day when the age-to-come arrives', and for sure Peter thinks of Jesus as the Agent of all these acts of God.

As we dig into this passage, something unique appears:

1. An 'out there' faith

In chapter 2 Peter conducts a powerful campaign against false teachers in the church and their 'deceptive words' which could lead his readers astray.[3] Here in chapter 3 it seems that his gaze has widened, for it seems very unlikely that those 'false teachers' would be mocking the faith of his readers as in verse 4. This is mockery from outside the church, and in this passage Peter is seeking to equip his readers with good responses. It is interesting that he does *not* say (in effect), 'What are you doing, throwing your pearls before swine in this way? Keep yourselves to yourselves – your faith is between you and God! These *scoffers* have just got it wrong – ignore them!' No: he accepts that they will be facing these challenges, and wants them to be 'stable': *You therefore, beloved, since you are forewarned, beware that you are not carried away with the error of the lawless and lose your own stability* (17) – unlike *the ignorant and unstable* who misinterpret the letters of Paul and end up in a total mess (16). The word translated *stability* here (with its negative counterpart, *unstable*) has the notion of being firmly fixed, able to take the strain: I'm thinking of the latest set of shelves I put up, and which I hope will take the strain of the books on them! Similarly Peter wants his readers to be well equipped, out there in the public arena, so that their convictions are stable, confidently maintained under the weight of all challenges.

So this passage is about having a *public faith*, one which is not hidden away but is contributing confidently in the public sphere, even if mocked. This is of huge importance for us today, when the temptation is strong simply to withdraw from the 'world' and leave it to its own devices. After all (so some argue), the world is under judgment and when Jesus comes again will be overthrown, so why should we bother with 'worldly' issues and questions?

---

[3] See 2 Pet. 2:1, 3.

Let's be clear: Peter will not let us agree with this. In this passage he encourages Christians to face into the difficult challenges and questions, and to think through and maintain a clear Christian response. The world we are in is very different indeed, but the issue is the same: the challenge of having a public faith which is ready to formulate Christian responses in the world, and not apart from it, and to engage in dialogue with all others, of whatever background or persuasion, who are also concerned. For us today, I'm thinking (for instance) of the issues of globalization and international relations, ecology and climate change, justice and poverty, distribution of resources, nationalism, war and the arms trade, feminism, religious violence, the growth of technology and the distribution of technological advances, social media, pornography, sexuality and gender, advertising . . . the list is endless! Only a handful of these were issues in Peter's world, but are so pressing now. I'm glad that Christians are speaking and writing into many of these areas, and seeking to formulate a confident public faith.[4]

2. 'Double listening'

John Stott, to whom The Bible Speaks Today series owes its origins, famously described this task as one of 'double listening': we have to listen on the one hand to *Scripture*, and on the other hand to *the world*, and seek to be shaped in our reactions by both. Here is the challenge in his own words: 'We are to listen carefully (although of course with differing degrees of respect) both to the ancient Word and to the modern world, in order to relate the one to the other with a combination of fidelity and sensitivity.'[5]

Fidelity to Scripture, sensitivity to the world. It's fascinating to see Peter prodding us in the direction of Stott's double listening in this passage. First and foremost, Scripture:

- Like Paul, Peter has clearly been influenced by Jesus' teaching – not least (for instance) in his reference to the Day coming *like*

---

[4] See for instance Miroslav Volf, *A Public Faith: How Followers of Christ Should Serve the Common Good* (Grand Rapids, MI: Brazos, 2011); Samuel Wells, *How Then Shall We Live? Christian Engagement with Contemporary Issues* (Norwich: Canterbury Press, 2016). An excellent book on a particular issue is Richard Bauckham, *Bible and Ecology: Rediscovering the Community of Creation* (London: Darton, Longman & Todd, 2010).

[5] John Stott, *The Contemporary Christian: An Urgent Plea for Double Listening* (Leicester: Inter-Varsity Press, 1992), p. 13. See also Tim Chester, *Stott on the Christian Life: Between Two Worlds* (Wheaton, IL: Crossway, 2020), esp. pp. 52–56.

a thief (10),[6] as well as his use of the word *parousia*. Peter wants them to remember that the appearance of *scoffers* was predicted by Jesus (2–3).[7]

- He draws on the story of the flood (6),[8] as well as on the biblical notion that creation takes place *by the word of God* (5).[9]
- There are many other detailed allusions to Old Testament scriptures, for instance to Habakkuk 2:3 (9), Psalm 90:4 (8), Isaiah 34:4 (10) and Isaiah 65:17 (13).
- And he includes Paul in the 'Scripture' category – see his reference to Paul's letters alongside *the other scriptures* (16)! There are many overlaps with and allusions to the letter of Jude as well, though more in 2 Peter 2 than in this chapter.
- These bullet points all develop his starting point in verse 2: he wants to remind his readers *that you should remember the words spoken in the past by the holy prophets, and the commandment of the Lord and Saviour spoken through your apostles.* Old Testament prophets and New Testament apostles speak with one voice, for Peter.

So Peter wants his readers to listen carefully to Scripture and to hold on to its truth in the face of contrary voices. But he is listening to other voices, too:

- Richard Bauckham makes a good case that Peter is drawing on a lost Jewish apocalypse in this passage. The details are complicated but the arguments are convincing.[10] In other ways, too, Peter is drawing on Jewish (and not just Christian) ideas here.
- Even more striking is the evidence that Peter is also connecting with Stoic philosophers and their views about the end of the world. They too believed that *the elements will be dissolved with fire* (10, also 12).[11] So if Peter's readers were familiar with Stoic thinking and language, they would have spotted this connection

---

[6] Cf. Matt. 24:43–44.

[7] He is probably thinking of sayings like Matt. 24:9 and John 15:20.

[8] Gen. 6 – 8.

[9] Gen. 1:3, 6, etc.; cf. Ps. 33:6.

[10] See Richard J. Bauckham, *Jude, 2 Peter*, Word Biblical Commentary 50 (Waco: Word, 1983), pp. 283–285.

[11] The evidence for this is set out by Edward Adams, *The Stars Will Fall from Heaven: Cosmic Catastrophe in the New Testament and Its World*, Library of New Testament Studies (London: T&T Clark, 2007), pp. 216–229.

and realized that he is trying to communicate biblical ideas in language that 'speaks' to the contemporary world and draws on contemporary thinking.

In other words, Peter is engaging in 'double listening'! This doesn't involve any compromising on biblical truth, but, as John Stott so wonderfully illustrates, it takes very seriously the context and the people around us. This is especially important in relation to the second coming of Jesus. We'll pursue this agenda as we look through the chapter, seeking to gain some insights into the key elements and basis of a public faith, as well as on the second coming.

In *Come, Lord Jesus!* I unpack a chiastic structure in verses 1–16, centred around the verses on God's patience (8–10).[12] However, it's also possible to understand the passage in a more linear way, because there is a connected line of thought that runs through it:

- Vv. 1–4 Foundations
- Vv. 5–7 The certainty of judgment
- Vv. 8–10 God and the passage of time
- Vv. 11–14 Getting ready: living well
- Vv. 15–18 Getting ready: thinking straight

We will look at each paragraph in turn.

3. Foundations (3:1–4)

Peter begins his section on the second coming and final judgment with a reminder of the basis of all Christian theology and engagement: Scripture. He says that in both his letters he has tried *to arouse your sincere intention by reminding you that you should remember the words spoken in the past by the holy prophets, and the commandment of the Lord and Saviour spoken through your apostles* (1–2).

We have a double foundation, the *holy prophets* of the Old Testament, and the *commandment* which comes to us both from *the Lord and Saviour* and from *your apostles* – the New Testament. Peter recognizes that we have access to the words of Jesus only through the teaching of the

---

[12] Motyer, *Come, Lord Jesus!*, p. 295.

apostles (especially the Gospel-writers), who also add their own teaching as Jesus' apostolic representatives. Peter's conviction is that Jesus' ministry and teaching makes 'the prophetic message more fully confirmed', and this combined message – Old and New Testament together – is like 'a lamp shining in a dark place, until the day dawns and the morning star rises in your hearts'.[13]

It is interesting that he calls the message of Jesus and the apostles a *commandment*. Biblical theology – the unified message of the prophets and the apostles, with Jesus himself at its heart – lays a discipline upon us, which calls for our obedience. This discipline faces us with a double challenge, which Peter unpacks in the whole passage: first to *hear the message clearly* (to understand exactly what Scripture means) and then to *live out the message vigorously* (14), *consistently* (17) and *progressively* (18). The *stability* Peter wants for them (17) does not mean *rigidity*, for he immediately encourages them to *grow in the grace and knowledge of our Lord and Saviour Jesus Christ* (18). He expects them to change!

This brings us to the specific issue Peter wants his readers to face, as they work out their obedience:

> *First of all you must understand this, that in the last days scoffers will come, scoffing and indulging their own lusts and saying, 'Where is the promise of his coming? For ever since our ancestors died, all things continue as they were from the beginning of creation!'*
> (3–4)

Indulging their own lusts is quite a 'tough' translation, implying that these *scoffers* are morally corrupt, and that's the real problem. 'Led by their own desires' would be a better translation, because the issue is the basis of their opinions: rather than be motivated by the teaching of the prophets and apostles, they are led simply by their instincts and inclinations, by what they *want* to believe. Hence they *deliberately* ignore the flood story in Genesis (5)!

But wait a minute. Is this not where we all are, fundamentally? Why do we believe what we believe? The rock-bottom answer is that generally we believe what we *want* to believe, even if our faith rests on a solid experience of the grace of God in Christ. This is why Peter begins as he does here.

---

[13] 2 Pet. 1:19.

He wants to *arouse your sincere intention* (1): in other words, he wants to motivate his readers, at this instinctual, feeling level, to attend to Scripture rather than just to their own desires. The issue is: what evidence counts for us, in order to shape our instincts and inclinations?

The *scoffers* want to have a solid, consistent world around them, and so they reject anything that points to the instability or impermanence of their environment. I can sympathize with that! Public faith starts with understanding the motivation of our dialogue partners. But we also have to communicate our key convictions:

4. The certainty of judgment (3:5–7)

They deliberately ignore this fact, that by the word of God heavens existed long ago and an earth was formed out of water and by means of water, through which the world of that time was deluged with water and perished.
(5–6)

In the first century, the general permanence of the world was easy to believe in. Disasters of various kinds (floods, droughts, etc.) are inevitable, of course, but the general reliability of the world seemed unquestionable. Its *impermanence* could be maintained only on the basis of texts like Genesis 6 – the ancient flood stories. Today, it is much easier: it has become part of public culture for people to know that the dinosaurs were wiped out by a massive asteroid strike, and that globally catastrophic events like that have happened regularly in earth's history, and could happen again.[14]

Global catastrophe has become a movie genre of its own – often recycling biblical imagery as Peter does here. For instance, in the movie *2012* the basic plot line is that a massive burst of solar radiation ignites the earth's core, creating worldwide earthquakes which in turn lead to huge tsunamis that overwhelm whole countries. Rescue is provided in the form of nine great arks (built of course by American know-how) in which the rich elite are saved, along with many animals. Facing imminent destruction, the American president broadcasts to the

---

[14] See Bill McGuire, *Apocalypse: A Natural History of Global Disasters* (London: Cassell, 1999); also Niall Ferguson, *Doom: The Politics of Catastrophe* (Dublin: Allen Lane, 2021).

nation and starts to recite the twenty-third psalm, only to be cut off as Washington is destroyed. One of the scientists remarks, 'Isn't it galling that those end-of-the-world nuts with their placards turn out to be right?'[15]

That illustrates the vital point here. The end-of-the-world nuts were warning not about coming disaster, but about coming *judgment*. In Peter's day, it was not difficult to persuade people that natural disasters were acts of judgment by irate deities. That was the cultural assumption – but that's the completely *counter*-cultural element today. The biblical imagery is recycled, but not the biblical message. God is cut out, just as in *2012* Psalm 23 is cut off after the first couple of lines. But his *word* is still the decisive factor: *But by the same word* [the word that both created the world and then decreed judgment through the flood] *the present heavens and earth have been reserved for fire, being kept until the day of judgement and destruction of the godless* (7).

Godless means specifically 'those who do not worship God'. In other words, God calls the world to account for our attitude towards him. Are we ready to bow in adoration, or do we want to tell stories which imagine the destruction of the world by fire (like *2012*) without any reference to him? Our public faith needs to be out there, showing us to be people who love and worship the God of our universe, and who expect all to be held accountable before him.

Peter comes back to this in verses 11–13, but first he wants to deal with an issue of special concern to his readers.

5. God and the passage of time (3:8–10)

It could well be that the *scoffers* of verse 4 are picking up on a specific worry that affected Christians in the late first century. As we saw earlier, the expectation that Jesus would return within one generation was widespread in the early church. Was this not what Jesus had said?[16] So when this didn't happen – especially after the destruction of the Jerusalem temple in AD 70 – Christians inevitably were puzzled and disturbed. The first part of the scoffers' words formed a question asked by many Christians: *Where is the promise of his coming?*

---

[15] *2012*, directed by Roland Emmerich (2009). One of the characters is called Noah!
[16] See Matt. 24:34.

So it could be that the scoffers are tapping into a Christian anxiety, something that makes them question their own faith, and Peter wants to respond to this, too – as well as equipping them to reply:

> But do not ignore this one fact, beloved, that with the Lord one day is like a thousand years, and a thousand years are like one day. The Lord is not slow about his promise, as some think of slowness, but is patient with you, not wanting any to perish, but all to come to repentance. But the day of the Lord will come like a thief, and then the heavens will pass away with a loud noise, and the elements will be dissolved with fire, and the earth and everything that is done on it will be disclosed.
> (8–10)

In verse 8 Peter is clearly drawing on Psalm 90:4, and his basic thought is that God does not count or experience time as we do. He stands outside it, so the notion of 'slowness' is meaningless in relation to God. The accusation that he is *slow* to keep his promise is therefore meaningless, too. Of course that observation does not help much if the Lord himself has promised a particular date and then doesn't turn up – and the first Christians (including Paul, it seems) gave Jesus' words their obvious meaning: he's coming again within one generation!

We thought about this earlier, and asked what Paul might have said if he had lived to see Jesus' prophecy about the destruction of the temple fulfilled, but *unaccompanied* by his return.[17] It's interesting that Peter here expresses the very thought which we imagined would be in Paul's mind: the vital thing is that there should be enough time for the preaching of the gospel (Matt. 24:14), because God *is patient* and wants *all to come to repentance* (9). If that means we have to reread Jesus' prophecy to allow more time, so be it. God's mercy is the completely determining foundation of the storyline, and *he does not want any to perish*. God lives by *kairos* – so if more time is needed to bring people to repentance, *chronos* has to step back and take second place!

We meet exactly this thought also in the risen Christ's letter to Thyatira in Revelation 2:18–29. He criticizes them for tolerating in their midst a 'prophetess' who is encouraging syncretism – teaching that it's OK for Christians to engage in pagan worship practices, including fornication in

---

17   See above, ch. 11, section 5 (pp. 141–142).

local temples. Jesus' message is, 'I gave her time [*chronos*] to repent, but she refuses to repent of her fornication', so now he warns of imminent judgment for her and her followers, 'unless they repent of her doings'.[18]

So we must wait while God is *patient*. But interestingly, we can also expect him to come *quickly*. There is a double perspective to hold on to here, with God's mercy behind both aspects. On the one hand, he holds back so that there is time for repentance. On the other hand, he does *not* hold back, but answers the cry of his people. The word that Peter uses here for 'patient' (*he is patient with you*, 9) is the same as the word 'delay' that we met in Luke 18:7–8:[19] 'Will not God grant justice to his chosen ones who cry to him day and night? Will he delay long in helping them? I tell you, he will quickly grant justice to them.'

This looks like a contradiction: how can both be true? How can God both come quickly and delay to give time for repentance? The answer lies in Peter's little comment *as some think of slowness* in verse 9. We have to take on board a different view of time. As far as *chronos* is concerned, there is a flat contradiction between these two impulses. But God relates to the world through his divine plan in which our whole history can be told as a single Day of Atonement,[20] expressed as a single unified action, a *kairos*-act of cosmic redemption which embraces *all* the individual moments in which he rescues us, both now (when we pray) and at the end. No contradiction here! This recalibrating of time is vital for our understanding of Revelation, as we will see in the next chapter.

Verse 10 looks like a physical description of cosmic destruction, until we get to the last line: *the earth and everything that is done on it will be disclosed*. God's whole action on that day is directed towards exposing the 'works' done on earth, so that judgment may follow. *Disclosed* is literally 'found' – that is, nothing can remain hidden, but everything done on earth is 'found out', its true colours revealed. The dramatic physical happenings simply underline this 'No Escape!' message, and we should not press Peter to be literal here.[21]

Peter may be drawing on Jesus' words encouraging the disciples to be confident on their mission: 'So have no fear of them; for nothing is covered

---

[18] Rev. 2:20–22.

[19] See above, ch. 6, section 5 (pp. 80–82).

[20] See the previous chapter on Hebrews, especially section 4b (pp. 197–198).

[21] Cf. 1 Cor. 3:13; 2 Thess. 1:8; Heb. 10:27; and Rev. 8:5 (etc.) for parallel uses of 'fire' as a symbol of judgment (and in the background, Ps. 18:8, 12).

up that will not be uncovered, and nothing secret that will not become known.'[22] This emphasis on moral accountability before God leads into the next two sections.

6. Getting ready: living well (3:11–14)

The last two sections of the chapter focus on consequences: what should be the impact on us, now, of believing in *the day of the Lord*? In different ways both paragraphs are concerned with our public life as believers. Both end with *Therefore, beloved . . .* (14, 17), underlining the consequences emphasized in each paragraph.

This first paragraph focuses on living well before the world as we 'wait for' the Day. The verb 'wait for' appears three times (12, 13, 14) and means 'expect', 'look forward to', rather than just 'wait'. Waiting can have very different qualities: this is waiting for the holidays, not for the dentist to shout 'Next!' It's the kind of waiting that says, 'I can't wait . . .', waiting that is *hastening* (12): in other words, we're longing for time to drop away and the moment to come. What we long for, says Peter, is *new heavens and a new earth, where righteousness is at home* (13): and if we're moving into that home, we must make sure that the furniture of our lives matches the decor . . .

> *Since all these things are to be dissolved in this way, what sort of people ought you to be in leading lives of holiness and godliness . . . ? Therefore, beloved, while you are waiting for these things, strive to be found by him at peace, without spot or blemish.*
> (11, 14)

To be found looks back to verse 10 and the 'finding' of everything done on earth when the Day cuts away all hiding places. Peter wants us to *strive* now so that we may be 'found' then *without spot or blemish* – that is, with no public stains on our character and record – and *at peace*, that is, living at peace with all people, as Paul puts it in Romans 12:18. There is something very important here about the public reputation of Christians, who cannot authentically represent faith in the coming Day unless they live 'holy' and 'godly' lives (11) – that is, lives marked by *attention to God* in every detail, including a focus on worship.

---

[22] Matt. 10:26.

The final paragraph (the second on 'consequences') focuses on doing good theology!

7. Getting ready: thinking straight (3:15–18)

We are all theologians! – not just the people who teach theology or write theology books. Peter's closing 'Therefore, beloved' gives us the steer:

> *You therefore, beloved, since you are forewarned, beware that you are not carried away with the error of the lawless and lose your own stability. But grow in the grace and knowledge of our Lord and Saviour Jesus Christ. To him be the glory both now and to the day of eternity. Amen.*
> (17–18)

Avoiding *error* (17) is secured by deepening *knowledge* (18). This follows on from his warning in verses 15–16 about the possibility of misinterpreting the letters of Paul. Those words are not just a fascinating curio, a throwaway comment irrelevant to his main theme. The interpretation of Scripture, and our consequent obedience to it, is basic to our present task of preparing for the Day. *Error* has terrible consequences and we must avoid it!

This lies behind Peter's encouragement in verse 15 to *regard the patience of our Lord as salvation*. As we've seen, his patience is that which delays the arrival of *the day of eternity*, so that people have an opportunity for repentance (9). Repentance – in Greek *metanoia* – is not just the initial turning to faith from unbelief, but is also that continuing 'thinking again', the changing of mind to which we are constantly called as disciples of Jesus Christ. 'Rethink' is the name of the game! – rethinking what salvation means for us (as Paul puts it, to 'work out [our] own salvation with fear and trembling').[23] In this sense *the patience of our Lord* is part of the process of *salvation* for us. We must do good theology, in concert with one another and with all who are interested, and then put that good theology into living practice. Developing and practising our faith publicly is vital to this process!

---

[23] Phil. 2:12.

Paul may be difficult, but he's worth working at! Peter's not that easy, either. But both are vital if our public faith is to be well founded, consistent, authentic – and glorifying to Jesus.

Public statements of belief in the second coming of Jesus are not often heard! – except (sadly) in connection with public statements about a coming Rapture, which in fact is a tragic diversion from a true biblical perspective. It is absolutely not part of our public faith to proclaim that one day (soon) all believers are going to be whipped away to heaven leaving the world bereft of their presence and ministry.[24] It *is* part of our public faith to say (and to show) that Christians are deeply committed to the world – to its peoples, its justice, its animals and its fabric – because the God of love who sent Christ to save it will one day call us all to account for our treatment of one another and the planet, when Jesus comes to complete his work and bring in the *new heavens and a new earth* (13).

That's our public faith! We need to be ready to 'confess' it openly and boldly.

---

[24] See above ch. 6, section 4 (pp. 78–80).

Revelation 22:6–21

17. 'See, I am coming soon!'

Our quest for key second-coming passages takes us now to the book of Revelation. Strangely it makes sense to start at the end, with the epilogue or concluding paragraph with which John rounds off the account of his vision, because from this vantage point we can look back over the whole book and get an overview which will prepare the way for the next two chapters as well as this.

At the heart of John's epilogue we hear the risen Christ say three times *I am coming soon* (7, 12, 20), and then the book ends with prayer: *Amen. Come, Lord Jesus! The grace of the Lord Jesus be with all the saints. Amen* (20–21). Revelation thus concludes with a strong expression of expectation and longing, voiced in words which reflect the early Aramaic prayer 'Maranatha!' – 'Our Lord, come!' Paul quotes this prayer in 1 Corinthians 16:22, reflecting the fact that it had become widespread even among Greek-speaking Christians: a deep yearning for the Lord to come, and alongside it (Rev. 22:21) a deep sense that we need his grace now, in the meantime, as we wait for his coming.

This paragraph serves as a wonderful and fitting conclusion not just to Revelation but to the whole Bible. The blessing pronounced in verse 7 by the risen Jesus – *Blessed is the one who keeps the words of the prophecy of this book* – refers (of course) just to the book of Revelation. But in God's providence this is the closing paragraph of the entire Bible. So even though John was thinking only of the prophecy he had written, these words can't help but look back over the whole Bible. Whatever is true for our 'keeping' of Revelation will be true for the rest of Scripture, too. As we wait for his return, how should we *keep* Scripture as a vehicle of *the grace of the Lord Jesus*?

Before looking closely at John's epilogue, we must set the scene.

1. The second coming in Revelation

a. The main theme of Revelation

Revelation begins, straight after the prologue (1:1–6), with a wonderful evocation of the second coming, drawing on our old friend Daniel 7:13 and other texts:

> Look! He is coming with the clouds;
>> every eye will see him,
> even those who pierced him;
>> and on his account all the tribes of the earth will wail.
> So it is to be! Amen.[1]

But in spite of this emphasis at both ends of the book, the second coming of Jesus is not the main theme of Revelation. Rather it is about *God's rule over, presence in, and plan for the world*, especially in the light of the many other 'powers' which seem so dominant – powers both secular and demonic. What does it mean to say 'Jesus is Lord!' when manifestly he is *not* Lord of the world as we see it? Revelation uses 'apocalyptic' to unpack an answer to this – essentially unfolding those much-loved theological prepositions of Paul which we met in Romans 11:36 ('For from him and through him and to him are all things. To him be glory for ever').[2]

How can God truly be the *source*, *means* and *goal* of all that is, when so much of what we see does *not* glorify him? 'Apocalypse' (the name of the book in Greek) means 'drawing back the veil', and Revelation seeks to look behind the scenes, uncovering the unseen realities behind the world, its past, present and future, so that we can see how Romans 11:36 is true. We thought already about how vital this 'unveiling' or 'unmasking' is when interpreting 2 Thessalonians 2:8, and how the second coming will mean

---

[1] Rev. 1:7. Most commentators agree that this verse refers to the second coming, but in fairness we must note that not all do. Those who are inclined to deny that other quotations of Dan. 7:13 refer to the second coming (e.g. in Matt. 24:30) deny it here also (for instance Paul, *Revelation*, pp. 63–64). But 'every eye will see him' seems to make the reference inescapable.

[2] See above, ch. 13, section 2 (pp. 162–163).

a final 'unmasking' of the powers of lawlessness.[3] In Revelation we get a sneak preview of this unmasking! – set into a theology of God's providence (his rule over his world), with Jesus now as the central figure through whom God is the *source*, *means* and *goal* of all things.

b. Second coming . . . and coming

Jesus' second coming is a vital element in this picture. Interestingly, however, Revelation begins with an emphasis not so much on his *second* coming as just on his *coming*. It is addressed to 'the seven churches that are in Asia' (1:4), engaging with the world as they experienced it, under the dominant power of the mighty Roman Empire. The whole book is a prophetic letter to all seven churches, but in chapters 2–3 each church receives a personal mini letter from the risen Christ. Each letter begins 'I know . . .' as Jesus reveals how intimately he knows their history, troubles, sins and future.[4] This follows from John's amazing vision of Christ in 1:12–20, whom he sees standing 'in the midst' of seven golden lampstands which turn out to be symbols of the seven churches.[5] He is in their midst, though they cannot see or hear him – except, of course, through John's eyes as he obeys Christ's command to 'write in a book what you see and send it to the seven churches'.[6]

During the course of the letters Jesus says three times 'I am coming', matching the three 'I am comings' in the epilogue: in 2:5, 2:16 and 3:11.[7] But notably these 'comings' are not his second coming. First he warns the church in Ephesus to 'remember . . . from what you have fallen; repent and do the works you did at first. If not, *I am coming to you* and will remove your lampstand from its place, unless you repent.'[8] This is a 'coming' that arises from his presence among the lampstands right now: he can see exactly what is going on, and he may come and snuff out the lamp in Ephesus unless they smarten up.

There's a similar message for the church in Pergamum, where some teachers are advocating the use of sacred prostitutes in pagan temples: 'Repent then. If not, *I am coming to you soon* and will make war against

---

[3] See above, ch. 11, section 6c (pp. 144–146).

[4] Rev. 2:2, 9, 13, 19; 3:1, 8, 15. The last four are all 'I know your works . . .' but the 'works' differ in each case.

[5] Rev. 1:20.

[6] Rev. 1:11.

[7] The 'I am comings' in 2:25, 3:3 and 3:20 use different verbs and tenses.

[8] Rev. 2:5. NRSV 'I will come to you' is misleading.

them with the sword of my mouth.'[9] This too is probably not his second coming in final judgment, but a specific intervention against these false teachers called 'the Nicolaitans' (2:15). He will not sit on the sidelines while bad teaching leads his people astray.

Third – and very differently – the church in Philadelphia hears Christ promise to keep them 'from the hour of trial that is coming on the whole world to test the inhabitants of the earth. *I am coming soon*; hold fast to what you have, so that no one may seize your crown.'[10] Is this the second coming? It could be . . . but the fact that it could be either the second coming or an earlier 'coming' to protect the church through 'the hour of trial' speaks volumes for our understanding of the second coming in Revelation. The risen Christ, we hear John saying, is not *absent* in heaven, away until the moment when his absence will end and he will be present again. He is already present to his church, and comes to us both now *and* then. We will return to this very important aspect of the second coming in chapter 19 below.

Interestingly, after the seven letters and the invitation in 4:1 which starts the rest of the vision, the voice of Jesus falls silent until the epilogue, *except* at one tiny point in the vision of the sixth 'bowl of wrath'.[11] In the middle of a horrifying picture of armies gathering for the battle of Armageddon, summoned by 'three foul spirits like frogs' coming from the mouths of the dragon and the two beasts, we suddenly hear Jesus' voice, in a quiet but wonderful intervention rightly put in brackets in NRSV: '("See, *I am coming* like a thief! Blessed is the one who stays awake and is clothed, not going about naked and exposed to shame").'[12]

It's as though he is underlining the promise made to the church in Philadelphia to keep them through the coming hour of trial – reminding us that, however bad it gets, he *knows* and *is coming*. But here, the words 'like a thief' and 'stay awake' remind us of Matthew 24 and Jesus' teaching about the coming of the Son of Man, and so this is definitely a promise of the *second* coming.[13] As in Matthew 24, the looming armies and the rumours of imminent war are a sign of his imminent appearance.[14]

---

9 Rev. 2:16; again, NRSV has 'I will come to you'.

10 Rev. 3:10–11.

11 Rev. 16:12–16.

12 Rev. 16:15.

13 Matt. 24:42–43.

14 Matt. 24:6–8.

So there is a fascinating pattern to these 'I am coming' sayings:

- There are seven of them in total,
- three in Christ's speech at the start, three in his speech at the end,
- and one in between, marking the only time we hear him in the body of John's visionary narrative.
- Five of the seven (all except numbers 1 and 4) are identical: 'I am coming soon.'
- Numbers 1, 2 and 3 are promises of his coming now, within the church's present experience.
- Numbers 4 to 7 are promises of his second coming.

This pattern is undoubtedly deliberate! There are several other instances of terms or phrases which occur seven times in Revelation, in addition to the headline 'sevens' (the letters, seals, trumpets, etc.).[15] We can see a progression through the seven 'I am comings' which roots Christ's second coming in his presence with his church *now*, and sees his second coming as the natural extension of that presence. This matches the way in which, in Revelation, God's ultimate, 'eschatological' rule over his world is not different from his rule over the world now, but simply a new (and very glorious) expression of it.

Within the story of John's vision (the whole book recounts a single visionary experience, with successive episodes building upon one another), there is only one vision of the second coming itself, in 19:11–16. We will look at this in the next chapter. For now, let's come back to the epilogue and see how John rounds up the account of his vision around the three *I am coming soon* sayings.

2. 'These words are trustworthy and true' (22:6)

The angel who has been guiding John[16] says this to him, expressing his verdict not just on John's description of the heavenly city in 22:1–5, but on the whole book. John has obeyed the command of Christ in 1:11 to 'write in a book what you see',[17] and the angel now assures him that the

---

[15] For details see Motyer, *Come, Lord Jesus!*, p. 308, n. 14.

[16] *He said to me* (6) looks back to 22:1 and beyond that to 21:15 and 19:9.

[17] John keeps reminding us of this command: see also 1:19; 2:1 (and the start of each of the letters); 10:4; 14:13; 19:9; 21:5.

result – like the words of God himself in 21:5[18] – is *trustworthy and true*. Then we immediately hear the voice of Christ himself endorsing the angel's opinion: *Blessed is the one who keeps the words of the prophecy of this book* (7). No book ever had a more prestigious back cover endorsement than this one! Written at Christ's command, stamped with Christ's approval.

This emphasis on the written word, the prophecy, runs right through John's epilogue. There are several ways of analysing it, and commentators tend to say that the epilogue is a random collection of miscellaneous thoughts, but I think it hangs together beautifully around this notion of 'the written word of prophecy'. And as we noted above, we can fittingly apply it to the whole of Scripture which comes to a conclusion with these verses. What role should Scripture play in our lives as we wait for the coming of the Lord?

- Vv. 6–9 The inspired book: keep it!
- Vv. 10–17 The open book: publish it!
- Vv. 18–21 The finished book: live it!

Each section begins with the phrase *the words of the prophecy of this book*, and each contains one of the *I am coming soon* sayings, giving a consistent 'second-coming' twist to the focus of each, and underlining the 'soon-ness' of his coming.

What does *soon* mean? More literally the Greek word means 'quickly', referring not to his velocity on the way back, but to the time lag between the present and his coming. A little embarrassed by this – because he *hasn't* come quickly – some suggest that *soon* means 'suddenly': he will burst upon the world without warning. This is certainly an emphasis we have met elsewhere, not least in the passage to which 'I am coming like a thief' (16:15) alludes,[19] but it is not the most obvious meaning for 'soon'. The whole of Revelation sits under this rubric, in fact: it is 'The revelation of Jesus Christ, which God gave him to show his servants *what must soon take place*; he made it known by sending his angel to his servant John.'[20]

The phrase 'what must soon take place' – repeated here in the epilogue (6) as John looks back over his whole experience – is drawn from Daniel,[21]

---

[18] See also 19:9.

[19] Matt. 24:42–44; cf. Luke 17:26–30; 1 Thess. 5:3–4.

[20] Rev. 1:1 (emphasis added).

[21] Dan. 2:29, 45.

where the emphasis is not so much on the quickness of fulfilment as on its *certainty*. There 'soon' means 'sure'. And that fits here, especially with verse 10: *And he said to me, 'Do not seal up the words of the prophecy of this book, for the time is near.'* This is looking back to 1:3, where a blessing is pronounced on those who 'hear and . . . keep' 'the words of the prophecy . . . for the time is near'. In both places *time* is our old friend *kairos*, not *chronos* – so the emphasis falls on the imminence of God's plan, not on the imminence of the date. In his plan the coming of Jesus is the next great moment, and he will not delay. He wants the whole thing wrapped up! And that wrapping-up is as sure as that the end always follows the beginning (see 13). As far as *chronos* is concerned, we have no idea when . . . but that *kairos*-moment is certain and *soon*, pressing in on us like dawn after darkest night.[22]

This gives urgency to our lives, and especially therefore to the ways in which we allow Scripture to shape our being-in-the-world.

3. The inspired book: keep it! (22:6–9)

And he said to me, 'These words are trustworthy and true, for the Lord, the God of the spirits of the prophets, has sent his angel to show his servants what must soon take place.'

'See, I am coming soon! Blessed is the one who keeps the words of the prophecy of this book.'

(6–7)

Putting verse 6 together with 1:1–3, we can reconstruct the journey taken by the 'revelation':

- It starts with God, who gives it to
- Jesus Christ, who passes it on
- through an angel
- to the prophet John,
- with a command to write it down in a book, so that
- God's servants (that's us) may hear and read it.

The assurance given in these verses is that there is no 'Chinese whispers' effect in this transmission – but that the written book *truly and*

---

[22] For this image, see Rom. 13:11–12 (where 'time', v. 11, is also *kairos*).

trustworthily represents the revelation God gave. John's own account is that he has 'testified to the word of God and to the testimony of Jesus Christ, even to all that he saw'.[23] Vital to this assurance is the description of God as *the God of the spirits of the prophets*: God makes sure that the *spirits* of the prophets are completely on board with the revelation, ready and able to transmit it without distorting or supplementing it. And the plural *prophets* encourages us to hear this as applying beyond Revelation to the whole of Scripture!

The beatitude in verse 7 (*Blessed is . . .*) matches the beatitude in 1:3, both of them pronouncing the 'blessedness' of those who *keep* the words of the prophecy.[24] The word *keep* is used twice in this section (7, 9), to underline its significance. What does it mean? The Greek word has a range of meaning, from 'guard' through 'treasure' to 'obey'. Pinning down its meaning here takes us into the strange little episode in verses 8–9:

> I, John, am the one who heard and saw these things. And when I heard and saw them, I fell down to worship at the feet of the angel who showed them to me; but he said to me, 'You must not do that! I am a fellow-servant with you and your comrades the prophets, and with those who keep the words of this book. Worship God!'

This is strange because John has done this before (with a different angel), and has already been ticked off for it in precisely the same terms – see 19:9–10. Why does he do it again? The answer appears when we consider how 'keeping' God's word can so easily be identified with defending it against attacks and mounting arguments to support a 'high' view of the Bible – defending its inspiration, or its 'inerrancy' or 'infallibility'. This is an important theological discussion, but here John is saying to us: don't focus on the *process* of the revelation so much that you ignore its *content*. The angel isn't important. His position doesn't need to be safeguarded. He's just a *fellow-servant*. To honour him is to fall into idolatry. G. B. Caird comments how insidious idolatry is – even John is tempted into it: 'a salutary warning to all crusaders not to mistake the cause they champion for the one true God'.[25] Ultimately, we 'keep' God's word not by guarding

---

[23] Rev. 1:2.

[24] Verse 7 contains no. 6 of seven beatitudes in Revelation; the seventh is in 22:14.

[25] G. B. Caird, *The Revelation of St John the Divine*, Black's New Testament Commentary (London: A&C Black, 1966), p. 237.

its status, but by treasuring and obeying its message: seeing its authority not as a cause to be defended, but as a calling to be lived.

Worship God! says the angel (9). All the honour goes to God, as his people give themselves to serving *him*, not *the Scriptures*. And at the heart of that living obedience is our joyful embrace of Jesus' *See, I am coming soon!* Living under the authority of that promise, and living out its implications day by day, is the touchstone of truly 'keeping' *the words of the prophecy of this book* – both Revelation and Scripture as a whole!

4. The open book: publish it! (22:10–17)

The central paragraph of John's epilogue unpacks in more detail what it means to 'keep' the words of the prophecy. Essentially, the task is *to let Jesus speak through us*: to let the world hear his voice.

One of the fascinating things about John's epilogue is that it is sometimes hard to tell who is speaking, whether the angel or John or Christ himself – but this is not surprising, granted that all are involved in the chain of revelation (see above), and all speak with one voice. In this section the angel begins, addressing John in verses 10–11, but then we hear Jesus' voice in verses 12–13 and in verse 16. It's not clear who is speaking in verses 14–15 and 17, although verse 17 imagines the joint testimony of the church and the Holy Spirit. The whole paragraph is about *getting the message out* – not keeping it to ourselves, but publishing it in the world. It falls into three mini segments.

a. Shining the light (22:10–13)

At the end of his prophecy, Daniel is told to 'keep the words secret and the book sealed until the time of the end'.[26] His visions are not for now, because the time is not yet. As a result, wickedness will increase, even though 'many shall be purified, cleansed, and refined'.[27] But it's very different for John:

> *And he said to me, 'Do not seal up the words of the prophecy of this book, for the time is near. Let the evildoer still do evil, and the filthy still be filthy, and the righteous still do right, and the holy still be holy.'*
> (10–11)

---

[26] Dan. 12:4.
[27] Dan. 12:10.

Now, *the time is near,* and so John's revelation must be published, and shine in the world. The point of verse 11 is probably that, with the light of the Word shining, evil and filthiness, as well as righteousness and holiness, are shown up in their true colours.[28] *Evil* means more specifically 'injustice', which can easily mask itself as something much more acceptable. One of the functions of faithful Christian discipleship in the world is to expose the hidden face of evil – which is precisely what John does in Revelation, in relation to the cruelty and injustice of Roman power. Then, if the unjust continue to practise injustice, and the filthy continue to be filthy, it is more obvious what their choice is.

But the continuation of injustice and filthiness is not the last word, by any means: *See, I am coming soon; my reward is with me, to repay according to everyone's work. I am the Alpha and the Omega, the first and the last, the beginning and the end* (12–13). The moment of judgment is coming, when each will be 'repaid' for his or her work. It really matters if we choose to stick with injustice and filthiness, rather than with righteousness and holiness. Jesus Christ is the exact Judge of all, his judgment precisely tailored to the *work* of each. But interestingly the *reward* here is his, not ours. Verse 12 draws on two passages in Isaiah where the coming Lord's 'reward' is to be greeted by his saved people[29] – so we cannot congratulate ourselves on our righteousness and holiness. It's all down to him.

His position as Judge arises from who he is, so beautifully summarized in verse 13. He takes charge of the End, because he is also the Beginning. The message we publish focuses upon him and the way in which, ultimately, everything is to be 'gathered up' in him, as Paul puts it.[30] To be open about this view of Jesus is at the heart of our 'public faith'. The three descriptions of him in verse 13 have a history in Revelation – three previous verses reach a climax here: compare 1:8 (where God is speaking) with 1:17 (where Christ speaks), leading to 21:6 (God speaks) and then 22:13 (Christ speaks). Again, Christ steps into the role and position of God himself.

b. The two ways (22:14–15)

Blessed are those who wash their robes, so that they will have the right to the tree of life and may enter the city by the gates. Outside are the dogs

---

28 See Eph. 5:11–14 for a similar thought.

29 Isa. 40:10; 62:11.

30 Eph. 1:10.

> *and sorcerers and fornicators and murderers and idolaters, and everyone*
> *who loves and practises falsehood.*

The 'two ways' have already been the focus in verse 11, and now they are unpacked more. The seventh beatitude (14) is a wonderful summary of the gospel offer: sin can be forgiven, we can be made clean,[31] and we may feed from the tree of life (which is 'for the healing of the nations', 2) and enter the heavenly city. Excluded from this blessing are all who cling to anti-God practices – who continue in 'evil' and 'filth'. But of course they may change: the offer of washing and life and home is open to all, unless and until the choice to inhabit verse 15 is locked in place.[32]

c. The great invitation (22:16–17)

Above all, we are commissioned to issue a glorious invitation to the world, a *testimony* which comes from Jesus himself: *It is I, Jesus, who sent my angel to you with this testimony for the churches* (16a).

The best way to understand this, I think, is that this is the *testimony* which Jesus lays upon the churches, so that we can speak it before the world. *For* is literally 'upon'. *This testimony* looks back to verses 14–15, but also beyond that to the message of the whole book. And here in summary the testimony has two key elements: a message about Jesus himself, and a consequent invitation:

> *'I am the root and the descendant of David, the bright morning star.'*
>> *The Spirit and the bride say, 'Come.'*
>> *And let everyone who hears say, 'Come.'*
>> *And let everyone who is thirsty come.*
>> *Let anyone who wishes take the water of life as a gift.*
> (16b–17)

The book ends with a call to *Jesus* to 'Come' (20), but this *Come* is addressed to the world. The Holy Spirit and the church in joint testimony[33] invite all to *come*, and encourage people to pass the invitation on (*let everyone who hears say, 'Come'*), and relate the invitation to the most vital

---

[31] John is looking back to 7:14.

[32] Cf. the very similar 'two ways' offers in 21:6–8 and 21:25–27.

[33] Cf. John 15:26–27.

human needs which can here be wonderfully met: *take the water of life as a gift!* The focus on Jesus is crucial: it is he who issues this invitation, and we simply speak on his behalf.[34]

5. The finished book: live it! (22:18–21)

We come full circle: the guarantee that *these words are trustworthy and true* (6) is matched now by a warning not to supplement them or subtract from them:

> *I warn* [literally, 'I bear witness to': this is part of the testimony] *everyone who hears the words of the prophecy of this book: if anyone adds to them, God will add to that person the plagues described in this book; if anyone takes away from the words of the book of this prophecy, God will take away that person's share in the tree of life and in the holy city, which are described in this book.*
> (18–19)

Again the speaker is unclear, but it doesn't matter! Behind this fearsome warning lie two passages in Deuteronomy, where the issue is the danger of idolatry and of being unfaithful to the Lord.[35] So this is far more than just a warning to the scribes, painstakingly copying out manuscripts of Revelation, to take care not to add bits or leave bits out. Broadening it out and thinking of the wider reference to the whole of Scripture, this is about being satisfied with the text, and being content to live in it, and to live it out, because it is our home. We don't want to throw out the furniture or build an extension. It is about letting Scripture be the sufficient parameter within which we think and move and have our being.

There is plenty of room in Scripture for delighted play and even for rival interpretations, and there is no prohibition here on using other realms of human knowledge to help us understand it better, and live it out more faithfully. It's about place, and roots, and home, and belonging – and about how passionately and knowingly we hold to the confession at the heart of scriptural faith, that Jesus is coming again as our divine Judge and Saviour:

---

[34] Matt. 11:28 and John 7:37–38 may lie in the background.

[35] See Deut. 4:1–4; 12:32 – 13:5. Cf. also Zech. 14:18.

The one who testifies to these things says, 'Surely I am coming soon.'
Amen. Come, Lord Jesus!
The grace of the Lord Jesus be with all the saints. Amen.
(20–21)

The last words of the Bible remind us that there is no authentic biblical faith that does not have the second coming of Jesus at its heart! – and that his *grace* (which is his gracious *presence*) will be with us as we wait. He patrols among the lampstands still! He sees us, he loves us, and he will *come* to us in our need and speak words of rebuke and encouragement if we keep our eyes on him.

Now we go back to look at the wonderful vision of the second coming in Revelation 19:11–16, and think about how it fits into the message of the book as a whole.

Revelation 19:1 – 22:5

18. The rider, the reign and the throne

Once again we enter holy ground as we approach this passage – the broad sweep of final visions that bring Revelation to a climax. I feel it as I come to write this chapter. We focus here on the mighty vision of the second coming in 19:11–16, which (as we will see) sets the scene for this whole final section of John's vision. Everything flows from it. Not that this is an easy section to interpret: there are many puzzles here and debates, and once again – rather than present and discuss them all – I have sought to find my way through them in order to present a clear sense of an ordered narrative with a powerful message, both for John's first readers and for us today.

It all starts back in the heavenly throne room,[1] and with an announcement so surprising that it's no wonder John falls before his angelic guide to worship him (19:10). He needs to be told (and later reminded, as we saw)[2] that the angel is just *a fellow-servant with you and your comrades*, and that what he has heard are the *true words of God . . . the testimony of Jesus*, which is *the Spirit of prophecy*.[3] All three persons of the Trinity are involved in issuing this staggering announcement! So *God* should be worshipped, not the messenger.

On the list of the surprising and the unexpected in Revelation (and that's a long list), this announcement is near the top: the Lamb is getting

---

married, and the invitations are in the post (19:7–9). Of all the things we might have expected the Lamb to do, this is surely the least likely.

1. Unpacking the surprise . . .

To understand this amazing turn in the drama of the book, we need to think about the structure of the last six chapters of Revelation (chs. 17–22) – and this will help us also to set 19:11–16 into its context.

The commentaries all notice how the last chapters of Revelation focus around two very contrasting but interestingly comparable women, who are both at the same time cities: on the one hand, a scarlet woman sitting on the beast (17:3–4), called 'Babylon the great, mother of whores and of earth's abominations' (17:5), and on the other, *the holy city, the new Jerusalem . . . prepared as a bride adorned for her husband* (21:2). Both are lavishly decorated with jewels and pearls,[4] and both offer sanctuary to 'the kings of the earth' – Babylon by ruling over them, fornicating with them and exploiting them to make herself luxurious,[5] new Jerusalem by opening her gates so that *the kings of the earth* can bring in *the glory and the honour of the nations*.[6] Let's look at each in turn.

a. 'Babylon the Great' (17:5)

John's readers would certainly have recognized Rome's profile in the picture of 'Babylon the Great', especially when her trade in luxury goods is described (18:11–13). But John is chiefly concerned to announce her *overthrow* – heralded in 14:8, proclaimed by a mighty angel appearing from heaven in 18:1–2, and then vividly described through the eyes of the kings, the merchants and the ship-owners who all profited from her (18:9–19).

That in itself is surprising enough. Rome's power seemed invincible to people living in first-century Asia Minor, where Revelation's seven towns had all, in different ways, prospered under Roman rule. But Rome didn't collapse, it went on prospering: in various incarnations, Roman power lasted in that part of the world until some decades before Constantinople finally fell to the Ottoman Empire in 1453. How should we understand

---

[4] 17:4; 18:16; 21:11, 19–21.

[5] 17:18; 18:3, 7.

[6] 21:24–26.

this? Revelation had quite a hard time being accepted as Scripture in the eastern, Greek-speaking churches, and one of the reasons for this was the non-fulfilment of its prophecies, most notably the prophecy of the fall of the Roman Empire.[7]

This is not a problem, for *Babylon is not Rome*. Paul helps us here, as we connect Revelation with his understanding of the 'rulers, authorities and powers' which Jesus will overthrow at his return, and which are already being 'disempowered' by the very presence of the gospel and church of Jesus Christ in the world.[8] Like Daniel's beasts,[9] Babylon represents all secular powers, not just Rome – and John's vision, like Daniel's, puts all such powers under notice of destruction, including all those so powerful in our world today. The very presence of Revelation in the world is *already* an undermining of their power – based on Daniel's ancient vision of the kingdom of God that expands until it fills the earth, displacing all other thrones.[10]

What an encouragement, in the twenty-first century as in the first! It's the heart of the message of the cross: the Lamb who was slain is now on the throne (5:6), and all who follow him are 'On the Victory Side',[11] however insignificant and powerless we may feel in the face of the 'kings', the 'captains' and the 'mighty'[12] who seem to have all the last words in this world.

John's vision of the destruction of Babylon is followed by an *After this . . .* (19:1), marking a shift to something new in the vision. It's the point at which the narrative moves from one woman to the other:

b. 'New Jerusalem', the bride of the Lamb

Revelation 19:1–10 is a transitional paragraph in which (with John) we are back in heaven again, hearing its worship as in chapter 5 and in 11:15–19. In response to an invitation from the throne to *Praise our God, all you his servants, and all who fear him, small and great* (5), John hears again *a great multitude*, the growling sound of all animate creation, last heard in 5:13. It is this cosmic crowd that announces the coming nuptials:

---

[7] See R. H. Mounce, *The Book of Revelation*, New International Commentary (Grand Rapids, MI: Eerdmans, 1977), pp. 36–39.

[8] 1 Cor. 15:24. See above, ch. 12, section 3b (pp. 154–156).

[9] See above, ch. 3, esp. section 3 (pp. 37–40).

[10] See Dan. 2:34–35, 44–45.

[11] To use the title of the chorus by Walter J. Main.

[12] See 19:18.

> *Hallelujah!*
> *For the Lord our God*
>   *the Almighty reigns.*
> *Let us rejoice and exult*
>   *and give him the glory,*
> *for the marriage of the Lamb has come,*
>   *and his bride has made herself ready;*
> *to her it has been granted to be clothed*
>   *with fine linen, bright and pure –*
> *for the fine linen is the righteous deeds of the saints.*[13]
> (19:6–8)

The angel then reacts: *And the angel said to me, 'Write this: Blessed are those who are invited to the marriage supper of the Lamb.' And he said to me, 'These are true words of God'* (9). Completely overwhelmed by this amazing announcement, John falls down to worship the angel, and gets firmly corrected (10).

Strangely, it all then goes quiet. There is no further mention of the wedding or of the bride until chapter 21, where John sees *a new heaven and a new earth,* replacing the old, and *the holy city, the new Jerusalem, coming down out of heaven from God, prepared as a bride adorned for her husband* (21:1–2).

As with the scarlet woman on the beast, *one of the seven angels who had the seven bowls* acts as a guide for John – *Come, I will show you the bride, the wife of the Lamb* (21:9)[14] – and then gives him a detailed guided tour of *the holy city Jerusalem coming down out of heaven from God* (10), the final episode of the vision.

There is not much that is bridal or nuptial about the description of the city, apart from the note that *the foundations of the wall of the city are adorned with every jewel* (19) – here *adorned* is the same word used of the bride in 21:2. In fact, the vision leaves us (not surprisingly) with some teasing questions. As usual, it is as we pursue answers to the puzzles that Revelation's meaning emerges:

---

[13] I think it is best to take the last half-verse (8b) as part of the voice of the great multitude (unlike NRSV and NIV, but in line with J. B. Phillips, Jerusalem Bible and *The Message*).

[14] Cf. 17:1 – identical wording.

- Who exactly is the bride? What's the tie-up between bride and city, and Jerusalem in particular?
- Why does *she* come down from heaven, rather than the Lord Jesus? Surely we are expecting him to come, not her!
- And when does she come down, anyway? At the start it looks like it's at the end, when the new heaven and new earth are created (21:1), but John is shown her *coming down* (present continuous tense),[15] and her gates are open for the kings and nations of the *present* earth to enter (21:24, 26). The nations walk by her light (21:24), and the leaves of the tree are for their healing (22:2). How is this possible?
- Along the same lines, the *water of life* flows through the city (22:1), but God offers it *now* in 21:6, and the offer is repeated in 22:17: a *present-tense* offer for all who hear the invitation to 'Come!' issued by 'the Spirit and the bride' – she speaks, *right now!* What's going on?
- And where is the wedding, and in particular the wedding feast, announced with such fanfare in 19:7, 9? It never happens! Why?
- And how do *we* fit into all this? It's a beautiful and inspiring vision, but what should we hear from it for ourselves today?

Some of these questions will occupy us in the next chapter. For now we will go back to look more closely at the visions that immediately follow the announcement of the wedding, and some light on these questions will begin to shine . . .

2. The rider on the white horse (19:11–16)[16] and what happens next

Revelation loves to surprise us. John constantly upsets our expectations, particularly as new episodes occur which contrast in some way with what precedes. Here, for instance, after the staggering announcement of the forthcoming wedding we see Jesus – yes, it is he, as revealed by the names he bears and the symbols associated with him – riding out of heaven not as a bridegroom but as a conquering warrior: *in righteousness he judges*

---

15 Both in 21:2 and 21:10.
16 See Motyer, *Come, Lord Jesus!*, pp. 317–330, for a much fuller exegesis.

and makes war (11). The *white horse* is a strong military symbol,[17] and this Rider is followed by *the armies of heaven*, also *on white horses* (14). This powerful image reaches a climax with a picture of irresistible judgment (15b–16): *He treads*[18] *the wine press of the fury of the wrath of God the Almighty. On his robe and on his thigh he has a name inscribed, 'King of kings and Lord of lords'.*

He bears the name of God and exercises the judgment of God (the wine press image goes back to Isa. 63:1–6). Final judgment has been heralded many times previously in the vision, but here it has a climactic quality, marked by the opening of heaven (11) and the actual issuing forth of the Lamb and his army. It leads into three key judgment episodes, involving all the main actors in the drama of the book:

- 19:17–21 The capture and destruction of the beasts
- 20:1–10 The capture and destruction of the dragon
- 20:11–15 The final judgment of all humankind and the destruction of death

The *lake of fire* features in all three episodes, appearing for the first time in Revelation.[19] Let's notice the order of these visions: it is notable that the judgment and destruction of these figures matches their arrival in Revelation, but in reverse order. Here's the plan – but notice how the appearance of the Rider from heaven seems out of place:

A. Large-scale death features (for instance) in the sixth trumpet (9:13–20) and the death of the witnesses (11:7)

   B. The dragon appears, assaulting the woman who bears the male child (12:1–17)

      C. The two beasts appear, representing and reinforcing the power of the dragon (13:1–18)

         D. The scarlet woman appears, sitting on the beast (17:1–18)

         D'. The scarlet woman is destroyed (18:1–24)

            E. Victory is proclaimed and the Rider on the white horse appears with the armies of heaven, to exercise the judgment of God (19:1–16)

---

[17] Cf. 6:2 – not the same rider!

[18] NIV. NRSV translates this with a future, *he will tread.*

[19] 19:20; 20:10, 14–15.

C'. The two beasts are destroyed (19:17–21)

B'.   The dragon is destroyed (20:1–10)

A'. The dead are raised to judgment and death itself is destroyed (20:11–15)

To make the pattern neat, we would expect the 'E' paragraph to appear between the two 'D' paragraphs. There's a special reason why it doesn't. The woman derives her power from the beast (she sits on it!) representing 'ordinary' secular power, like Rome and the Roman Empire. God certainly judges her,[20] but John actually portrays the beast and other secular powers as the cause of her downfall.[21] Great empires like Rome are inherently unstable, we hear him saying; they bring about their own downfall, albeit under God's sovereign plan.

To get a good handle on the three destruction passages (C'–A'), we need to look more closely at the army following the Rider.

3. The followers of the Lamb

One of the questions we posed above was: who exactly is the bride of the Lamb? John gives a hint as he describes *the armies of heaven* following the Rider. Amazingly, they are dressed not in military garb bristling with swords and spears, but in *fine linen, white and pure*: in other words, wearing the bridal garments given to the bride of the Lamb in 19:8. Maybe the wedding hasn't vanished after all! Is this army on its way to a war, or to a wedding – to *their* wedding? What's going on?

These 'followers' of the Lamb have appeared before, in chapter 14:

Then I looked, and there was the Lamb, standing on Mount Zion! And with him were one hundred and forty-four thousand who had his name and his Father's name written on their foreheads . . . These follow the Lamb wherever he goes. They have been redeemed from humankind as first fruits for God and the Lamb.[22]

It's important to realize that the 144,000 are indeed an *army*: they first appear when the tribes are numbered in Revelation 7:4–8, and the

---

[20] See 18:8, 20.

[21] See 17:16–17.

[22] 14:1, 4.

'numbering' of the tribes is for military purposes in the Old Testament.[23] And in chapter 14 they are also doing very unmilitary things, specifically turning themselves into a choir to sing the unique song which is theirs alone, as the 'redeemed from the earth' (14:3). This army doesn't fight, it sings! The point about bearing the name of the Lamb and of his Father is that they carry his name *and not the name and number of the beast*.[24]

So here they are again in chapter 19, dressed like a bride on the way to her wedding. We can immediately connect this with Paul's vision that, when Jesus comes, 'God will bring with him those who have fallen asleep'.[25] Maybe that's it: this army is the company of the already redeemed, the 'first fruits' of the cross, those who have died in Christ and now come 'with him' when he returns as Judge and Saviour.

Looking ahead, we meet this group again in 20:4–6, where John sees thrones and it turns out that those sitting on them are

> those who had been beheaded for their testimony to Jesus and for the word of God, and those who[26] had not worshipped the beast or its image and had not received its mark on their foreheads or their hands. They came to life and reigned with Christ for a thousand years . . . This is the first resurrection. Blessed and holy are those who share in the first resurrection. Over these the second death has no power, but they will be priests of God and of Christ, and they will reign with him for a thousand years.

The most natural interpretation of this, I think, is that Revelation is filling out what Paul means by being 'in' or 'with' Christ after death. It means 'reigning' with Christ. The dead are not in some vacant state just waiting for the final resurrection. Because they are 'in' Christ they share his rule, throughout the period while the gospel is spreading and the 'powers' are being gradually disempowered. John calls this life-after-death *the first resurrection*, ahead of the final resurrection and the 'second death' – see 20:13.

---

[23] See Num. 1:20ff.: the numbering is of 'everyone able to go to war'.

[24] Cf. 13:16–17.

[25] 1 Thess. 4:14.

[26] I've adjusted the NRSV here, following NIV margin, N. T. Wright and Jerusalem Bible. The issue is whether those reigning with Christ are just the martyrs, or include all who have refused to worship the beast. I think the latter! See Greg Beale, *The Book of Revelation*, New International Greek Testament Commentary (Grand Rapids, MI: Eerdmans; Carlisle: Paternoster, 1999), p. 1001.

So then the 'coming down' of the bride in 21:2 fills out the picture even more: now she is not just a following army but the star of the show (as brides usually are!), her preparation complete, fully adorned and ready to be seen: the full people of the Christ, all those whose names are *written in the Lamb's book of life.*[27] She is Jerusalem because that is the place where God's people live with God himself – or rather, where God comes to live in the midst of his people, as he emphasizes so wonderfully in 21:3–4. People and place come together because they and it are the spot where God has chosen to live in glory-filled relationship with humankind – that's us – and there has to be a whole new creation (21:1) for that to be fully and finally a reality.

So 21:2 is also a picture of the second coming! – except that Jesus allows the focus now to rest on his beloved bride, as she comes to be united with him for ever.

4. The beasts, the dragon and death – RIP

Let's go back now to look at 19:17 – 20:15 (C'–A' on the analysis above), where the beasts and the dragon meet their deserved end, and the final judgment takes place. All the enemies of God's redemptive purposes are done away with, so that the new creation can burst forth in all its glory and beauty. This section has its own interesting structure:

- A. 19:17–21: The birds are invited to feast on the slain, and the beasts who deceived their worshippers are captured and thrown into the lake of fire and sulphur.
  - B. 20:1–6: The dragon is bound and Christ reigns for a thousand years with the souls of those who refused to worship the beast.
- A'. 20:7–10: The dragon is released, the final war with Gog and Magog takes place, and the dragon who deceived the nations is thrown into the lake of fire and sulphur.
  - C. 20:11–15: The present heaven and earth are banished and all the dead are raised to judgment. Death itself is thrown into the lake of fire, with all whose names are not written in the book of life.

---

[27] 21:27; cf. 3:5; 13:8; 17:8; 20:15.

a. The beasts and the dragon – the great battle (A, A', 19:17–21; 20:7–10)

A and A' match each other, not just because of the parallel fate of beasts and dragon in the *lake of fire and sulphur,* but because the same passage in Ezekiel lies behind both, uniting the symbolism of the passages. After his powerful 'Valley of Dry Bones' vision of Israel's restoration in chapter 37, Ezekiel hears from God a terrible warning that the restored Israel is going to be attacked by 'a great horde, a mighty army'[28] from the north, under the command of 'Gog, of the land of Magog, the chief prince of Meshech and Tubal'[29] – but God will repulse the attack and destroy this enormous army spread across the mountains of Israel. In God's name Ezekiel issues an invitation 'to the birds of every kind and to all the wild animals'[30] to come and enjoy a huge banquet, feasting on the flesh of the fallen soldiers:

> You shall eat the flesh of the mighty, and drink the blood of the princes of the earth . . . And you shall be filled at my table with horses and charioteers, with warriors and all kinds of soldiers, says the Lord GOD.[31]

This is the passage on which John draws in the rather gruesome 19:17–18. In the second instalment of the battle (A'), in addition to the specific mention of Gog and Magog (20:8), the sheer size of the invading army is what connects John's narrative to Ezekiel 38,[32] and – fascinatingly – the notion of *deception.*[33] Here in Revelation it is the dragon who *will come out to deceive the nations . . . in order to gather them for battle . . . as numerous as the sands of the sea* (20:8). But in Ezekiel it is the Lord who deceives. He draws this massive horde together and brings them against Israel. Their desire is to 'seize spoil and carry off plunder'.[34] But God's plan is to inflict terrible judgment on them, including judgment by 'fire and sulphur',[35] to make known his greatness and holiness.[36] In Revelation we

---

[28] Ezek. 38:15.

[29] Ezek. 38:2. These were shadowy tribes living in eastern Anatolia; see the map and article in J. D. Douglas and N. Hillyer (eds.), *The Illustrated Bible Dictionary* (Leicester: Inter-Varsity Press, 1980), pp. 985–986.

[30] Ezek. 39:17.

[31] Ezek. 39:18, 20.

[32] 'Like a cloud covering the land . . . many peoples with you' (Ezek. 38:9, 16).

[33] Though it is mentioned in A as well, 19:20.

[34] Ezek. 38:12.

[35] Ezek. 38:22.

[36] Ezek. 38:16, 23; 39:21, 27.

already know that God's purposes lie behind the actions of the dragon and the beasts – and in particular behind this final battle: in 16:12–16 it's the pouring of the sixth 'bowl of wrath' which prompts the dragon and the beasts to summon 'the kings of the whole world, to assemble them for battle on the great day of God the Almighty'.[37] The dragon only operates under the sovereignty of 'God the Almighty'.

So one great battle in Ezekiel (and indeed in Rev. 16:12–16) is presented as *two* battles here. John's careful use of Ezekiel gives our interpretation a steer: we should not think that he is imagining two separate battles, either side of the thousand-year rule of Christ, overcoming first the beasts and then (a thousand years later) the dragon. This is one great overcoming – in line with Paul's expectation that 'every ruler and every authority and power' will be destroyed when Christ comes again.

b. The end of death (C, 20:11–15)

As in Paul, so here: the destruction of the 'powers' is completed by the destruction of death, the 'last enemy'.[38] The lake of fire and sulphur is doing sterling work here in Revelation 20 – swallowing up not just the beasts and the dragon, but *Death and Hades* along with all who finally do not belong to the Christ. The dead are raised to judgment *according to their works* (13), which in Revelation will specifically be about whether they have borne the mark of the beast or resisted loyalty to the beast and followed the Lamb instead.

The final words in 20:15, *anyone whose name was not found written in the book of life was thrown into the lake of fire*, make us reflect on the ultimate destiny of the 'lost'. We wondered about this when looking at Philippians 3:19, 'their end is destruction'.[39] Does *the lake of fire* entail the extinction of all thrown into it – does Revelation envisage that they cease to exist at that point? Or are they, like the beasts and the devil in 20:10, to *be tormented day and night for ever and ever*? This is a topic related to the discussion about 'evangelical universalism', because the definition of Paul's 'alls' (Rom. 11:32, 36; 1 Cor. 15:28; Phil. 3:21; etc.) will be affected *either* if some people end up in eternal conscious torment *or* if some people end up not saved and eternally extinguished. Either way, not 'all' numerically are saved.

---

[37] 16:14.

[38] 1 Cor. 15:26, 54b.

[39] See above, ch. 14, section 7c (p. 184).

This is a terrible topic to discuss, and I'm glad that we don't have to enter into it fully because it is at a tangent to our main focus on the second coming. So far as Revelation is concerned, we can make three points:

- In spite of reference to 'torment' in 20:10, the imagery of *the second death, the lake of fire* (14b) is more naturally understood as a symbol of destruction, rather than of punishment.
- The fact that Hades (the place of the dead) is destroyed as well as death (14a) means that the dead no longer have a place in which to continue to exist.
- It is a principle of biblical prophecy (including Rev. 20:11–15) that its purpose is not just *prediction* but also (and even more so) *deterrence*: paradoxically, one of the points of prophecy is to stop itself from coming true – in this case, by impelling readers to make sure that they and their loved ones have their names inscribed in the book of life.

We simply have to leave all this in the hands of our returning Lord, merciful Judge and Redeemer. The basic principle to apply here is expressed in Abraham's prayer: 'Shall not the Judge of all the earth do what is just?'[40]

c. The thousand years (B, 20:1–6)

The interpretation of the thousand-year reign – the millennium – is much argued about, although in large parts of Christendom the debate has been settled in favour of a literal interpretation and expectation: that after Christ comes again he will rule for a thousand years on earth, while the dragon is bound; then a final showdown will take place at the battle of Armageddon.

But two features of the passage noted here incline me against this interpretation.

i. The background in Ezekiel (not to mention 1 Cor. 15)

As noted above, this background prods us to see the two battles here as one battle (Jesus' final victory over all powers) presented in two aspects. Maybe this is simply because of the structure we noticed above: that the

---

[40] Gen. 18:25.

powers are introduced separately in Revelation 12 – 13, and therefore it gives a sense of completeness to picture them being overcome separately. Revelation 20:7–10 is not therefore *temporally subsequent* to 20:1–6, nor is 20:1–6 temporally subsequent to 19:17–21 – nor 19:17–21 to 19:11–16. It is easy to be misled by the repeated 'then' in translations like the NRSV, which give the impression of successive events.[41] But the Greek simply has 'and . . .', leaving *us* to decide how the elements of the vision relate to one another. It seems clear that there is one act of judgment here, and so it's unlikely that we should understand the thousand years as a literal period in earth's history.[42]

ii. The identity of those who share the throne with Christ

As we saw, these are most naturally understood as those who have already died in Christ: a growing company, of course, throughout this age of the church. But if this is right, then again we must see the thousand years as not literal, but as a symbol of the age of the gospel – a period known to God but not to us. So the binding of the dragon (20:1–3) will be about God's restriction on the power of Satan to hinder the preaching of the gospel. This looks like a follow-on from 12:13–17, where Satan comes down to earth raging against God's people, and a natural question would be: why don't we see him directly trying to destroy us? The answer is, because he has been bound by God throughout this age. He is not allowed to *deceive the nations* (20:3) – that is, to rouse them up in concerted violent opposition to God, his Christ and his people. But if that should ever happen – as indeed it sometimes does – then we can apply Ezekiel 38 – 39 to that situation, and know that God is in control and that even the most appalling threats will turn out to serve his purpose of redeeming love.

5. And finally . . .

Let's come back to the vision of the triumphant Christ storming out of heaven to judge and make war (19:11). This powerful image is softened, not just by the strange picture of the following army wearing bridal gowns, but also by the extraordinary language in 19:15: *From his mouth comes a*

---

[41] In 19:6, 11, 17; 20:1, 4, 11; 21:1 (and regularly throughout the book).

[42] In addition we must note that all numbers in Revelation have symbolic rather than literal meaning, as explored for instance by Paul (*Revelation*, pp. 34–39, 326f.) and others. One thousand years (a perfect cube, like the heavenly city in 21:16–17) symbolizes the full story of God's reign on earth.

sharp sword with which to strike down the nations, and he will shepherd[43] *them with a rod of iron.* On the one hand, he 'strikes down' the nations, on the other hand, he 'shepherds' them. In that they join with the beast, he strikes them down. In that they respond to the wedding invitation, don the wedding garments and climb on white horses behind him, he shepherds them. 'Shepherding with a rod of iron' is one of Revelation's gloriously paradoxical images, like 'making their robes white in the blood of the Lamb' and 'the Lamb will be their shepherd'.[44]

Many of us could testify to this as Jesus' typical style of dealing with us. He wields a rod of iron, never letting us off the hook or sparing us the feelings and the consequences of being human and making human mistakes, of being the embodied creatures we are. But he doesn't beat us with the iron rod – he shepherds us, using it to prod, to guide and to protect us along the difficult path which is our life. His is 'A Severe Mercy', to use the title of Sheldon Vanauken's remarkable book.[45] Apparently this will be his typical style after he comes again, too, when he rides out of heaven and continues to deal with the nations in this way. But Paul had seen it already, noticing God's 'kindness and . . . severity' in dealing with Israel and the nations.[46]

So once again his coming *then* will be of a piece with his coming *now*: and this will be the focus of our interest in the next chapter.

---

[43] Following NRSV margin. The Greek says 'shepherd'.

[44] 7:14, 17.

[45] Sheldon Vanauken, *A Severe Mercy* (London: Hodder & Stoughton, 1977). The expression 'a severe mercy' was used by C. S. Lewis in a letter to Vanauken to capture God's action towards him in and through the death of his wife at a young age.

[46] Rom. 11:22.

Part 5
The second coming and the Christian life

Revelation 3:14–22;
1 Corinthians 11:17–34

19. Eating with Jesus

We look at two apparently not-very-related passages in this chapter. There is not space in the chapter to display the texts at length, so it would be good to read them now so as to have them clearly in mind. They bring us face to face with what it means to live in the 'in-between' space, between the ascension and the second coming of Jesus. Putting it bluntly, this is the space in which

- The gospel says that we have been delivered from death, but we still have to face it (both our death and the deaths of others), and the reality of bodily weakness as well as mortality;
- We believe that Jesus is 'the way, and the truth, and the life',[1] but it is still agonizingly difficult sometimes to feel that our lives make sense;
- Relationships are completely vital for our well-being, but are often places of great pain and loss, and we cannot escape ultimately bearing our pain and death – and those of others – *alone*;
- The responsibility to act well and wisely can lead to despair if we take bad decisions we have to live with – and we have to 'look forward' to being judged by God for our choices and actions.

This in-between space is puzzling and tough (to put it mildly)! These bullet points pick up the four great life-anxieties identified by Irvin Yalom,

---

[1] John 14:6.

on which we touched above.[2] I think he is fundamentally right, but I'm a Christian, so I add to his analysis a theology which says that *God's in charge*: so God must have arranged things like this. He *chose* not to bring in the kingdom straight away as the disciples expected,[3] and (as we saw above)[4] that creates the gospel age, the time when the end is postponed so that the gospel can be proclaimed, and *only when that is accomplished* will Jesus come and bring the kingdom. We must not downplay the impact of this: our lives are stretched over these huge interlocking challenges which are like mountain ranges towering between us and home.

How can we cope well in this in-between time? These passages help us with some great equipment to sustain us over the mountains.

1. The invitation

The letter to the church in Laodicea in Revelation 3 is an excellent example of Jesus' shepherding with a rod of iron![5] They think they are doing fine, but in his eyes they are deeply self-deceived, and he leaves them in no doubt about his feelings and verdict:

> *So, because you are lukewarm, and neither cold nor hot, I am about to spit you out of my mouth. For you say, 'I am rich, I have prospered, and I need nothing.' You do not realize that you are wretched, pitiable, poor, blind, and naked.*[6]

Jesus doesn't mince his words. He is disgusted by them. They knew about disgusting water: though it was a wealthy place, with vigorous local industries and trade, Laodicea was not blessed with a good water supply, unlike nearby Hierapolis which had medicinal hot springs, or Colossae which had beautiful cold sources. Laodicea piped its water from a hot spring, and it arrived lukewarm and sulphurous.[7] Jesus' image would have spoken with powerful irony. But he *doesn't* spit them out immediately:

---

[2] See above, p. 165 (ch. 13, section 2b): death, meaninglessness, isolation and freedom.

[3] Acts 1:6.

[4] See above, ch. 5, section 3 (pp. 62–64).

[5] See the end of the last chapter (p. 238).

[6] Rev. 3:16–17.

[7] The background to all the letters (revealing that 'I know your works' builds on exact local knowledge) has been brilliantly explored by Colin Hemer, *The Letters to the Seven Churches of Asia in Their Local Setting*, JSNTSup 11 (Sheffield: JSOT Press, 1986). He deals with Laodicea's water on pp. 186–191.

first, he makes a series of offers (18 – again drawing on local imagery), based on the principle that *I reprove and discipline those whom I love. Be earnest, therefore, and repent* (19). Then he backs up this encouragement with two final offers, which seem designed to conclude all seven letters and to be a 'standing invitation' to all churches that seek to *listen to what the Spirit is saying* (22):

> *Listen! I am standing at the door, knocking; if you hear my voice and open the door, I will come in to you and eat with you, and you with me. To the one who conquers I will give a place with me on my throne, just as I myself conquered and sat down with my Father on his throne.*
> (20–21)

Disgusting they may be, but he is not abandoning them. *Standing* and *knocking* both have a 'continuous action' flavour: he has taken his stand outside the door of their church and is constantly knocking, constantly inviting them to open up and enjoy true fellowship with him again.

Here's another irony: the language of 'eating with' probably refers to the Eucharist, the 'Lord's Supper', the fellowship meal that all early Christians celebrated. The Greek word translated *eat* is literally 'feast', used of the Eucharist in Luke 22:20 and in 1 Corinthians 11.[8] Undoubtedly they were regularly celebrating this fellowship meal in Laodicea . . . except that they weren't. Jesus wasn't there. He was on the wrong side of the door. They *thought* that he was there, just as they *thought* that they were 'rich . . . prosperous . . . needing nothing' (17), but they were wrong about both.

It was the same in Corinth. Such was the poor quality of spiritual life in the church (detailed below) that Paul says roundly to them, *When you come together, it is not really to eat the Lord's supper* (1 Cor. 11:20). They thought that was what they were doing, but the Lord was not involved – it was just bare 'supper', their own meal: *each of you goes ahead with your own supper* (21). Paul tries to call them back to true worship, just as Jesus does with the Laodiceans.

So both churches need to get their feeding habits in order. But how does the invitation in Revelation 3:20 relate to the second coming, to which there is no reference in the letter to Laodicea? There is however a

---

[8] 1 Cor. 11:20, 21, 25. Also in John 13:2, 4 and 21:20. Both the noun and verbal forms of the word are used, sometimes translated 'supper'.

three-word allusion in 1 Corinthians 11:26: *For as often as you eat this bread and drink the cup, you proclaim the Lord's death until he comes* – and the connection between this and the invitation to eat with the risen Christ in Revelation gives more than enough reason for us to link these two passages and to include them in this book, as we'll see. Let's look more closely.

2. 1 Corinthians 11:26: 'until he comes'

In the Eucharist (says Paul) *you proclaim the Lord's death until he comes*. It's easy to see how the Eucharist looks back to the cross: it's a visible action in which the breaking of the bread and the pouring of the cup represent the breaking of his body and the pouring out of his life, and the eating and drinking express intimate faith and 'sharing in' him.[9] The whole action 'proclaims' the gospel through its symbolism, and pulls us into fellowship with one another as we connect with him and 'remember'[10] his death for us.

But what about *until he comes*? Does celebrating the Lord's Supper look forward as well as back? How? The answer is almost certainly that Paul is thinking of the fellowship meal as an anticipation of the messianic banquet. Luke does the same – he alone includes Jesus' words at the institution of the Lord's Supper: 'I have eagerly desired to eat this Passover with you before I suffer; for I tell you, I will not eat it until it is fulfilled in the kingdom of God.'[11] Then all three Synoptic Gospels include Jesus' similar words after giving the cup: 'I tell you that from now on I will not drink of the fruit of the vine until the kingdom of God comes.'[12]

Undoubtedly his disciples would connect this with the expectation of a great banquet at which the Messiah would preside over the whole gathered company of God's redeemed people. We meet this expectation in Matthew 8:11–12:

I tell you, many will come from east and west and will eat with Abraham and Isaac and Jacob in the kingdom of heaven, while the heirs of the

---

[9] 1 Cor. 10:16.

[10] The distinctive command 'do this in remembrance of me' is shared by Paul and Luke (Luke 22:19; 1 Cor. 11:24, 25).

[11] Luke 22:15–16.

[12] Luke 22:18; Matt. 26:29; Mark 14:25. Matthew and Mark have 'until [that day when] I drink it new in the kingdom of God / my Father'.

kingdom will be thrown into the outer darkness, where there will be weeping and gnashing of teeth.

Jesus is redefining the guest list, but not disputing the event. Crowds of previously excluded Gentiles are going to be drawn in, while some who presumed on their place at the table will find themselves shut out. The expectation of the messianic banquet also underlies parables like the great dinner[13] and the wedding feast.[14]

So for Paul, the Eucharist shows forth Jesus' death *until he comes* because that is the point at which the meal which it foreshadows will finally take place.[15] It will then have served its purpose as a foretaste proclaiming his coming, as well as his death. And there is something very wonderful to gather here about *the way in which* the Eucharist looks forward to the messianic banquet: as a foretaste, *it already contains the reality which it foreshadows*, the real and wonderful presence of Jesus at the meal, in and through his body which can truly be 'discerned' there.[16] More on this below!

3. Revelation 3:20: eating with Jesus

The lovely invitation to allow the risen Jesus through the door into the Laodicean church helps us beautifully to address some of the questions with which we were left by the vision of the new Jerusalem in Revelation 21.[17] In particular, we noticed the extraordinary *absence* of the wedding banquet from the vision of the coming-down bride. The marriage was announced in 19:7, and in 19:9 we heard the blessedness of 'those who are invited to the marriage supper of the Lamb'. But no feast ensues. The only 'supper' that takes place after that point is the ghastly feeding of the birds on the flesh of the Lamb's fallen enemies (19:17–18) – as G. B. Caird says, 'a grim contrast to the wedding feast of the Lamb'.[18]

So why do we not actually see or hear of the Lamb's wedding feast, when the bride appears? Eating and drinking are hinted at, in the picture of 'the

---

[13] Luke 14:15–24.

[14] Matt. 22:1–14.

[15] So e.g. Thiselton, *Commentary on the Greek Text*, p. 888, and Pastoral Commentary, p. 186.

[16] 1 Cor. 11:29.

[17] See above, p. 229. Of the bullet points there, I'm thinking now especially of numbers 2, 3 and 4.

[18] Caird, *Revelation*, p. 247.

river of the water of life' beside which grows the tree of life 'with its twelve kinds of fruit . . . and the leaves of the tree are for the healing of the nations' (22:1–2). But this is not obviously a wedding feast or a messianic banquet.

This is an extraordinary absence. We need to take a step back in order to understand it.

In our list of questions we also noticed that the offer of the water of life is *contemporary* – an evangelistic offer made by 'the Spirit and the bride' to all John's readers and to all to whom they might pass it on (22:17).[19] 'Living water' is not just an expectation for the new creation, where the river flows through the new Jerusalem. 'The bride' speaks *now*, giving her testimony alongside the Spirit in offering the water to all who will 'come'.

So I think there is clear evidence that, in John's mind, the new Jerusalem is already in existence, already 'coming down' from heaven, and already welcoming the nations through her wide-open gates, even though the 'new heaven and new earth' are yet to be. Technically, this is 'inaugurated eschatology' – a terrible expression beloved of New Testament scholars, meaning that the kingdom of God is both 'already' and 'not yet', both *present* in God's people right now as they experience the reality of the Holy Spirit, and *yet to be* because the resurrection and the second coming have not yet taken place.[20] The new creation is already present within the old.

Paul's dramatic words in 2 Corinthians 5:17 – 'If anyone is in Christ, there is a new creation: everything old has passed away; see, everything has become new!' – are very similar to God's words in Revelation 21:4–5: '". . . for the first things have passed away" . . . "See, I am making all things new!"' A process of new-making is already under way! *I think that this is why there is no description of the wedding feast in the heavenly city: because the feast is already happening, whenever God's people fling open the door and 'feast' with him right now.* The invitation is issued in the preaching of the gospel, and we do not have to wait for the new heaven and new earth to hand it in at the door and enter the event. The door is right here, too, and in fact *Jesus* is the one knocking and asking for admittance. The feast is not described in Revelation 21 because it is already under way in Revelation 3 (at least, potentially!).

---

[19]   See also ch. 17, section 4c (pp. 222–223).

[20]   See for instance G. E. Ladd, *A Theology of the New Testament* (Grand Rapids, MI: Eerdmans, 1974), esp. pp. 68–69, and Ian Paul's very useful overview, *Kingdom, Hope and the End of the World: The 'Now' and 'Not Yet' of Eschatology*, Grove Biblical Series 82 (Cambridge: Grove Books, 2016).

Both passages, therefore, are looking forward to the messianic banquet when Jesus comes again, and both are telling us we don't have to wait, but can sit and eat with him now. In Revelation the worship theme continues into chapters 4–5, where we hear the worship of heaven in a way that inspires worship on earth. This is the worship which Jesus will bring with him, if we let him in! It's fascinating to notice how prominent the imagery and themes of Revelation 4 – 5 are in contemporary worship songs.

And so both these passages have a lot to say about life in the in-between space, while we both enjoy the new age and wait for Jesus to come. We will look more closely at them now through the lens provided by Irvin Yalom, summarizing their message in relation to the deep anxieties of our human life. In each case these passages pose a challenge, and a decision for us to take.

4. Death: die with Jesus!

Whether we like it or not – and none of us do, though most of us manage to push the thought out of awareness and live as if it were not true – the Grim Reaper waits for all of us. The fear of death sinks into our unconscious and can motivate behaviours which at first sight seem to have nothing to do with death. The challenge of these passages is not to deny our death but to face it, to know it, and to *live it* now: to hold our death consciously in awareness and to thank God for it as we embrace it with Jesus.

As we look ahead into our future, the moment of our death is (1) the only absolute certainty, and (2) the only moment which – as Christians – we *know* will be a *kairos* of encounter with God. Hopefully there will be many such moments in our future. But this is the only sure one!

The Lord's Supper is not just about the death of Jesus: it's about our death, too. As we look back to the cross, we celebrate a death which was 'for' us.[21] 'For' means 'on behalf of': Jesus died *in our place*, bearing and defeating the death which otherwise will destroy us. By taking into our bodies (doomed to die) these symbols of his death (broken bread, poured-out wine), we unite ourselves with him by faith so that our death becomes *his* death. *His* death is a death-unto-life, a death swallowed up by resurrection, and so united to him our death will also be 'unto life'. Of course,

---

[21] 1 Cor. 11:24.

the Holy Spirit is crucial for this: it's the *Spirit* who brings us into union with Christ's death and resurrection.[22]

But 'eating with Jesus' covers much more than just celebrating the Lord's Supper with him truly present. If he is truly with us, that will mean that we have opened the door to him – and therefore have overcome all that was keeping the door locked against him. What was hindering true 'feasting' with him in Laodicea and in Corinth? We can learn from their example.

5. Meaning: give up money!

Yalom believes that we passionately seek sources of meaning which can give us a reason to live, and at the same time blank out the horror of death. We certainly need our lives to make sense, but Scripture encourages us to seek meaning *as we face* the fact of our death, not in order to escape it! In both Corinth and Laodicea money was significant in giving a sense of meaning – but in both cases it was actually endangering their lives, not securing them.

In many societies money confers status, as well as security: to have wealth gives social standing and significance, and is often seen as a sign of being blessed by the gods or by God. In many places, therefore, money brings with it honour, and a leadership role and position. All this seems to have been true in Corinth and Laodicea. In Corinth the problem Paul addresses (though it's a little hard to reconstruct with complete certainty) is that at the fellowship meal wealthy members of the church were going ahead on their own, not sharing what they had with poorer members, and not waiting for everyone to be present. So

> *when the time comes to eat, each of you goes ahead with your own supper,* *and one goes hungry and another becomes drunk. What! Do you not have* *homes to eat and drink in? Or do you show contempt for the church of God* *and humiliate those who have nothing?*[23]

Paul then recounts the words of the institution of the Lord's Supper in order to underline Jesus' example of self-giving, and to show how it is

---

[22] See Rom. 8:11; 1 Cor. 12:13.
[23] 1 Cor. 11:21–22.

impossible to *do this in remembrance of me* in this self-centred way (23–26). The wealthy members of the church – who might be called upon to host the fellowship meal – have a duty to care and provide for the poor members (many of whom will have been slaves). Otherwise, *when you come together, it is not really to eat the Lord's supper* (20). So they must give up their sense of rank and status – abandoning that on which they relied to give their lives significance – and find it simply in a true connection with Jesus: which will mean dying to self[24] and living by his example of sacrificial self-giving. It's not surprising that, when Paul goes on in the next chapter (1 Cor. 12) to describe the gifts of the Spirit, he makes no mention at all of social status, gender or importance: *anyone* can be a prophet or a teacher in the church of Jesus Christ, including a slave or a woman.

Similarly in Laodicea, the church's wealth – built on the wealth of the city – had completely skewed their self-awareness and stifled their spiritual life. The city had a lucrative clothing industry and a famous eye salve which made it a lot of money. They prided themselves on their wealth, which had meant that they did not need to seek help from the Roman Empire when the area was last devastated by an earthquake (a not infrequent occurrence in that part of the world). But the Laodicean church must live by a different power. They need to discover the gold, the white clothes and the eye salve that *Jesus* will provide,[25] because only his will count for anything in the long run.

These churches challenge us today to make sure that our deepest sense of value and significance rests in, and arises out of, our connection to Jesus Christ. For his life in us is the life of the new age, the life of the city of God whose streets are paved with gold[26] and whose lamp is the Lamb,[27] and where we human beings truly make sense. That's where our citizenship lies!

That leads us to Yalom's third great 'anxiety':

6. Isolation: discern his body![28]

Yalom's point is that we all yearn for satisfying relationships, ever since we spent nine months inside another human being and emerged dependent

---

[24] See Gal. 2:19–20.
[25] Rev. 3:18. The 'white clothing' image looks ahead to Rev. 7:14 and to the wedding garments in 19:8, 14.
[26] Rev. 21:21.
[27] Rev. 21:23.
[28] On this point and the last, see above, ch. 12, section 1 (pp. 148–151).

and enmeshed. Though so often relationships become unsafe for us and we withdraw, we still need deep connection and can look for it in other ways than through open, trusting and committed engagements. Paradoxically, says Yalom, we eventually have to die alone and cannot escape that fate.

Both the Laodiceans and the Corinthians had rich relationships – but only with people of their own social group. Paul underlines to the Corinthians how much is at stake when he urges them to *examine yourselves* before eating the bread and drinking the cup, *for all who eat and drink without discerning the body, eat and drink judgement against themselves.*[29]

Paul suggests that this is why *many of you are weak and ill, and some have died* (30). Clearly *discerning the body* is really important, and the Corinthians have not been doing it! Probably Paul is deliberately ambiguous here, because *the body* has a double reference in this context. On the one hand, it is Christ's body represented by the bread, as in verse 24: *This is my body that is for you. Do this in remembrance of me.* On the other hand, it is Christ's body the church, the topic that Paul will develop next – 'you are the body of Christ and individually members of it'.[30] To 'discern the body' means both recognizing what the bread and wine stand for, in the context of the Lord's Supper, and also recognizing that those who 'share in' the bread and the cup are his body spiritually, 'baptized into one body' by the Spirit, whether 'Jews or Greeks, slaves or free'[31] – in other words, whatever their ethnic, social or economic status.

To 'discern the body' means knowing to whom we are connected in Christ and by the Spirit, and acting effectively on that connection, letting it shape how we are in the world. We are *not* isolated! But we need to cross boundaries, and to embrace the connections the Spirit forges for us – chiefly, of course, with Jesus himself, but also with all for whom he died, however different from us they may be. After all, these are the ones who will gather around the Table when he comes. It would be tragic if we were excluded from that Meal because we did not truly 'discern' them, like the 'heirs of the kingdom' who forfeit their place at the table and are thrown into outer darkness.[32]

---

[29] 1 Cor. 11:28–29.

[30] 1 Cor. 12:27.

[31] 1 Cor. 12:13.

[32] Matt. 8:12.

The challenge to discern the body is thus the same as the challenge to *hear my voice and open the door* (Rev. 3:20). The Laodiceans are observing the fellowship meal, but Jesus is not there – and he will not be there, until they

- Recognize themselves as he sees them (*wretched, pitiable, poor, blind, and naked*, 17), and
- Take consequent action to repair themselves (18). This will entail reaching out to those who, in the world's eyes, are indeed *wretched, pitiable, poor, blind, and naked.*

Then they will truly enjoy table fellowship with the risen Lord – in fact, they will enter *now* into the experience of the feast at which he celebrates his love for his bride. Nothing less than that. Inaugurated eschatology! And then, when the end comes, they will have 'conquered' (21). That brings us to . . .

7. Freedom: obey his word!

Yalom suggests that the challenge of taking decisions (in the light of the other three anxieties) can be so great that it can be disabling in itself. I have sometimes felt completely overwhelmed by the choices available in the supermarket aisle – which I deal with by short-circuiting the decision and always choosing the same things. Sometimes we limit our freedom because it is too big to handle.

That's why it's always more comfortable to stick with the people we know and the social environment in which we feel at home. But Jesus will not let us do that: the Jesus who gives himself to us in fellowship in the Eucharist calls us out of the comfortable and into the unfamiliar – into new ways of seeing both ourselves (*wretched, pitiable*, etc.) and the world around. Laodicea's civic self-confidence stinks! The *you say* in 3:17 is the voice not just of the church but of the whole town. Their wealth is *not* a sign of blessing by the gods or God. *Be earnest, therefore, and repent,* Jesus says, just as Paul says to the Corinthians, *if we judged ourselves, we would not be judged.*[33] Here *judged* is the same word as that translated 'discern' in 11:29 (*discerning* the body). This is about seeing truly both ourselves

---

[33] Rev. 3:19 and 1 Cor. 11:31.

and the Lord and those with us in fellowship. This true seeing comes from him: *buy from me . . . salve to anoint your eyes so that you may see* (Rev. 3:18).

This freedom is about taking charge of our lives and grasping our responsibility for ourselves. This can be frightening. But Jesus wants us to 'judge ourselves', to examine ourselves in the light of his word, and take appropriate action – which, at heart, is to fling open the door and welcome him in.

It's not just an individual thing! *Be earnest, therefore, and repent* is a command addressed to the whole church – it's a 'you singular' imperative, addressing the church as a corporate entity. How interesting: in the very way in which he frames the encouragement, Jesus wants the Laodicean church to act in openness and fellowship *with one another*, taking *shared* action to repair their ways of being. Inviting the risen Christ in through the door starts with recognizing that there is something about their shared life which excludes him, and therefore something they need to do *as a church* to put things right. Their whole culture needs to shift.

How can he come into fellowship with us at the end if we don't welcome him into fellowship with us now? This is deeply challenging, and in our next chapter we look at a series of passages which will help us to 'be ready'.

1 John 3:2–3; James 5:7–11; Titus 2:11–15; Colossians 3:1–4

20. Be ready!

1. Please remember, don't forget!

The second coming is part of a whole range of topics and themes that go under the collective title 'eschatology' – defined in the *Concise Oxford Dictionary* as 'the doctrine of death, judgement, heaven, and hell'.[1] It's impossible to overestimate what a focus there is on eschatology in the New Testament. Jesus is the New Testament's core and centre, of course – the 'Lord' of all.[2] But because human life (the world, the universe, everything) is now apparently carrying on without its Lord, the New Testament is very concerned for us to know that this 'apparently' is illusory. Jesus really is the heart of human destiny (the world, the universe, everything), and one day this will be clear to all. And we need to be ready! Eschatology rules, in the New Testament – and the fact of the second coming needs to bear upon our everyday life in very practical ways.

For a long period in recent church history the second coming (indeed, eschatology generally) has not been a widespread focus of interest, except in circles where teachings about the Rapture and a literal millennium have been influential. There have been some bright spots, most notably N. T. Wright's great and deservedly popular book *Surprised by Hope*,[3] but generally speaking mainstream Christian churches have included 'the last things' under 'Any Other Business' rather than at the head of the agenda.

---

[1] H. W. Fowler and F. G. Fowler (eds.), *The Concise Oxford Dictionary of Current English*, 5th edn (Oxford: Clarendon Press, 1964), p. 412.

[2] See 1 Cor. 8:6; 12:3; etc.!

[3] N. T. Wright, *Surprised by Hope* (London: SPCK, 2007).

Leading evangelical theologians have underlined this 'also-ran' approach to eschatology. For instance, the great summaries of Christian doctrine by Louis Berkhof, Millard Erickson and Wayne Grudem all deal with eschatology at the end of their huge books, *after* apparently exhaustive treatments of God, Christ, creation, human being, the Holy Spirit and salvation.[4] In each case (with a one-page exception in Berkhof) the long sections on the person and work of Christ do not include the second coming. But this is like writing a history of the Second World War that ends in June 1944 with the D-Day landings. It seems that eschatology (including the second coming) is an add-on, *after* 'the basics' have been properly explored.

Similarly at a more popular level, eschatology has not been a particular focus in church preaching programmes and evangelism. For instance, the very popular and effective British *Alpha Course* – now used worldwide[5] – presents its survey of Christian ideas and life without mentioning the second coming.

This is not where the New Testament would be! As we've seen, Paul gave teaching on the second coming and on eschatology in Thessalonica right at the start, when he first preached the gospel there.[6] This is because *hope* and the linked virtues of *patience, endurance* and *steadfastness* are vital in Christian believing and living, as we will see again below. None of the main topics in Christian theology can be properly treated if this 'where-it's-all-going' focus is blurred. The story of Jesus himself, and therefore the story of our salvation in him, is incomplete without the second coming, the final judgment and the new creation.

I'm very glad that in recent years the second coming has been creeping back into worship, with some excellent new hymns and worship songs that celebrate it.[7] It's making a comeback! Often our theology follows our worship, so there are glimmerings of hope that the second coming will re-emerge as a focus in thinking about the Christian life.

---

[4] Louis Berkhof, *Systematic Theology* (London: Banner of Truth Trust, 1958; first published in the 1930s); Millard J. Erickson, *Christian Theology*, 2nd edn (Grand Rapids, MI: Baker Academic, 1983); Wayne Grudem, *Systematic Theology: An Introduction to Biblical Doctrine*, 2nd edn (Downers Grove, IL: InterVarsity Press, 2020).

[5] See <https://alpha.org.uk>.

[6] See 1 Thess. 1:8–10.

[7] E.g. Timothy Dudley-Smith, 'When the Lord in Glory Comes'; Gerald Coates and Noel Richards, 'Great Is the Darkness'; Nathan Fellingham (Phatfish), 'There Is a Day That All Creation's Waiting For'.

In line with the New Testament's emphasis on the fact of the second coming, the challenge to be ready for it is also consistent, as we have already seen. In this chapter we look at four short passages which illustrate this challenge in four very different ways, and which make the second coming a *practical focus* for our living and believing.

In each case the call to be ready for Jesus the Lord to come is linked to two things:

- a 'because': a *reason why* the coming of the Lord should be a practical focus that impacts our daily living as Christians; and
- a 'therefore': a *consequent Christian behaviour* that follows from the reason, something to shape our everyday lives.

2. 1 John 3:2–3: we will be like him!

Beloved, we are God's children now; what we will be has not yet been revealed. What we do know is this: when he is revealed, we will be like him, for we will see him as he is. And all who have this hope in him purify themselves, just as he is pure.

This passage beautifully illustrates how essential the second coming is to the whole story of salvation. Right now, we are in a dilemma. On the one hand, *we are God's children now*: we have a deep feeling of connection, an awareness of being adopted into God's family – so cleverly captured by Paul in Romans 8:15–16: 'You have received a spirit of adoption. When we cry "Abba! Father!" it is that very Spirit bearing witness with our spirit that we are children of God.' We find our hearts moved towards God with a powerful sense of relational belonging – an inner 'cry', says Paul, using the ancient and intimate term 'Abba' to express that feeling of family attachment spoken into being by the Holy Spirit in us. This is the heart of prayer!

But on the other hand, *what we will be has not yet been revealed*. What exactly does it mean to be God's children? Glorious though it is, we don't understand ourselves in this experience of belonging to God as Father. We can say a great deal about what makes human beings tick, and whole sciences are devoted to exploring ourselves in multiple dimensions (physical, neurological, anthropological, sociological, psychological, spiritual, etc.). But the energy behind all these sciences lies in *not knowing*. In spite of huge advances in understanding (for instance, in brain science), we are a mystery to ourselves. Theologically, this is related to being made in God's image: God himself is a mystery, finally beyond our comprehension, even though we still strive to capture understanding of him as well as of ourselves. So if he is beyond our grasp, and we are in his image, it is hardly surprising that we don't know ourselves!

So when it comes to the search for meaning (see the last chapter), we are on a hiding to nothing in this life. We must learn to live with not knowing (completely). But here's the glory: because we are in his image – which means being *made* like Christ through the process of redemption – we will see *ourselves* as well as him when he returns. *When he is revealed, we will be like him, for we will see him as he is*. At last we will understand ourselves, when we see ourselves finally 'in' the glorified Christ. I think this applies both to the general question – 'What are we – what is this thing called "human being"?' – and also to my particular corner within it: 'Who am I, why am I the way I am, how do I make sense of me as a creature in God's universe?' John suggests that we already know the heart of the answer: we are *God's children*. So when the Son of God appears, the family likeness will reveal our true nature as well as his.

This is a deeply resonant and powerful *hope in him* which will already begin to transform us as we embrace it. It's the 'because'! We need to be ready *because* our *present* needs to line up with our *future*, like strangely shaped jigsaw pieces that make sense only when they fit into the picture. We need to be in the right shape!

The 'therefore' follows: *all who have this hope in him purify themselves, just as he is pure*. We need to do our best to be *pure* now, because that's what he is, and so we must prepare for his return by maximizing the family likeness as much as possible.

The word translated *pure* is closely related to the word 'holy', one of the great descriptions of God in the Bible. It summarizes his uniqueness, rather than specifically his moral perfection. Hannah's prayer begins with it:

My heart exults in the LORD . . .
There is no Holy One like the LORD,
   no one besides you;
    there is no Rock like our God.[8]

---

[8] 1 Sam. 2:1–2.

God's holiness consists in his being uniquely himself – 'no one besides you'! Unique, and therefore beyond our capacity to grasp. But we can know enough: his uniqueness consists not in stern moral uprightness, but in being the kind of God who hears agonized prayer like Hannah's, so that she can call him a 'Rock' on which she can rely. And of course his holy uniqueness is now 'fleshed out' wonderfully (and literally) in the person of Jesus Christ. God is now uniquely 'the God and Father of our Lord Jesus Christ'[9] – that is now his *identity*, the stamp on his name badge, and he is acting to bring us into that same family.

Against this background, 'purity' is that collection of qualities in us which display a family likeness to the God who is revealed as the Father of Jesus Christ. What will that mean? Loving like Jesus, praying like him, trusting like him, serving like him, bearing adversity like him, obeying like him, worshipping like him, and ultimately facing death like him. *Seeking to be like Christ* – that's John's keynote as we prepare for his 'appearance'. In becoming like him, we move towards the meaning of our whole existence!

Our next passage colours in even more what 'purity' looks like:

3. James 5:7–11: the Judge is near!

> *Be patient, therefore, beloved, until the coming of the Lord. The farmer waits for the precious crop from the earth, being patient with it until he receives the early and the late rains. You also must be patient. Strengthen your hearts, for the coming of the Lord is near. Beloved, do not grumble against one another, so that you may not be judged. See, the Judge is standing at the doors!*
> (7–9)

The reason why we must be ready (the 'because') is obvious here: *the coming*[10] *of the Lord is near . . . the Judge is standing at the doors!* We know how to understand 'nearness' now. It's a *kairos*-nearness, about urgency rather than about timetable. His coming has always been *soon*, and always will be, irrespective of its date on the calendar. Similarly we have no idea when our death will intervene, cutting across the course of our lives.

---

9 See 2 Cor. 1:3; Eph. 1:3; Col. 1:3; 1 Pet. 1:3.

10 James uses our old friend *parousia* (Matt. 24:3, 27, 37, 39; 1 Cor. 15:23; 1 Thess. 4:15; 2 Pet. 3:4; etc.).

Whatever our age, it is always *near*, always something to prepare for – and is therefore a good analogy for the 'nearness' of the Lord's coming. But actually – as we've seen in earlier chapters – the two might coincide anyway: the moment of the death of each of us, I believe, *is* the moment of the second coming, the point at which the *chronos* of our lives collapses into the *kairos* of God's End, and the Judge who is *standing at the doors* steps through them and we are called to account.

James' 'therefore' is equally clear in the light of this nearness. He gives three commands:

- *Be patient*, like the farmer waiting for harvest (7).
- *Strengthen your hearts* (8).
- *Do not grumble against one another* (9).

All these 'therefores' arise, for James, from the nearness of the Lord's coming. An interesting collection! Why these? I think the answer is that James already has in mind the example of the prophets and of Job, which he goes on to describe:

> As an example of suffering and of patience, beloved, take the prophets who spoke in the name of the Lord. Indeed we call blessed those who showed endurance. You have heard of the endurance of Job, and you have seen the ultimate purpose of the Lord, how the Lord is compassionate and merciful.
> (10–11)

I have added the word 'ultimate' to NRSV here (following N. T. Wright's translation) because James is thinking of the end of the story of Job – how it all turned out.[11]

The example of the farmer's patience until harvest doesn't seem to fit at first sight: surely, if the Lord is near, we ought to get busy, not sit around waiting patiently! But farmers usually have to work very hard for their crops. Job illustrates what 'patience' really looks like: it's *endurance*, keeping going in the face of terrible odds. And as he endured, Job didn't *grumble*. He questioned God's purposes, but from a place of ultimate trust in God's goodness. His so-called friends, however, certainly 'grumbled

---

11 Cf. NIV: 'what the Lord finally brought about'.

against' Job, criticizing him and accusing him of being a closet sinner who was getting his just deserts. They were *anticipating* the judgment of the Lord, speaking it in advance (that's what criticism does), rather than patiently waiting for it, like Job.

Because *the Lord is compassionate and merciful*, his judgment is something to be longed for, not feared. We prepare for his judgment, not by polishing up our righteousness like Job's friends, and thinking how well we're doing compared with others, but by knowing how wretched we are, how needy and weak, how much in need of his compassion and mercy. If we stay in *that* place – which is where Jesus wanted the church in Laodicea to be![12] – then not only will we be ready for the Judge to come, but we may even find ourselves speaking his word right now, like the prophets whose example we are following (10). That's how it was for Job: he thought he was simply voicing his own agonized questions out of his awful perplexity, but God's verdict was that '[he has] spoken of me what is right', unlike his friends.[13] Job 'strengthened his heart' by resisting his friends' criticisms and holding on to God in *questioning* trust. Interestingly there was 'compassion and mercy' also for Job's friends, when they offered the sacrifice the Lord asked for, and Job prayed for them.[14]

So James' message is to keep going, strengthen our resolve, and make sure that we leave all judgment to God, because *the Judge is standing at the doors!* There is a beautiful twist around the name of the Judge here: *the Lord* in whose name the prophets spoke (10) was Yahweh, the God of Israel, but *the Lord* who is imminently coming as Judge is the Lord Jesus. Without any sense of inappropriateness, the identity of 'the Lord' shifts, and with it the terror around judgment. The Judge who comes is our *compassionate and merciful* Saviour.

This shift in God's identity also pops up in our next passage:

4. Titus 2:11–15: expecting the glory!

For the grace of God has appeared, bringing salvation to all, training us to renounce impiety and worldly passions, and in the present age to live lives that are self-controlled, upright, and godly, while we wait for the blessed

---

[12] See above, pp. 242–244 (ch. 19, section 1).

[13] Job 42:7.

[14] Job 42:8–9.

hope and the manifestation of the glory of our great God and Saviour,
Jesus Christ. He it is who gave himself for us that he might redeem us from
all iniquity and purify for himself a people of his own who are zealous for
good deeds.

Declare these things; exhort and reprove with all authority. Let no one
look down on you.

This is such a rich passage! Paul wants Titus to have solid and clear perspectives on the Christian life, so that his teaching (15) will be authoritative and effective. These verses hinge around the repetition of the word *appeared* (11), which is also translated *manifestation* in verse 13. It's the same word in Paul's Greek, the verb in verse 11 and the related noun in verse 13. God's *grace* appears in verse 11 and his *glory* in verse 13 – although it's fascinating to see that the *glory* is that of Jesus Christ, who is here directly called *God*. The glory of God and the glory of Jesus Christ have merged.[15] Between the two sits the word *wait* (13a) – the activity which bridges the gap between the appearance of the grace and the appearance of the glory.

Wait for is not a good translation: 'expect' would be better, because 'waiting' is passive whereas 'expecting' is much more active. 'We're expecting a baby!' means that life has been turned upside down, and is now full of plans, purchases and paintbrushes – not to mention a plethora of medical appointments! Definitely not passive. After the coming of the grace, and before the coming of the glory, there is an appropriate 'expecting' which is much more than just 'waiting for' like a queue at a bus stop.

This is because God's grace appeared with a purpose. Paul summarizes the purpose in verse 11b and then unpacks it in verse 12. Again *bringing salvation to all* (11b) is not a great translation: it reads more like the result of the appearing than its purpose. 'With saving intent for all people' would be a better paraphrase. The intent? That we (that is, we humans – the 'all people' of v. 11) should learn two things:

- Negatively, to reject the world's way of being human, centred on our own desires and ignoring the call of worship (12a); and

---

[15] NRSV has an alternative translation (possible, but less likely) in the margin: 'the glory of the great God and our Saviour Jesus Christ'. But even if the alternative is right and Paul does not explicitly call Jesus 'God', still the glory of the one is the glory of the other: just one glory (*God's*) is revealed when *Christ* appears.

- Positively, to live well in this world in the three relational dimensions of human life (12b):
  - inwardly with ourselves (*self-controlled*);
  - outwardly with others (*upright* – that is, with justice, rightly);
  - upwardly with God (*godly* – lives centred on worship).

Paul gives another summary of the purpose of God's grace in verse 14, which begins with a 'who' describing what Jesus was doing. Again there is a negative and a positive:

- He rescues us from lawlessness, from living contrary to his design for human life; and
- He purifies us to be his own special people *zealous for good deeds*.

Again we can see this is no passive 'waiting for'! As we 'expect' his appearance manifesting his glory, we work at being what his first appearance aimed to achieve: we seek to be a *people* who reject bad ways of being in favour of belonging to him, and who show their connection with Jesus by doing good things with zeal. In other words, we try to be *now* what he came to make us, so that his work as *Saviour* is well on the way to completion when he comes in glory! His glory arises from the success of his work. The question will be: has he truly created a people clinging to him, redeemed from the world and keen to do the good deeds he loves? And the answer will be: Yes!

It's fascinating to reflect on the implication that he wants us to be *a people . . . zealous for good deeds* not only now, but also in the new creation after his return: what will *good deeds* look like there?

So what about the 'because' and the 'therefore' in this passage? We must 'be ready' for Christ's return *because* being ready for him is the whole purpose of his work of salvation! There is nothing else, nothing apart from this. There is no version of the Christian life which makes sense without this emphasis on being ready for his coming in glory – at least, no authentic New Testament account of the Christian life. We are to be a people prepared for him!

And *therefore . . .*

- Get cracking! Let's get stuck into the *good deeds* that sit before us, and let's undertake them as *a people* who belong to him, consciously living by different values (where necessary) from those of the world around us.

- Let's talk about it! Paul encourages Titus to make the second coming and its practical implications a clear focus in his teaching (15). He could be speaking directly to us, too. For Paul, the ethics of the Christian life and the commitment of the church to practical service in Christ's name are *directly* related to his coming in glory. His glory as Saviour is that he has truly created this special people – his work has worked! We need teaching in the church that unpacks this connection.

Our fourth passage digs further into this sense of being a special people who already belong elsewhere:

5. Colossians 3:1–4: alive with Christ!

So if you have been raised with Christ, seek the things that are above, where Christ is, seated at the right hand of God. Set your minds on things that are above, not on things that are on earth, for you have died, and your life has been[16] *hidden with Christ in God. When Christ who is your life is revealed, then you also will be revealed with him in glory.*

We can see in verse 4 similar ideas to those we met in 1 John 3 above (that *we* are going to be *revealed* as well as Jesus, when he comes again), with the addition of the idea of *glory*. Paul attaches the word 'glory' to this future revelation of ourselves also in Romans 8:18: 'I consider that the sufferings of this present time are not worth comparing with the glory about to be revealed to us' – and here 'to us' does not mean that we will be mere spectators of someone else's glory, as when watching a show. We are to be participants in it – 'glorified with him', in fact.[17] So *in glory* in Colossians 3:4 means that the glory covers us: it's Christ's, but ours as well because we are *with him*. This is describing an experience which it is impossible to unpack further, granted our present cognitive capacity! What will that be like, to be 'in' his glory? What is this 'glory'? We will know it when we see it – or rather, when we see *him*, and ourselves at the same time.

---

[16] NRSV has *is hidden*, but 'has been hidden' is more accurate: a perfect tense pointing to a past act with present consequences.

[17] Rom. 8:17.

Verse 4 also reminds us of 1 Thessalonians 4:14, where Paul writes about the dead in Christ coming 'with him' at his return.[18] As we saw when we looked at that passage, the key to Paul's teaching is that the dead are already 'in' Christ, and therefore must come 'with' him when he returns. How can they be anywhere else? But what Paul said about the dead in 1 Thessalonians 4 he says about the living here! The Colossians are still living and breathing, but Paul tells them that they must think of themselves as dead already, because *your life has been hidden with Christ in God* (3). It's the same point the other way round: in 1 Thessalonians the dead are alive because they are in Christ, while here the alive are dead because they are in Christ. Either way, whether physically alive or physically dead, *Christ . . . is your life* (4).

This is an incredibly radical view of human being. We have no life apart from Christ, and when he appears we will truly see what our life is, because *he is our life*. Indeed, our present life is *hidden with Christ in God* (3) – we are not what we appear to be! We are so much more – already 'raised . . . up with him and seated . . . with him in the heavenly places in Christ Jesus'.[19] It seems as if we are in two places at once! Can we get our heads around this?[20]

Behind it lies the Old Testament perspective that God breathes his breath, the breath of life, into human beings, so that the 'spirit' in us – our livingness – is a gift of God and a presence of *his* 'spirit' within us. All human beings have this 'breath': it's not enough to form a 'soul' that keeps us alive after death, but it makes us distinctively human, in God's 'image', and capable of entering into special relationship with God by his grace (like Israel in covenant with him). And some are given extra 'doses' of Spirit to make them kings or prophets or wise. In the New Testament this giving of God's Spirit to human beings is gloriously expanded, so that it is no longer restricted to kings or prophets,[21] but the basic perspective remains. God's Spirit within us is not an extra, separate gift added to our basic humanity. God's Spirit-breath is the very basis of our humanity, the aliveness of our bodies, but now brought into intimate connection with Christ – because amazingly the Spirit of God is now the Spirit *of Christ*.[22]

---

[18] See above, ch. 10, esp. section 3 (pp. 125–128).

[19] Eph. 2:6.

[20] See the reflections above on time and eternity – ch. 9, section 4 (pp. 113–115).

[21] See Joel 2:28–32 quoted and fulfilled on the day of Pentecost (Acts 2:16–21)!

[22] This is all very helpfully explored in John R. Levison, *Filled with the Spirit* (Grand Rapids, MI: Eerdmans, 2009).

The Spirit of Christ is that life of God animating all human beings, but *savingly* present within all who open themselves to Christ in faith and respond to his promise of 'abundant life'[23] – a life that opens up glorious new possibilities in knowing him and following him day by day. He *is* our life, and one day we will see him face to face.

So the 'because' is clear: we must 'be ready' for his return because he is already the life within us, and in a deep sense therefore our life is *not here* but *there*, where Christ is. *You have been raised with Christ* is Paul's starting point (1). This principle of resurrection with Christ has a kind of spatial component for Paul: to be raised *with* him means truly being *with* him where he is, and therefore we can't truly see ourselves while we can't see him. *[Our] life has been hidden with Christ in God* (3).

And the 'therefore'? *Seek the things that are above, where Christ is, seated at the right hand of God. Set your minds on things that are above, not on things that are on earth* (1–2). It would be possible to interpret this as a call to mysticism and to visionary experiences, but this would be far from Paul's mind. He has just been encouraging the Colossians not to listen to people who emphasize such experiences – they are actually a distraction from 'holding fast' to Jesus, he says.[24] No – because Jesus is our *total* life, and not just a spiritual life added on top of our humanity, we need to seek him in everything: in all our relationships and all the embodied behaviours and activities that occupy us daily. This is what the rest of Colossians 3 unpacks – reaching a climax in 3:17: 'And whatever you do, in word or deed, do everything in the name of the Lord Jesus, giving thanks to God the Father through him.'

This is what it means to *seek* or 'think on' *the things that are above*: seeking to live our embodied life now, in every detail, 'in the name' of Jesus (that is, knowing that his identity rests on us and defines who we are), and using our minds to give thanks to God, because the voice of worship is the breath of his Spirit within us.

6. And so . . .

In different ways, these passages all unpack the same message: we need to 'be ready' for Christ's return by bringing our lives into line with what we

---

[23] John 10:10.
[24] Col. 2:18–19.

will be when we see him – in fact, with what we *already are* because his life is already in us. That means purifying ourselves, enduring suffering patiently and leaving all judgment to him, getting cracking on the 'good deeds' which mark us out as his people, and focusing on him in worship because all our life is 'hidden' in him. Our very life-breath is Jesus within us,[25] and one day that will no longer be hidden!

We are nearly at the end of our journey through the second coming. We have one more passage to look at, which forms a fitting finale to the book. We started with a psalm in which David looks back over his life, and we end with a passage in which Paul is doing the same, and showing us how the second coming has shaped him and currently gives him hope as he faces death. It's not over yet!

---

[25] Cf. Gal. 2:19–20.

2 Timothy 4:1–8

21. The final charge

We cannot do better, at the end of this book, than sit with Timothy as he reads Paul's final charge to him – maybe the last words he ever heard from Paul his great mentor and father in Christ:

> *In the presence of God and of Christ Jesus, who is to judge the living and the dead, and in view of his appearing and his kingdom, I solemnly urge you: proclaim the message; be persistent whether the time is favourable or unfavourable; convince, rebuke and encourage, with the utmost patience in teaching. For the time is coming when people will not put up with sound doctrine, but having itching ears, they will accumulate for themselves teachers to suit their own desires, and will turn away from listening to the truth and wander away to myths. As for you, always be sober, endure suffering, do the work of an evangelist, carry out your ministry fully.*
>
> *As for me, I am already being poured out as a libation, and the time of my departure has come. I have fought the good fight, I have finished the race, I have kept the faith. From now on there is reserved for me the crown of righteousness, which the Lord, the righteous judge, will give to me on that day, and not only to me but also to all who have longed for his appearing.*

We can never know what impact these words had on Timothy, but we can allow them to impact us today. What feelings and reactions rise within you?

I'm struck by what an incredible *campaigner* Paul was. Reviewing his life, it's not writing letters that stands out! It has been a *fight* and a *race* (7), and he has kept going with huge energy and determination, and now urges Timothy to do the same. In his exhortations to Timothy in verse 2, we can see a picture of how Paul himself pressed urgently onward in his ministry. We've touched on some of the underlying reasons for this passion. In particular, he thought that the gospel had to be taken to the whole Gentile world within one generation, and then Jesus would come.[1] Would he expect us to live with less passion, because it has turned out that both the world and the task are much bigger than he thought?

There's no doubt that the fact of the second coming underlies and energizes Paul's passion here. Notice how the paragraph begins and ends (1, 8) with Jesus' *appearing*, which is the basis of Paul's solemn appeal to Timothy (1). *I have kept the faith*, he says (7), thinking particularly of faith in *this* Christ, the one who will appear as *judge* of *the living and the dead*. Notice again how *the Lord* in verse 8 is the Lord Jesus, who (as in v. 1) takes over God's prerogative to exercise judgment over God's world.

This is a kind of 'last will and testament' from Paul to Timothy, as Paul passes on the *key passions* that have underlain his life as an apostle. His passion, fuelled by the coming of the judge, has three practical focuses here:

1. It's all about ministry

Paul's last encouragement to Timothy is to *carry out your ministry fully* (5). He wants to leave Timothy well equipped – as he has just said, 'proficient, equipped for every good work'.[2] Two things stand out in his encouragements to Timothy about his ministry here:

a. There's no distinction between evangelizing and pastoring

We tend to distinguish quite clearly between these. Evangelists are those who preach the gospel to non-believers, and pastors and teachers then take over, to nurture converts in the faith. But Paul never made such a distinction, although he lists them separately in the 'ministries of the Word' in Ephesians 4:11. He did both himself, and encourages Timothy to do the same, because both are about 'proclaiming the message' (2) and encouraging people to understand it and then live by it.

---

[1] See particularly ch. 11, section 5 (p. 142).

[2] 2 Tim. 3:17.

b. There's no distinction between the life and the work of the minister

Paul's encouragement to *do the work of an evangelist* is preceded by *always be sober, endure suffering* (5) – as though Timothy will not be able to preach the gospel if the practices of his life, away from the public arena, do not match the message. He may mouth the message, but it won't be the gospel if his life doesn't fit.

Always be sober means never using artificial means to dull the pains of the ministry, whatever they are – and so it goes closely with the paired encouragement to *endure suffering*. Ministry is tough, demanding every resource we have. It takes us into close connection with all the horrors of the fallen world, and Paul encourages Timothy (and us) truly to feel the pain of this. We must be ready to 'weep with those who weep',[3] and to deal with whatever internal or external strategies we might have for pulling back and not really allowing ourselves to be touched by the pain of others. Once again Job's friends come to mind: at the heart of their 'grumbling' against Job (which was dressed up as pastoral care!) was their own comforting theology which enabled them to feel good about themselves and gave them a clear, uncomplicated world in which the good are rewarded and the wicked punished.[4]

Which leads us neatly into the next of Paul's focuses:

2. It's all about theology

Paul's passion is for the true gospel, what he calls *sound doctrine* in verse 3. *Doctrine* here is more precisely 'teaching', and this expression 'sound teaching' is a favourite in the letters to Timothy and Titus.[5] 'Sound' means more literally 'healthy', and this connection with health comes out in Titus 2:1–2, where Paul encourages Titus to 'teach what is consistent with [healthy] doctrine', and then immediately urges that 'elders' should be (among other things) 'healthy' in faith – using the same word. So here in 2 Timothy 4:3 'health-giving teaching' would not be an inappropriate translation. N. T. Wright translates it with 'healthy teaching'. There is teaching that nourishes our spiritual, moral and emotional health, and there is teaching that undermines it.

---

[3] Rom. 12:15.

[4] See above, ch. 20, section 3 (pp. 258–259).

[5] See 1 Tim. 1:10; Titus 1:9; 2:1; and the closely related 'sound words' in 1 Tim. 6:3; 2 Tim. 1:13.

The trouble is, theological junk food is often cheaper, more attractively packaged and easier on the tongue, like the theology of Job's friends. But it leaves us ill-nourished and it compromises our spiritual immune system – our capacity to discern good from bad. Such is its attractiveness that Paul doesn't just warn Timothy against it as a possibility, he *predicts* that he will have to deal with it: *the time is coming when* . . . (3). Here *time* is *kairos*, and for sure Paul is not thinking of just *one* time when this will happen. This is going to be a constant issue – and isn't that true?

Paul gives Timothy a way of spotting bad theology. The problem with junk-food teaching is its motivation: it aims to *suit their own desires* and to tickle *itching ears* (3). *Myths* (4) lead people astray because they don't challenge people's desires, but give people good reasons for believing what they want to anyway. People go off hunting for teaching that confirms their own inclinations. But as we saw in Titus 2:11–15, the whole purpose of the work of salvation is to rescue us from 'worldly desires' and to 'cleanse' us so that we become a new people, specially shaped for the new creation and 'zealous for good works'[6] that match it. 'Healthy teaching' is all about retraining our desires precisely so that they become focused upon Christ and the 'expectation' of his coming.

We saw in chapter 16, too, how Peter emphasizes the training of desire ('sincere intention') as basic in our engagement with the world and the development of a public faith.[7] The development of a capacity for spiritual discernment is so important, and is a theme beloved by Paul.[8]

So Paul is also providing us with a definition of *good* theology. Good theology doesn't pander to our instincts, giving us easy reasons for feeling good about ourselves, but it faces us with the difficult questions we don't want to ask. Indeed it rubs our noses in them. We've faced a few in the course of this book – most notably the question that underlies the whole *raison d'être* of Paul's ministry: why, if Jesus came to save the world, do we have to *wait* for the salvation of the world? Why does he ascend to heaven rather than bring in his kingdom straight away? Why does he make it necessary for there to be evangelists and pastors who embrace lives of intense suffering in order to spread the message of Christ?

---

6 See above ch. 20, section 4 (pp. 259–262). NRSV has 'worldly passions' in Titus 2:12, but the Greek word is the same.

7 2 Pet. 3:1–4: above, ch. 16, section 3 (pp. 203–205).

8 See Rom. 12:2; Eph. 1:17–18; Phil. 1:9–10; also Heb. 5:14.

We've wrestled with this and some answers have appeared: at the heart of them, the value of this 'gospel' period, when people like Paul urge us (the church) to grow in faith, learning to strengthen our trust in the coming kingdom and the Lord who will bring it, and in the meantime learning to extend his love into all the world. Faith, hope and love expand while he does not come – but it's tough. Right now, faith hope and love need to grapple with the huge issues of climate change and the international relationships that make tackling it so difficult. No easy answers, no simple solutions, no quick affirmation of our own pet ideas. Just tough commitment – faithful, hopeful, loving.

Good theology keeps the focus on Jesus, but then allows new thoughts about God and the world and the outworking of his purposes. *I have kept the faith* (7) does not mean never questioning it, but precisely (like Job!) asking the difficult questions out of trust in God's goodness and Christ's love, and not sticking to the stock answers. In this way *the faith* is *kept* from being irrelevant and other-worldly. Why should we continue to believe in the second coming of Jesus Christ? It would be easy to give it up, or just tacitly ignore it. But – good theology says – it is the basis of hope in a hopeless world, and hope vanishes if all we have are differently phrased versions of the worldly answers around us.

3. It's all about judgment

Here's another unpopular idea. But Paul's passion is deeply driven by his belief in coming judgment – again, notice how Christ is called the *judge* in verses 1 and 8, forming an *inclusio* around the passage with the word *appearing*.[9]

How does Paul think of this coming judgment? What does he expect? Since he has invested so much in his ministry, we might expect that (like other high achievers) he might be anxious in case he hasn't done enough. The drive to achieve more can be relentless. But he is clearly not worried that the Judge will be critical of him and point out his shortcomings: *From now on there is reserved for me the crown of righteousness, which the Lord, the righteous judge, will give to me on that day* (8). Is he being presumptuous?

---

[9] An *inclusio* is a literary feature often found in the Bible whereby a passage begins and ends with the same words or ideas, thus marking (1) its extent, and (2) its key ideas, or some of them.

No: because he is not expecting a reward for his labours. The same prize (*the crown of righteousness*) is to be given not to 'all who have laboured hard for the Lord' (or some such language), but to *all who have longed for his appearing* (8). The qualification for the prize is to *long for* the appearance of the Judge – hardly a sign that the judgment is going to be fearful! Actually *longed for* here is the Greek word 'love', which to my mind is even stronger: 'all who have loved his appearing'. This *agape*-love is the distinguishing mark of Christian service and ministry,[10] and it's what holds together the hard work and the confidence facing judgment: love of Jesus motivates both. We serve because we love him, we love him because he loves us, and we love the thought of his coming because we will see him face to face, and the *crown of righteousness* will be the final, wonderful capstone on the story of our salvation.

Righteousness is what God gives us in Christ when we are 'justified by faith',[11] and *the crown* of righteousness is that final entering into the glory of his kingdom, in which rule is shared. *Crown* in verse 8 connects with *kingdom* in verse 1 (another element of the *inclusio* in these verses). Paul looks forward to sharing the rule with Christ and with all who 'love' *his appearing* – we are reminded of the saints who rise to rule with Christ in Revelation 20:4.[12] So judgment for Paul is definitely not something he fears, but not because he knows he's done well enough to get through! The crown is the final gift sealing his 'justification by faith', and he *loves* the thought of Christ appearing with it in his hand.

At one time Paul talked about 'we who are alive, who are left'[13] when Jesus comes, implying that he thought he would still be living. But now it is clear that his death is close: *the time of my departure has come* (6). He knows he will not live to see the second coming. But his expectation of the *appearing* and of *the crown of righteousness* seem to be just as vivid as if it *were* the second coming that was about to happen, rather than his death. In fact, *that day* (8) is somewhat ambiguous: does it refer to the day of his death, or the day of the second coming, or (most likely) both?

I think we are finding further scriptural support for the idea that the moment of our death *is* the moment of the second coming for us: immediately we are there, at the last judgment, receiving *the crown of righteousness*.

---

[10] See John 13:34–35.

[11] See Rom. 4:1–8; Phil. 3:8–9.

[12] See above, ch. 18, section 3 (p. 232).

[13] 1 Thess. 4:17. Cf. 1 Cor. 15:51, 'We will not all die, but we will all be changed.'

There is an interesting coming together of our two time perspectives here. From a *chronos*-perspective, we reign with Christ for a thousand years until the end comes. From a *kairos*-perspective, the end is already with us and the new creation is already in place,[14] implicit in Jesus' resurrection and ascension and the gift of the Spirit. And in Christ we are already reigning.[15] Either way, the crown comes with our death, whether we reign with him after death and *prior to* the final resurrection and judgment, or whether we shoot straight to the final resurrection and judgment at the moment of death. Both perspectives are equally scriptural and equally encouraging!

This is a fitting place at which to 'draw stumps' on our journey: sitting with Timothy as he reads these words, gives thanks for his wonderful father in Christ, hears his encouragements for his ministry, and shares his excitement and thankfulness for the end of the journey that lies immediately ahead. By the time Timothy read them, possibly some weeks after Paul wrote them, the crown could have been firmly in place on Paul's brow at the appearing of his Lord, the righteous judge!

---

[14] Remember 2 Cor. 5:17.
[15] See Rom. 5:17, 21.

Epilogue

In this book we have focused on the second coming, but 'eschatology' is much bigger. As we met them we have touched on other eschatological themes also, such as judgment, heaven and hell, and the new creation; but all of these need much fuller treatment (especially judgment), and some 'eschatological' themes have hardly appeared at all (sanctification, for instance, and the great Hebrews theme of 'perfection', and the theme of the kingdom of God). Many of these biblical themes, of course, are studied in other volumes in The Bible Speaks Today series. But we've managed to gather all the main 'second coming' passages and look at them in their context, with an eye to letting them speak for themselves as clearly as possible. I hope your journey as a reader has been as much fun as mine in writing!

For me the challenge to *live it* is the standout message: to *live* the second coming in such a way that it truly impacts my everyday ways of being.

We have travelled a long way in this book, matching the long journey that we are all on towards the Heavenly City. It would be appropriate to finish with one of Paul's glorious prayers, which is certainly my prayer for all who make it this far through this book!

> As for you, may the Lord make you increase and overflow in love for one another and for all (just as we overflow with love for you), so that your hearts may be strengthened and made blameless in holiness before our God and Father at the coming of our Lord Jesus with all his saints![1]

---

[1] 1 Thess. 3:12–13, my translation.

The Message of the Second Coming

We can do nothing better to live out the second coming than to learn to 'abound in' love for one another in his name, and to let that experience of love point beyond our present to the future we have in him. The little phrase 'and for all' is fascinating (12): this is an expansive love, one which reaches beyond the bounds of the Christian fellowship and stretches outwards. It 'overflows' in ways that touch the lives of 'all' – and at this point in our history there's no doubt that this must especially include all who suffer the effects of climate change and who are victims of war and refugees from conflicts worldwide. Our 'blamelessness' and 'holiness' before God, when Jesus comes, will be shaped by their needs.

I'm writing this Epilogue on Advent Sunday 2021 – the annual reminder in the calendar of how vital it is to keep hope alive, focused on him. It so happens that COP26, the world summit on the response to climate change, took place here in the UK just a few weeks ago. For a brief moment, world attention was grabbed by the vital issues at stake through potentially catastrophic global warming in this century. 'Love for all' will be shaped in us by these issues, as the decades unfold from now. Let love be the life-breath of the Spirit in us, strengthening us in faith, hope and holiness for all that lies ahead, and finally for his coming!

Study guide

Introduction

Many Christians either find the subject of the second coming of Jesus impossible to understand, or they have accepted one particular interpretation which prevents them from approaching this topic with an open mind.

The purpose of this study guide is to enable you as a group (or an individual) to study a wide range of biblical texts from both the Old and New Testaments on this crucial doctrine, using *The Message of the Second Coming* as an aid. Steve Motyer makes clear his own interpretation. The aim is that his understanding will enrich the discussion of the Bible rather than pushing the discussion into a dispute as to whether or not he has got it right! Since this is a relatively rapid journey through the subject, discussion of minute detail and interpretations will not be possible – which may not be a bad thing!

The guidelines expect the leader to have read this book and that a few copies will be available for use in the discussion time. Obviously the more members who have read the book, the better. The leader will need to have prepared well but it is hoped that all members will also come prepared, having read the relevant Bible passages.

At the end of these studies each member should have a much better understanding of the second coming. Also, their hopes and fears for the present and future will be viewed far more from God's perspective. Pray that this will be so.

PART 1: THE SECOND COMING IN THE OLD TESTAMENT

ⓠ Psalms 89 – 90
1. History and time (pp. 7–18)

1 How do you respond to the stories behind these psalms – Ethan's experience of the destruction of Jerusalem, and Moses' experience of exile and lostness in the desert?

2 Which verses in these psalms touched you most, and why?

3 Do you know anyone who is facing disappointment like Ethan at the moment? What would Ethan say to this person, do you think?

4 Why did Moses have to wait so long (forty years) before he met God in the burning bush? Was God punishing him for his sins?

5 Why do you think God has structured our experience of him in this way – so that we have to live in *hope* of seeing and being with him, rather than experiencing him fully right now?

ⓠ Psalm 18
2. Presence in power (pp. 19–31)

1 In what ways can you echo David's experience of being rescued by God in desperate situations?

2 How do you think we should interpret, and apply to ourselves, what David writes about victory in battle? (See verses 37–42.)

3 Under what circumstances could we echo David's words that 'the Lord has recompensed me according to my righteousness' (24)? Compare Isaiah 64:6; Psalm 14:2–3; Romans 7:14–25. Does God reward us for being good in this life? or in the life to come? or not at all?

4 How do you imagine the second coming of Jesus taking place? What will it look/feel like for those alive at the time?

5 If we read the psalm with Jesus in mind, how should we understand verses 40–42?

ⓠ Daniel 7:1–28
3. The beasts and the Son of Man (pp. 32–43)

1 What thoughts and emotional reactions does Daniel 7 inspire in you?

2 As you review your reading of Daniel 7, what features of his vision stand out for you – and why?

3 Where do you think we see the 'beasts' in the world today? How does Daniel 7 help us to interpret the powers under which people live?

4 Read Matthew 8:19–20; 9:6; 12:40; and 24:27–30 (four 'Son of Man' sayings). How does Daniel 7 help us to understand these sayings?

5 What difference might it make to our prayers, to address Jesus as 'Son of Man' rather than as 'Lord'?

ⓠ Zechariah 14:1–21
4. 'A day is coming for the LORD'! (pp. 44–55)

1 How would you summarize the message of Zechariah 14 for today? What stands out for you?

2 Steve Motyer's exposition defends a 'non-literal' reading of Zechariah 14. What do you think of this, bearing in mind that others want to understand these prophecies much more literally? Should we expect a literal remodelling of the Mount of Olives, and a literal reinstatement of the feast of Tabernacles?

3 What does the image of 'living waters' mean to you?

4 Can we think of all our tools and possessions as 'holy to the LORD', like the horse bells and cooking pots in verses 20–21? What difference might it make to think of our 'things' in this way?

5 Zechariah's vision is truly universal, with the Lord as the future 'king over all the earth' (9). What are the key features of his coming universal rule, both in this chapter and elsewhere in the Bible? In what ways should we prepare for it?

PART 2: THE SECOND COMING IN THE GOSPELS AND ACTS

ⓠ Acts 1:6–11; 3:17–21
5. Refreshments to follow (pp. 59–70)

1 Can you remember (and describe, if you are in a group) a 'time of refreshing' in your life? Spend time praying for people who need refreshment.

2 Luke's emphasis is strongly on the task of 'evangelism' – spreading the gospel worldwide. How should we be doing this today?

3 In what ways should we, like the disciples, wait for the Holy Spirit to empower us for mission? What would this 'waiting' look like?

4 New human beings are constantly joining the race. How will it ever be possible to have fully proclaimed the gospel to the whole world? What will this look like?

5 Steve Motyer writes: 'Our witness *at home* is still our primary responsibility' (p. 64), referring to the way in which the disciples will have to return to Galilee to bear witness there. What are the special challenges of witnessing 'at home'? How can we do it better?

ⓠ Luke 17:20 – 18:8
6. Will he find faith on the earth? (pp. 71–82)

1 Faith is a prominent theme in this passage. As you respond to it, how would you define the 'faith' that the Son of Man will look for when he comes?

2 Steve Motyer argues strongly against expecting a 'Rapture' ahead of the second coming. Do you agree? What impact should Luke 17:34–35 have on our expectations and our lives?

3 Where do you see the kingdom already working in the world? In what, particularly? How do you respond?

4 There is a strong impetus here against materialism and the piling up of possessions that claim our attention and focus, so that we are distracted from longing for 'one of the days of the Son of Man'. How can we avoid falling into this trap?

5 The chapter in the book ends with a challenging question: 'How might – should – this passage impact our prayer?' What response do you give?

ⓠ Matthew 24:1–44
7. The coming of the Son of Man (pp. 83–95)

1 How can each of us play our part in the task of 'proclaiming the gospel to all the nations'?

2 Jesus warned his disciples against being led astray by 'false messiahs and false prophets' during the period of terrible disturbance and suffering leading up to the fall of Jerusalem (24), and he makes this warning general for all of us in verses 4–5 and 11. What does this mean for us today? What or whom should we avoid?

3 Read again Jesus' predictions of the coming sufferings, both international (6–7) and personal (9–13), which are all signs of the end like the first labour pains (8). How do you respond to his words?

4 Can we definitely say that the good news has not yet been 'proclaimed throughout the world' (14), and therefore Jesus will not come tomorrow?

(Q) Matthew 24:45 – 25:46
8. Parables of preparation (pp. 96–107)

1 Jesus wants us to 'keep awake' and to 'be ready'. What do you think these two commands mean for us practically, in everyday life?

2 What dangers does Jesus warn against in these parables? How can we avoid them?

3 What 'talents' has the Master left with you, to put to work for him until he returns? Do a little audit: how are you getting on? Let others help you with the audit, if possible.

4 The 'sheep and the goats' parable seems to give an absolute priority to practical social action and care, rather than preaching the gospel to convert people. Is that a correct impression? How do 'evangelism' and 'social action' fit together?

5 Do you think 'the righteous' (25:37 etc.) are *all* who engage in compassionate action for the poor, the sick and the despised, or are they just the followers of Jesus who do this?

(Q) John 14:1–31
9. At home with the Lord (pp. 108–117)

1 What do you expect to experience after death? How does this passage help you to imagine it?

2 How do we experience Jesus 'coming' to us here and now? What does it look and feel like?

3 The 'home' that Jesus makes among us with his Father (23) seems to be his answer to Judas' implied question about how he will reveal himself to the world (22). According to this passage, what will (or should) the world see that will show that Jesus is at home with us? How do you feel about that?

4 What do you think about Steve Motyer's speculation about time and eternity (section 4), which means that (a) our death is the moment when we experience the second coming, and (b) that we will be

immediately united not just with the Lord but with all who belong to him, including future generations? Do you agree?

PART 3: THE SECOND COMING IN THE LETTERS OF PAUL

ⓠ 1 Thessalonians 4:13 – 5:11
10. The coming of the Lord: Part 1 (pp. 121–132)

1 Which aspect of Paul's teaching in this passage do you find most exciting or challenging – and why?
2 See 1 Thessalonians 5:8: why are faith, love and hope vital as armour to help us be ready for the second coming?
3 What questions would you like to ask Paul about life after death, or about the second coming? Does this passage help at all with answers to your questions?
4 How can talking or thinking about the second coming 'encourage' us (4:18; 5:11)?
5 Paul is clear that we will be 'together with them' (4:17), that is, united with those who have already died. Who are you especially looking forward to meeting or being reunited with?

ⓠ 2 Thessalonians 2:1–12
11. The coming of the Lord: Part 2 (pp. 133–146)

1 There are so many different views of the 'last things', including many who say that we are in the very last days and Jesus is surely coming very soon. How should we evaluate such views?
2 Steve Motyer suggests that Paul's teaching is building on Jesus' prediction of a coming 'abomination of desolation' or 'desolating sacrilege' (see Matt. 24:15), and that this was partially fulfilled in the events leading up to the Jewish War in AD 67–70. How do you think we should apply this prophecy today? What do you think a 'desolating sacrilege' looks like in today's world?
3 Do you think that we Christians have a responsibility to 'unmask' evil and injustice in the world around us, or should we leave this to the Lord?
4 Is it part of God's plan that his people (the church of Jesus Christ) should be dominated by anti-God 'powers' and suffer persecution?

Why? And how can we cope? A look at Colossians 1:24 and
2 Corinthians 1:3–7 will help your thinking.

ⓆⓆ 1 Corinthians 15:20–28
12. 'He must reign until . . .' (pp. 147–158)

1 There are some quite complicated ideas but great richness in this
passage. What stands out for you from your reading? What is God
highlighting for you?

2 What do you think about the idea that 'the powers' are already being
'dethroned' or put out of commission in the church? Steve Motyer
writes, 'National, racial and economic barriers must tumble in him
as we foreshadow the new world coming' (p. 156). What should be the
practical outworkings of this?

3 Steve Motyer asks, 'What will this look like?' – to live in a world in which
all 'powers' have surrendered their rule to God and he has become 'all
in all' (15:28; see section 4, p. 158). What do you imagine it will look like?

4 Give some space to meditating on the *spirituality* of your body – your
body as a 'limb of Christ' (see 1 Cor. 6:15). How do you feel about this?
What difference might it make to your everyday life, to know that your
body is a 'limb of Christ'?

ⓆⓆ Romans 11:25–36
13. Mercy on all (pp. 159–171)

1 What do you think about the issue of 'evangelical universalism' as Steve
has represented it in this chapter?

2 On the basis of Romans 11:26, many believe in a 'mass conversion' of
Jews to Christ in the period just before his return. As you'll gather from
the chapter, Steve Motyer is not convinced that this is the right
interpretation. What do you think?

3 Is it really possible to praise God for the uncertainty that surrounds
our lives? What's the balance between being confident in who God is
(see 2 Tim. 1:12) and not knowing what he is up to (Rom. 11:33b)?

4 Do you think that, when Jesus comes again, people will *at that moment*
be offered a final opportunity to repent and receive the forgiveness of
their sins? If so, what are the implications of this?

5 Paul's whole purpose in this passage is to stop the Gentile believers
in Rome from being 'conceited' (11:25). How does the message of this
passage prevent conceit?

(Q) Philippians 3:1–21
14. The Saviour from heaven (pp. 172–184)

1 Steve Motyer writes about Philippians 3:12, 'In his grip we are secure, however tough the way' (p. 183). How have you experienced security in Christ when going through tough times in your life?

2 Why does Paul want to share the sufferings of Christ 'by becoming like him in his death' (3:10)? Is this a healthy desire?

3 Paul is deeply ambitious here: read again his words in verses 13–14. Can this passionate ambition for 'the prize of the heavenly call' fit with ordinary ambitions – for success in exams, family, career? How? Will such 'ordinary' ambitions always fall into the category he criticizes in verse 19 – 'their minds are set on earthly things'?

4 The Roman citizens in Philippi knew that they really 'belonged' elsewhere – in Rome. How do you feel about 'really belonging' in heaven (3:20)?

5 How can we live 'now in a transformed way that anticipates "the day of Jesus Christ"' (Steve's summary of Paul's message in Phil. 3, p. 176)? What are the main features of that 'transformation'?

PART 4: THE SECOND COMING IN THE LATER NEW TESTAMENT

(Q) Hebrews 9:23–28
15. The high priest reappears (pp. 187–198)

1 What's your overall response to the message of Hebrews 9:23–28 as Steve Motyer has unpacked it in this chapter?

2 How helpful do you find Hebrews' use of the Day of Atonement rituals as a way of understanding the work of Christ, including the second coming?

3 What impact does it have on you to imagine Jesus 'interceding' for us in heaven right now? See also Romans 8:34, and Romans 8:26–27 where Paul applies the same idea to the Holy Spirit.

4 Steve says that Christ's ministry to cleanse the heavenly sanctuary (9:23–24) is 'a beautiful message to encourage sinners of all shapes and sizes' (p. 191). Probe your own heart to discover any ways in which you have felt, or still feel, that God is distant from you because of your sins. Seek to apply this message to yourself.

5   In the Day of Atonement picture, the people are 'eagerly waiting' outside the sanctuary for the high priest to reappear (9:28). How well does that describe the attitude to the second coming that you see (a) in the church generally, (b) in your own fellowship, and (c) in yourself?

2 Peter 3:1–18
16. The day of the Lord (pp. 199–211)

1   2 Peter 3 is quite a complex chapter. What stands out for you from reading it? What particularly strikes you? What questions are left for you?

2   Steve Motyer suggests that Peter is engaged in 'public theology' in this chapter, seeking to equip his readers to argue *for* the second coming and the fact of coming judgment 'out there' in the world, in the public sphere. Do you think we should do the same? How should we do it?

3   It's not fashionable now to denounce 'error' — we tend to 'live and let live' when it comes to people's beliefs. Is this right? Peter spends chapter 2 of this letter denouncing false teachers in the church, and warns his readers here not to be 'carried away with the error of the lawless' (3:17). Should we be more like Peter, or are there good reasons today for living with the existence of many false ideas, both within the church and outside it?

4   Think about the expectation summarized in verse 13. This is very different from simply 'going to heaven when we die'. What do you expect to see in the 'new heavens and . . . new earth'?

5   How can we make the most of the Lord's 'patience' (3:15)? What should we be doing, above all, so that it is 'salvation' for us?

Revelation 22:6–21
17. 'See, I am coming soon!' (pp. 212–224)

1   Once again there is huge richness in this Bible passage. Having read it and Steve Motyer's chapter on it, what stands out for you? Does anything in particular speak to you?

2   Steve underlines the *urgency* implied by Jesus' words 'I am coming soon'. Do you think that we regard the second coming as something happening *urgently*? How should it impact us?

3   How well do verses 10–17 work as a summary of the gospel message we have to share with people?

4 Steve suggests that this paragraph also serves to conclude the whole of Scripture, and thus prompts us to reflect on how well we 'keep' Scripture at the heart of our faith. What does the Bible mean to you? Do you want to add anything to it, or take anything away from it? How does its authority function for you?

5 'Let everyone who is thirsty come' (22:17). Spend some time identifying your deepest longings, and bringing them to Jesus.

ⓠ Revelation 19:1 – 22:5
18. The rider, the reign and the throne (pp. 225–238)

1 This chapter is a little longer than others and covers a great deal of ground. As you review it in your mind, what stands out for you to take away as encouragement or challenge?

2 Steve Motyer suggests that the thousand years (20:1–6) are not a literal future reign of Christ on earth after his second coming, but a picture of the present gospel age during which Satan is bound and the dead in Christ are already 'reigning' with him. What do you think of his interpretation?

3 Steve does not say much about the vision of the new Jerusalem coming down from heaven in chapter 21, except to say that it represents the full company of God's people redeemed by Christ, now pictured as a city in which God and the Lamb dwell (cf. John 14:23). How do you respond to this vision? What encouragements do you find in it?

4 Read again the basic 'second-coming' vision in 19:11–16, from which the whole final part of Revelation flows. How do you respond to the picture of Christ presented in this vision?

5 What do you make of the notion of 'the wrath of God' (19:15)? How do you understand God's 'wrath'?

PART 5: THE SECOND COMING AND THE CHRISTIAN LIFE

ⓠ Revelation 3:14–22; 1 Corinthians 11:17–34
19. Eating with Jesus (pp. 241–252)

1 Once again, review your reading of the two biblical passages and the chapter in the book by reflecting on what particularly stands out for you: has anything here held a particular message for you?

2 Think about the church to which you belong in the light of Jesus' words to the church in Laodicea. What do you think he might say to your church?

3 What has been your theology of the Lord's Supper (the Eucharist)? What do you think happens when we consecrate and eat bread and wine together in remembrance of Jesus? Has this chapter challenged or changed your thinking?

4 Can you give any instances in your experience where Jesus has 'shepherded you with a rod of iron'? What does it feel like to sit at table with him in the light of this history?

5 Steve Motyer uses Irvin Yalom's analysis of the four 'anxieties' of human life as a framework in this chapter. Which of these speaks to you most personally and pressingly?

6 Reflect on any ways in which you think that Jesus may be calling you to 'judge yourself' and take action to grasp your freedom in him. What is he calling you to do?

1 John 3:2–3; James 5:7–11; Titus 2:11–15; Colossians 3:1–4
20. Be ready! (pp. 253–265)

1 What are the absolutely key features of the 'family likeness' that God's people (his children) need to be showing in their lives?

2 And what are the absolutely key activities (the 'good deeds') for which God wants us to be 'zealous' as we wait for him (Titus 2:14)?

3 Many Christians want to emphasize our responsibility to care for the planet as at the heart of Christian witness and engagement today. As we 'wait' for Jesus to come, how vital is this ecological commitment to repairing the damage we have done to the world and caring for it – and how does this fit in with our responsibility to preach the gospel?

4 Steve Motyer emphasizes that we cannot know or understand ourselves fully in this life. How do you feel about that?

5 What's wrong with a good grumble? Some people recommend it as an emotional release, and counsellors encourage honest expression of our frustrations. Why does James say we shouldn't grumble, and how does this fit in with his commendation of Job who certainly did?

2 Timothy 4:1–8
21. The final charge/Epilogue (pp. 266–274)

1 What last will and testament would you like to pass on to those you leave behind? What would be your key message or encouragements?

2 Steve writes about the dangers of theological junk food. What bad theologies can you identify – wrong ideas which leave us 'ill-nourished and . . . compromise our spiritual immune system – our capacity to discern good from bad' (p. 269)?

3 Why is the 'crown of righteousness' reserved for those who 'love his appearing'? Don't you think that other achievements or qualities ought to be recognized more? To whom would you give 'the crown of righteousness'?

4 At several points in the book Steve Motyer underlines the special importance of the issue of climate change for Christian discipleship today. Is this just his bright idea, or do you think that this really is a key 'good deed' for Christians to embrace as we prepare ourselves for the coming of the Lord?

5 Has reading this book changed you? How do you feel now about the second coming of Jesus? Review before God the reactions you have felt in reading this book, and decide what (if any) lasting takeaways there are for you.

The Bible Speaks Today:
Old Testament series

The Message of Genesis 1 – 11

The dawn of creation

David Atkinson

The Message of Genesis 12 – 50

From Abraham to Joseph

Joyce G. Baldwin

The Message of Exodus

The days of our pilgrimage

Alec Motyer

The Message of Leviticus

Free to be holy

Derek Tidball

The Message of Numbers

Journey to the Promised Land

Raymond Brown

The Message of Deuteronomy

Not by bread alone

Raymond Brown

The Message of Joshua

Promise and people

David G. Firth

The Message of Judges

Grace abounding

Michael Wilcock

The Message of Ruth

The wings of refuge

David Atkinson

The Message of 1 and 2 Samuel

Personalities, potential, politics and power

Mary J. Evans

The Message of 1 and 2 Kings

God is present

John W. Olley

The Message of 1 and 2 Chronicles

One church, one faith, one Lord

Michael Wilcock

The Message of Ezra and Haggai

Building for God

Robert Fyall

The Message of Nehemiah

God's servant in a time of change

Raymond Brown

The Message of Esther

God present but unseen

David G. Firth

The Message of Job

Suffering and grace

David Atkinson

The Message of Psalms 1 – 72
Songs for the people of God
Michael Wilcock

The Message of Psalms 73 – 150
Songs for the people of God
Michael Wilcock

The Message of Proverbs
Wisdom for life
David Atkinson

The Message of Ecclesiastes
A time to mourn, and a time to dance
Derek Kidner

The Message of the Song of Songs
The lyrics of love
Tom Gledhill

The Message of Isaiah
On eagles' wings
Barry Webb

The Message of Jeremiah
Grace in the end
Christopher J. H. Wright

The Message of Lamentations
Honest to God
Christopher J. H. Wright

The Message of Ezekiel
A new heart and a new spirit
Christopher J. H. Wright

The Message of Daniel
His kingdom cannot fail
Dale Ralph Davis

The Message of Hosea
Love to the loveless
Derek Kidner

The Message of Joel, Micah and Habakkuk
Listening to the voice of God
David Prior

The Message of Amos
The day of the lion
Alec Motyer

The Message of Obadiah, Nahum and Zephaniah
The kindness and severity of God
Gordon Bridger

The Message of Jonah
Presence in the storm
Rosemary Nixon

The Message of Zechariah
Your kingdom come
Barry Webb

The Message of Malachi
'I have loved you,' says the Lord
Peter Adam

The Bible Speaks Today:
New Testament series

The Message of Matthew
The kingdom of heaven
Michael Green

The Message of Mark
The mystery of faith
Donald English

The Message of Luke
The Saviour of the world
Michael Wilcock

The Message of John
Here is your King!
Bruce Milne

The Message of the Sermon on the Mount (Matthew 5 – 7)
Christian counter-culture
John Stott

The Message of Acts
To the ends of the earth
John Stott

The Message of Romans
God's good news for the world
John Stott

The Message of 1 Corinthians
Life in the local church
David Prior

The Message of 2 Corinthians
Power in weakness
Paul Barnett

The Message of Galatians
Only one way
John Stott

The Message of Ephesians
God's new society
John Stott

The Message of Philippians
Jesus our joy
Alec Motyer

The Message of Colossians and Philemon
Fullness and freedom
Dick Lucas

The Message of 1 and 2 Thessalonians
Preparing for the coming King
John Stott

The Bible Speaks Today: Bible Themes series

The Message of the Living God
His glory, his people, his world
Peter Lewis

The Message of the Resurrection
Christ is risen!
Paul Beasley-Murray

The Message of the Cross
Wisdom unsearchable, love indestructible
Derek Tidball

The Message of Salvation
By God's grace, for God's glory
Philip Graham Ryken

The Message of Creation
Encountering the Lord of the universe
David Wilkinson

The Message of Heaven and Hell
Grace and destiny
Bruce Milne

The Message of Mission
The glory of Christ in all time and space
Howard Peskett and Vinoth Ramachandra

The Message of Prayer
Approaching the throne of grace
Tim Chester

The Message of the Trinity
Life in God
Brian Edgar

The Message of Evil and Suffering
Light into darkness
Peter Hicks

The Message of the Holy Spirit
The Spirit of encounter
Keith Warrington

The Message of Holiness
Restoring God's masterpiece
Derek Tidball

The Message of Sonship
At home in God's household
Trevor Burke

The Message of the Word of God
The glory of God made known
Tim Meadowcroft

The Message of Women

Creation, grace and gender

Derek and Dianne Tidball

The Message of the Church

Assemble the people before me

Chris Green

The Message of the Person of Christ

The Word made flesh

Robert Letham

The Message of Worship

Celebrating the glory of God in the whole of life

John Risbridger

The Message of Spiritual Warfare

The Lord is a warrior; the Lord is his name

Keith Ferdinando

The Message of Discipleship

Authentic followers of Jesus in today's world

Peter Morden

The Message of Love

The only thing that counts

Patrick Mitchel

The Message of Wisdom

Learning and living the way of the Lord

Daniel J. Estes

The Message of the Second Coming

Ending all things well

Steve Motyer